EAST TEXAS
TROUBLES

EAST TEXAS
TROUBLES

THE ALLRED RANGERS'
CLEANUP OF SAN AUGUSTINE

JODY EDWARD GINN

FOREWORD BY ROBERT M. UTLEY

UNIVERSITY OF OKLAHOMA PRESS : NORMAN

Publication of this book is made possible through
the generosity of Edith Kinney Gaylord.

Library of Congress Cataloging-in-Publication Data

Names: Ginn, Jody Edward, 1969– author.
Title: East Texas troubles : the Allred Rangers' cleanup of San Augustine / Jody Edward Ginn.
Description: Norman : University of Oklahoma Press, [2019] | Includes bibliographical references
    and index.
Identifiers: LCCN 2018052927 | ISBN 978-0-8061-6291-1 (hardcover : alk. paper)
Subjects: LCSH: Law enforcement—Texas—San Augustine—History—20th century. | Texas
    Rangers—History—20th century. | Allred, James V., 1899–1959. | Vigilantes—Texas—San
    Augustine—History—20th century. | Criminals—Texas—San Augustine—History—20th
    century. | Violence—Texas—San Augustine—History—20th century. | San Augustine
    (Tex.)—Social conditions—20th century.
Classification: LCC HV8148.S298 G56 2019 | DDC 363.209764/17509043—dc23
LC record available at https://lccn.loc.gov/2018052927

Copyright © 2019 by Jody Edward Ginn. Published by the University of Oklahoma Press,
Norman, Publishing Division of the University. Manufactured in the U.S.A.

In memory of
Daisy May (Hines) Carr
and
Cherry Hale (Hines) Harrison,
without whom this story might never have been told

CONTENTS

ILLUSTRATIONS

Map

FOREWORD

Jody Edward Ginn's *East Texas Troubles* recounts early 1930s violence that roiled San Augustine, a community located deep in the Texas Piney Woods, surrounded by distinctively red clay soil, near the Louisiana border. The culmination of the disorders coincided with landmark events in the history of Texas and its elite law enforcement body, the Texas Rangers. The elevation of liberal, reform-minded attorney general James Allred to the governorship in 1935 is said to have marked the beginning of the transformation from "horseback Rangers" to "motorized Rangers." Allred would oversee the replacement of thousands of political appointees—Rangers appointed during the governorship Miriam "Ma" Ferguson—with professional Rangers. Ginn effectively describes how the "Allred Rangers" shoved out the "Ferguson Rangers" and brought honest law enforcement to crime-ridden San Augustine.

Ginn's book is the first to deal in depth with the transition from the old-style Texas Rangers to the new, professionalized Rangers that Allred launched with the creation of the Texas Department of Public Safety. While Allred intended for the new Rangers to be insulated from politics of the past, a change from the Ferguson era, he had to resort to some heavy-handed politics to accomplish his reforms. Ginn shows how this worked in bringing honest, effective lawmen to San Augustine.

Allred's secretary, Ed Clark, a native of San Augustine, brought his hometown violence to the governor's attention, which led to Allred dispatching his earliest appointees to clean up the town. After the events described in the book, Allred lasted the customary two terms as governor, then failed at two bids for a US Senate seat and finally settled for an appointment to a federal judicial post. Meanwhile, Clark rose to become President Lyndon Johnson's ambassador to Australia and one of the most influential Democrat power brokers of the twentieth century.

Ginn has devoted almost two decades to researching the San Augustine "troubles" that culminated in the arrival of the Allred Rangers in 1935. He has delved into sources hitherto untapped, especially court records of the many trials that resulted from the Allred Rangers' investigations. These, combined with newspaper reporting of the time and interviews with some surviving participants and eyewitnesses, provide a solid foundation for a factual and interpretive account of this significant episode in Texas history.

A vivid and exacting portrayal of those events has emerged from these years of study and reflection. Jody Edward Ginn has published a valuable and enduring contribution to the history of law enforcement in Texas—and to local history that has long disturbed the citizens of San Augustine.

—Robert M. Utley

ACKNOWLEDGMENTS

This book is the product of eighteen years of research performed across Texas and beyond. In an effort such as this, success depends on the guidance, assistance, and encouragement of a host of people. My work has benefited immeasurably from such support, from beginning to end. A comprehensive list of all those who aided me would require more space than is available. Nevertheless, there are some key people I must publicly recognize, since their involvement has been crucial. Each deserves credit for their contributions to this book, while any shortcomings are mine alone.

This project owes its origins to Daisy May (Hines) Carr, elder sister of Texas Ranger Daniel J. Hines. Daisy was my great-grandmother, and I was very close to her. She lived to be ninety-six years old, passing away in 1990, when I was twenty. I grew up listening to stories about the changes that she experienced during her lifetime, which spanned from riding into Houston in a horse-drawn wagon through the Space Age and into the Computer Age. She often shared stories about her "baby brother" Dan, of whom she was very proud. While I could not recall many details when in 2000 I set about researching Dan Hines's career, I eventually homed in on her oft-repeated tale about how he became a Texas Ranger during the Great Depression and "cleaned up" a town in East Texas that had been overrun by criminals. Daisy noted that he had been given a set of engraved pistols in appreciation for his part in restoring peace and order to that

community, so I set out on a family research project to see if I could locate those
pistols and any records of Dan Hines's activities as a Ranger. Little did I know
at the time that my great-grandmother had catalyzed a new career for me and a
life-changing quest that would culminate with this book. My love and respect
for her are immeasurable, and I remain forever in her debt.

As I embarked on my research, I quickly learned about Cherry Hale (Hines)
Harrison, the youngest daughter of Dan Hines. Cherry was my first cousin twice
removed, and I had never met her until I contacted her out of the blue in 2000 to
ask whether she had any records or recollections of her father's service as a Texas
Ranger. Cherry invited me to her home in Alleyton, Texas, where she provided me
with primary source materials, including the engraved pistols given to her father
by the citizens of San Augustine. Over the ensuing years, Cherry and her husband,
Dittman Harrison, regularly hosted me to discuss my progress. In the process we
became friends, and I will always cherish memories of our get-togethers. Cherry
and Ditt consistently encouraged and supported my efforts until Cherry passed
away at the age of eighty-two in 2016. My one regret regarding this book is that
it was not published during her lifetime, but Cherry and Ditt's children, Holly
Waligura and Hines Harrison, have continued to support me and encourage my
efforts since their parents' passing.

As I expanded my research, I was made aware of San Augustine native and
local historian Harry Noble, former vice president of Lamar University, who has
published numerous books and countless articles in the *San Augustine Tribune*
on his hometown's history. Harry, who had been a young child at the time of the
cleanup and knew most of the people involved in the story, generously took me
under his wing, pointing me to potential sources and introducing me around
town to those who remembered or possessed some knowledge of those 1930s
events. Harry was also responsible for securing grant funding to digitize local
court records and the archives of the *San Augustine Tribune*, both of which proved
invaluable resources for me. He even arranged for the *Tribune* to run an article
about my research, leading to contacts from several individuals with exclusive
information regarding those events, including a key eyewitness. All told, the value
of Harry's guidance and support cannot be overstated.

I must also recognize the guidance and encouragement of three mentors:
Robert M. Utley, James L. Haley, and the late Al Lowman. Their encouragement
and guidance throughout this process has been invaluable to me. It is unlikely that
I would have ventured into what became a midlife career change and written this
book were it not for these three wise and generous souls. By sharing their expertise

and providing me with opportunities to work with them in the field, Bob and Jim each instilled in me the confidence to grow this effort beyond a mere family project and into a new career path. Al took me under his wing, inculcated me with his passion for both history and the books in which it is recorded, and introduced me to virtually everyone who is anyone in Texas and western US history today.

Additionally, a number of people with personal ties to the 1930s events in San Augustine provided me with access to privately held primary source materials. They include Arlan and Stephen Hays, owners and editors of the *San Augustine Tribune*; Edward Boone Brackett III and Bismarck Brackett, grandson and great-grandson respectively of Edward Boone Brackett Sr.; Chip McCormick, grandson of Texas Rangers captain J. W. McCormick; John and Betty Oglesbee, San Augustine historians; and Suzanne Sowell, San Augustine historian and genealogist.

I owe special thanks to the late Sidney "Tut" Lister Jr., the only documented eyewitness to the event that hastened the assignment of the Allred Rangers to San Augustine. Despite never before having recounted out loud what he witnessed on the day of the infamous shoot-out at the Thomas hardware store, Sidney shared with me a detailed account of that event, shedding light on what has long been a heavily mythologized episode in local history. He also told me much about what life was like in San Augustine during and after the troubles. Many others who recalled the troubles and cleanup (or were personally connected to those involved in them) also shared personal stories, including Jamie (Burleson) Dougherty, Arlene and Patsy Thomas, Jack and Josephine (Montgomery) Hollis, Panella (Curl) Davis, Exa Clark, J. L. Mathews, Mr. and Mrs. Morris Thompson, Maurine Fussell, Nelsyn Wade, and Curtis Haley. I am forever indebted to all herein who honored me by sharing their time, efforts, and often delicate family history in support of this project.

I would also like to thank the many archivists who assisted me. In chronological order of my earliest visits to each: the Briscoe Center for American History at the University of Texas at Austin; what is now the Tobin & Anne Armstrong Texas Ranger Research Center at the Texas Ranger Hall of Fame and Museum in Waco; the Texas State Library and Archives Commission (now-retired archivists Donaly Brice and John Anderson, in particular); Jean Wallace at the Terrell Historical Library in Beaumont; the San Augustine Public Library; the National Archives and Records Administration, College Park, Maryland; the East Texas Research Center at Stephen F. Austin State University in Nacogdoches; and Special Collections at the M. D. Anderson Library, University of Houston.

This book is a revised and expanded version of my 2014 doctoral dissertation, and substantial revisions were based largely on the advice of my dissertation committee at the University of North Texas. I must thank Richard B. McCaslin, major professor; Randolph B. Campbell; F. Todd Smith; Andrew Torget; and Scott Belshaw of the Department of Criminal Justice for their continued guidance and encouragement.

I also want to thank the editorial staff at the University of Oklahoma Press (OUP), including Chuck Rankin and director Byron Price, who first invited me to submit my manuscript and then waited patiently for many years until it was completed. Chuck and OUP's Rowan Steineker also reviewed an early draft and provided invaluable insights that guided my post-dissertation revisions and shaped the final manuscript. I also could not have hoped for a more knowledgeable and patient guide to the publishing process than my acquisitions editor, J. Kent Calder. Additionally, managing editor Steven Baker, marketing and publicity agents Amy Hernandez and Katie Baker, and freelance copy editor Chris Dodge have all been consummate professionals and a pleasure to work with. Finally, the editorial committee members and outside readers (peer reviewers) all provided constructive guidance that has enhanced the book. I am honored to join the author ranks of such a prestigious publisher focused on the history of the US Southwest.

I must also thank the Texas State Historical Association for the 2001 Fred White Jr. Research Fellowship in Texas History, which partially funded my first research foray into San Augustine that year.

Finally, the support of family throughout this process was essential. Researching and writing this book would have taken several years even if I had focused on that full-time, but during the first half of this undertaking I worked as a law enforcement investigator. For years it was a self-funded passion that I pursued during evenings and days off, whenever possible. I cannot thank my wife, Lesli, enough for her support and patience throughout. Further, as a first-rate legal writer, Lesli has always been my first editor, helping me to hone and polish my work prior to submission. I also want to thank my mother, Sheiran Pudifin, for her unwavering support and encouragement. After I ventured into graduate studies in history, my father and stepmother, Russell and Beverly Ginn, generously provided essential financial and moral support. They even read and provided feedback on early drafts of my dissertation from the layperson's perspective. Finally, I must also thank my children, Spencer and Katherine, who have never known a time in their young lives without their father regularly being away (traveling for research, commuting to classes) or needing quiet around the house while studying and writing. I hope that this book instills in each of them a sense of pride and the value of perseverance.

—Jody Edward Ginn

EAST TEXAS
TROUBLES

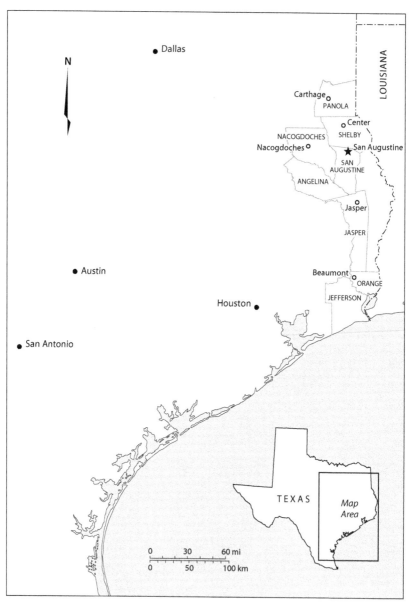

East Texas communities and counties discussed in the narrative.
Cartography by Bill Nelson Maps.

INTRODUCTION

In 1935 and 1936, during the Jim Crow era and "behind the Pine Curtain" in the heart of East Texas, three all-white juries found white defendants guilty of felony crimes against African Americans. The time and place of those convictions are all the more notable because they were based exclusively on the testimony of black victims and witnesses, who testified that the unprecedented prosecutions were the product of investigations by Texas Rangers sent by newly elected governor James V. Allred. Known as "Allred Rangers," they were sent to resolve the "troubles" that had plagued San Augustine County for more than a decade. The sworn testimony of numerous African American San Augustinians (corroborated by many additional sources) revealed that a group of local white criminals led by members of the McClanahan and Burleson families had been exploiting Jim Crow culture to abuse and extort the minority community. Anyone who attempted to defy the McClanahan-Burleson gang, black or white, faced violent reprisals, including murder. The Allred Rangers' year-and-a-half-long effort to bring about a reckoning for the gang on behalf of its victims, both black and white, eventually came to be known as the "cleanup of San Augustine."[1]

The troubles originated as routine bullying and extortion of black citizens but developed into an unsophisticated but brutal organized crime ring that oppressed the entire community. Over time, the ring's crimes escalated from robbing and extorting black citizens to murdering anyone who dared to challenge the gang, including white residents who stood up for their black neighbors or otherwise questioned the criminals' exploitation of the community. Eventually the gang became so brazen as to instigate shoot-outs and carry out assassinations in broad daylight on the town square. One such shoot-out, days before Christmas in 1934, finally drove local white community leaders to seek state intervention in the violence that had accelerated out of control. After the shoot-out, journalists became aware of what they soon dubbed the "San Augustine Crime Wave."[2]

The unassuming hamlet of San Augustine is situated deep in rural East Texas along State Highway 21, approximately thirty miles east of Nacogdoches and thirty miles west of the Louisiana border. This region, known as the Redlands because of its dark-red clay soil, is in the portion of Texas most closely connected culturally to the "Old South," particularly where race relations are concerned. San Augustine was founded in 1827 on the Ayish Bayou by Anglo-Celtic farmers from the Cotton Belt of the southern United States, including uninvited immigrants whose arrival predated those of Stephen F. Austin's colonists. Many brought their African American slaves, descendants of whom still lived alongside their white neighbors at the time of the 1930s troubles, under the segregationist strictures of post-Reconstruction Texas (and elsewhere in the South).[3]

From the town's founding through the early twentieth century—except for a moment of prosperity in the antebellum period—San Augustine was isolated and economically stagnant and thus prone to conflict and vulnerable to criminal activity. The community developed in a region long plagued by political controversy and neglect by the governments of rival colonial powers. First colonized and then abandoned (more than once) by the Spanish, the border region between Texas and Louisiana was the subject of recurring disputes over several centuries. American and Spanish military commanders in 1806 entered into an agreement that declared the region "Neutral Ground" and forbade settlement in or near it, but unauthorized immigration escalated from both Mexico and the United States.[4]

As US and Mexican authorities had also agreed not to station troops in the area, the settlers found themselves left to settle their own disputes. By the time the Texas Republic asserted official authority over the region, the local population was loath to acquiesce. As a result, in 1840 Sam Houston, president of the Republic, sent General Travis G. Broocks to quell a long-running, bloody feud over fraud and land disputes. After the Regulator-Moderator War, as the disputes were known, Broocks remained in San Augustine, and some of his descendants there were involved in later disturbances, including the 1930s troubles. From the Mexican colonial period through the Jim Crow era, African American San Augustinians remained a marginalized people who were easily victimized. These circumstances, combined with a failure to repudiate informal, extralegal methods of "justice" (such as feuding and vigilantism), produced the environment that facilitated the McClanahan-Burleson gang's rise to power.[5]

"Jim Crow" originated as the name of a minstrel caricature of African American men, played by Antebellum era white entertainers in blackface. The precise origins of how the term came to refer to the cultural and systemic practices of racial segregation that originally developed in the northern and midwestern United States are lost to history. During the late eighteenth and early nineteenth centuries, northern states slowly abandoned the practice of chattel slavery in favor of unregulated industrial wage labor. Despite this shift, most white northerners still subscribed to the core tenets of white supremacy and avoided interacting with blacks in social, professional, and political settings. Further, they created laws and cultural practices to prevent any unnecessary engagement with individuals they regarded as inherently inferior. Slavery precluded the need for most such restrictions in the antebellum South, but after the emancipation of enslaved blacks and the adoption of federal legislation to promote political equality, the South embraced Jim Crow statutes and customs to maintain white supremacy over black people.[6]

Anglo-Texans followed this pattern. Many emigrants from slave-holding states brought slaves and the plantation culture to Texas while it was still a province of Mexico. When Texas became an independent republic, it passed laws prohibiting free blacks from obtaining land grants or otherwise residing in the new nation. The admittance of Texas into the United States was delayed due to its slaveholding status, which continued after annexation. Despite the efforts of many post-Reconstruction Texans to identify more closely with the American Southwest, its racial dynamics belied such efforts at reinvention. East Texas, in particular, remained more southern than western in demographics and race relations through the nineteenth and twentieth centuries. Jim Crow political and cultural strictures of segregation, discrimination, and deference were in full force across Texas, including San Augustine. Perceived violations of that social order resulted in vicious retaliation by white Texans, including riots, arson, torture, and lynching. Black Texans inclined to resist any aspect of Jim Crow risked those consequences not only for themselves but also for their families, friends, and local community. Resistance, if it happened at all, was limited primarily to individual acts for several generations and rarely involved collaborative efforts between different racial groups.[7]

This history makes it surprising that in 1935 a legal and cultural anomaly emerged behind the Pine Curtain. Most of the descendants of former slaves in the region were sharecroppers. As such, they relied on white landlords and community leaders for protection from those inclined to capitalize on the lack of due process and other civil rights afforded to black citizens during this period. This meant that blacks received little protection from the unscrupulous whites who subjected them to all manner of criminal abuses. This oppression eventually escalated into white-on-white violence by the 1930s, when some white landowners began to push back against the abuse of their black tenants. But as some white San Augustinians began to interfere with the loosely organized, race-based rackets, the perpetrators were emboldened by weak and often corrupt law enforcement. Some officers had received their commissions for their political patronage, enabling the gang to expand into a wider spectrum of criminal activities, including bootlegging and gambling. Like others involved in organized crime, the McClanahan-Burleson gang began with low-level offenses and escalated to more significant crimes, controlling the community through violence and intimidation.[8]

While various acts of violence against white San Augustinians garnered the most press attention at the time and the most historical attention from later generations, the gang's core criminal activities primarily involved robbing and extorting local black sharecroppers. The gang eventually consolidated its power over the broader community by expanding into hijacking, counterfeiting, and racketeering, the latter in order to control local gambling and bootlegging. Black citizens in and near San Augustine lived in perpetual fear during the troubles, and the only whites they could turn to for help—until the arrival of the Texas Rangers sent by Governor Allred—were landlords, who were typically just as afraid of the McClanahan-Burleson gang. In the end, as has often been the case throughout the history of the United States, it took the violent deaths of whites to bring attention, and an effective response, to a situation that had long plagued the black community.[9]

During the decade that the McClanahan-Burleson gang cultivated their East Texas brand of organized crime that reached its apex in the 1930s, they did so with the support of state officials. Some of the gang's leaders gained government authority after gaining state-level "special Ranger" commissions from Governor Miriam A. "Ma" Ferguson, wife and political stand-in for impeached former governor James E. "Pa" Ferguson. The Fergusons were notorious for their use of both "regular Ranger" and "special Ranger" commissions for political purposes. Long-time and widely respected Ranger captain Manuel T. "Lone Wolf" Gonzaullus once quipped that the Fergusons "had to pardon their rangers before they appointed them." This referred to the Fergusons' practice of selling pardons to convicted criminals who supported their campaigns.[10]

Special Ranger commissions, like those for Texas Rangers of the time, came with statewide law enforcement authority, including the right to carry a handgun and make arrests. They had originally been intended for people with law enforcement experience engaged in security-related tasks for ranches, railroads, and oil companies. The Fergusons, however, gave them to just about any political supporter who requested one, including those with criminal convictions. Therefore, most "Ferguson Rangers" lacked effective oversight, a circumstance that allowed criminals like the McClanahans and Burlesons to use the commissions to expand their criminal activities. While there were dozens of white and even some black men with varying degrees of involvement in the McClanahan-Burleson gang, a smaller core group of men actively worked together to abuse black San Augustinians and suppress any white residents inclined to interfere with their crimes.[11]

Tensions were so thick and violence so pervasive during the troubles that one person who grew up during that period, looking back decades later, commented, "I was eighteen years old before I realized that Ford motorcars did not come standard with a Colt .45 in the glove box." This provides a stark perspective on how dangerous the community had been for a decade, if not longer.

The extent of the abuse of African Americans by the McClanahan-Burleson gang is illuminated through the detailed testimony of black victims and witnesses. Such testimony provides unprecedented insights into the experience of the African American community in San Augustine during that time. Black San Augustinians explained how gang members came to their homes and accosted them on local highways to rob and extort those who had no law enforcement officials to protect them. Their testimony reveals that the San Augustine troubles were the product of an organized and continuing criminal enterprise.[12]

All of this changed after Allred sent his Rangers to San Augustine. In two cases that had occurred prior to the arrival of Allred's Rangers, black victims later specified that they had never reported the crimes against them—neither to local authorities nor to anyone else outside the black community. With the Jim Crow restrictions of the time, black citizens were not allowed to bring charges against whites or testify against white defendants. In addition, leading members of the gang held law enforcement positions in San Augustine, and they coerced and intimidated other law enforcement officers and other public officials who attempted to oppose them. The black victims in these two cases later explained to white judges and juries that Allred's Rangers had sought them out, investigated and believed their allegations, and then filed charges on their behalf in the courts.[13]

It is important to note that the Rangers did not secure access into the black community in Jim Crow–era San Augustine on their own. A well-regarded member of that community with whom the Rangers managed to establish trust most likely assisted them in their investigations. Although no records have surfaced to prove this, the supposition is well-founded. The first two black victims and witnesses in cases that went to trial noted in their testimony that they had never reported the crimes against them outside of their own families or community. This suggests that a member of that community alerted the Rangers.[14] Additionally, both the victims in their testimony and other members of the community who lived through that time noted their mistrust of white law enforcement officials, reflecting similar circumstances across the Jim Crow South. Therefore, they likely would not have risked confiding in unknown white officers from outside the community without having a member of that community convince them that those officers could be trusted. Finally, one of the crimes at issue occurred several months after the arrival of Allred's Rangers but prior to the trials for the earlier crimes. The victim in this case reported the crime immediately after it occurred—to a new local law officer known to have been working directly with the Rangers, who collaborated with him to investigate the case and arrest the offenders. This case demonstrates a dramatic change in the relationship of blacks in San Augustine to law enforcement in just a few months. After years of abuse and neglect of their circumstances, local black citizens had found allies among white law enforcement officials.

The three 1935 and 1936 jury trial convictions of whites for crimes committed against black San Augustinians did not comprise the entirety of Allred's Rangers' cleanup of San Augustine. Many other white men pled guilty to similar offenses against black San Augustinians, but the adjudicative process did not produce transcripts and other documents that preserved the details of their respective crimes and surrounding circumstances. Those cases were likely among the sources of the numerous accounts passed down in the local collective memory. While not flawless or as detailed as the written record in primary accounts, community memory of the troubles and cleanup has been largely affirmed by the extant primary sources.[15]

The most egregious example of the McClanahan-Burleson gang's abuse of those from outside San Augustine is also one for which the fewest particulars have survived in the collective memory: an attack on a US Secret Service agent. That incident has long been among the most mysterious stories passed down orally about the 1930s troubles because many facts became lost or muddled over time. Regardless, the attack on a federal agent demonstrated how bold the McClanahans and Burlesons had become in openly using violence to oppress the community, having reached the pinnacle of their power. One notable yet long-forgotten fact about the assault was that Allred's Rangers were integral to the Secret Service's subsequent investigation of it. Also, the prosecution of the agent's attackers was founded on what was a new statute that made it a federal crime to assault an agent of the federal government in the execution of one's duties.[16]

Due to the escalating nature of the violence by the McClanahans and Burlesons, the citizens of San Augustine suffered in silence for a decade or more. The breaking point was a December 1934 shoot-out at the local hardware store that was reminiscent of the wild and dangerous times of the "Old West." When the bullets stopped flying and the dust settled, three men lay dead, and a fourth, the primary shooter, would die shortly thereafter. A bystander was also wounded, though not fatally. It was at least the third public murder in as many years, a bloody indication of how bold the local criminal element had become.[17]

Several murders occurred in daylight and before dozens of witnesses, but no one could be convinced to testify against the gang. Citizens' ever-increasing fear only strengthened the gang's illicit grip on the community. While many such murders appeared to be white-on-white violence, disagreements at their roots often entailed the gang's abuses of their white victims' African American sharecroppers or other associates. Details surrounding many of the countless crimes committed during the troubles reveal how pervasive the McClanahan-Burleson gang's corruption was throughout the community. In particular, accounts describing the aftermath of the murders sometimes illuminate the personal toll those crimes took on multiple generations of the victims' families. Many of those crimes are still infamous among locals, although the community's collective memory often lacks details necessary for a comprehensive and nuanced assessment of the events.

Finally, more angered than frightened at how out of control their community had spiraled, leading citizens of San Augustine reached out to lame duck governor "Ma" Ferguson for help before Allred entered office in January 1935. Unfortunately, she had packed the Texas Rangers with political cronies instead of experienced lawmen. As already noted, several of the culprits in the troubles carried Ferguson special Ranger commissions, which they used to establish a thin veil of legitimacy over their criminal operations. Instead of protecting the local community from those who had run roughshod over it, Ferguson's Rangers only put on a show of enforcing the law. It also appears that they betrayed the confidence of those who complained to the governor, causing those individuals to be subject to retaliatory harassment and threats.[18]

Ferguson's term ended, however, and progressive Democrat James V. Allred succeeded her as governor. A former district attorney and attorney general of Texas, Allred had run for governor in 1934 as an anti-Ferguson, pro–law enforcement candidate, advocating a massive overhaul of state law enforcement, specifically to end gubernatorial abuses in the granting of law enforcement commissions and to professionalize the Texas Rangers. On January 18, 1935—the day after Allred's inauguration—four newly minted Rangers drove into San Augustine with orders from Allred to take control and "clean up" that community.

Once the citizens of San Augustine, black and white, understood that the McClanahan-Burleson gang and its associates had been deposed and no longer presented a threat to the community, Allred's Rangers shifted their focus from establishing order to investigating countless criminal cases, many dating back years. In addition to contacting dozens of victims and witnesses, the Rangers worked with prosecutors to prepare the cases for indictment and trial. The San Augustine County criminal courts were revitalized by the successful collaboration of local black and white citizens with the Rangers and also reassured by the Rangers' commitment to the security of victims, witnesses, jurors, and court officers. Two corrupt local elected officials were also ousted as a result of the cleanup. The concomitant revitalization of the local criminal justice system enabled prosecutors in San Augustine to proceed with many other contemporary cases that had stalled prior to the arrival of Allred's Rangers.[19]

Most of the charges filed as a result of the cleanup were adjudicated through plea agreements, meaning that the prosecution and defense came to an agreement on punishment, and the defendant pled guilty. This was, and is, commonplace in the criminal justice system, and it leaves little for future researchers to analyze. However, a handful of cases went to trial and resulted in convictions and were subsequently appealed, which meant that records about the cases were preserved in the state archives. Detailed accounts extracted directly from trial transcripts of three of those cases show that the victims, who were black and had never reported the crimes, were contacted by the Rangers in the course of their investigation and agreed to testify. Those cases resulted in successful convictions by white juries, an unprecedented turn of events during the Jim Crow era in East Texas. The conspiratorial nature of the crimes is revealed throughout much of the surviving witness testimony, which exposed the fact that the local gangsters engaged in all manner of common criminality. The lengths to which Allred's Rangers went in their investigations to locate African American victims in cold cases—people who had previously never had any hope of securing justice for crimes against them—is also illuminated throughout those transcripts.[20]

By the end of March 1935, numerous indictments had been issued, several murder trials had been held in cold cases, and victims and witnesses finally felt safe enough to relate their traumatic experiences of the previous years, first to Allred's Rangers and then to judges and juries. Community leaders and average citizens began openly expressing their gratitude to the Rangers for restoring order in San Augustine, holding what would be the first of several gatherings and celebrations in their honor on March 22, 1935. Despite that early stage of the cleanup, the Allred Rangers considered the situation to be sufficiently under control, and only one of them remained assigned to the area full-time to complete the cleanup.[21]

The success in San Augustine was heralded as a high spot in Texas Ranger history and cited as evidence of the triumph of Allred's renovation of state law enforcement policies and practices. However, the events held to celebrate the community's deliverance from the clutches of the McClanahan-Burleson gang served as stark evidence that the interracial cooperation that defied Jim Crow cultural norms did not extend beyond the courtroom. Black citizens were only allowed to attend such events on designated days, during which most whites stayed away. Despite their willingness to buck Jim Crow limitations and permit black citizens to bring criminal charges against whites, most white San Augustinians remained unwilling to fully embrace their black neighbors as equals in other aspects of community life.[22]

Not only did the community hold multiple events to celebrate their liberation from the McClanahan-Burleson gang, many local business, government, and other community leaders expressed their gratitude in local newspaper notices and public statements. This is evidence that, notwithstanding perhaps a few McClanahan and Burleson family members and close associates, the citizens of that beleaguered community, black and white, had opposed the oppressive reign of the gang and approved of and appreciated the actions of Allred's Rangers. The only documented criticism of any aspect of the cleanup I found was a self-published memoir written decades later by a corrupt former sheriff who was ousted in the process. That book includes complaints about "unfair" treatment by unspecified Rangers, although the author offered no defense of any members of the McClanahan-Burleson gang and did not generally denounce the cleanup. I unearthed no other publications or documents recording any voices of dissent during my nearly two decades of research on those events.

Out of the hundreds of indictments and convictions in San Augustine County during 1935, the court of last resort in Texas, the Court of Criminal Appeals, heard less than a dozen of those cases. The cases they did consider form the foundation of this study, providing never-before-examined insight into the events of the period. These involved various key players in a variety of roles, and they shed light on the circumstances unfolding in San Augustine at the time. With the eyewitness accounts and contemporary news articles, a well-rounded and thorough examination of those events is possible. The Allred Rangers' success in San Augustine throughout 1935 and 1936 marked a turning point for an organization that had come under increasing criticism over the preceding three decades, and these events played into the Rangers' absorption into the newly created Texas Department of Public Safety, which was the final step in their evolution from a paramilitary frontier defense force into modern law enforcement investigators.

By the time of the Texas Centennial celebrations in 1936, the San Augustine cleanup was effectively complete. However, over eighty years have passed without a well-documented history of the affair being published. The few previously published accounts are primarily based on limited oral testimony or are too brief to provide the detail necessary to debunk longstanding myths and provide a clear understanding of all that occurred and how those events affected—and were perceived by—the people who actually experienced them.

East Texas Troubles is a story of race, power, and resistance that is uncommon in Texas history scholarship. Black and white citizens collaborated with the Allred Rangers to dismantle a pseudo-regime built by local gangsters on the foundation of Jim Crow racism and enforced against all challengers, black and white, with brutal violence. It is important to note that, while the participation of all three groups—white citizens, black citizens, and the Allred Rangers—was integral to the success of the San Augustine cleanup, the effort did not result in a comprehensive local overthrow of Jim Crow segregation in that community. Nonetheless, local blacks and whites uncharacteristically allied with each other and the Allred Rangers in putting aside Jim Crow restrictions on black access to due process in local criminal courts, leading to convictions that were upheld by the Texas Court of Criminal Appeals. As a result, the San Augustine cleanup represents one time when those who had exploited Jim Crow prohibitions on black access to the courts were eventually held accountable for their transgressions.

As noted by Robert M. Utley, former chief historian of the National Park Service and prolific author on the history of the American West, Texas Rangers traditionally stood for law and order and opposed vigilantism and violence. Utley acknowledges that, as white Texans in the Jim Crow era, most Rangers at the time generally accepted the notion that blacks were inherently inferior to whites and took for granted the accompanying tenets of segregation. Nevertheless, Rangers did confront racist lynch mobs and used deadly force when necessary to defend the due process rights of minority Texans accused of crimes, particularly when local officials were unwilling and perhaps afraid to do so. The extent of such actions in the nineteenth and twentieth centuries is difficult to ascertain, due to a lack of research on the topic. However, such instances are documented in the historical record to varying degrees, enough to justify the theory that they were more common than many scholars currently believe them to have been.[23]

This is not to say that examples of color-blind altruism by some Texas Rangers should be used to negate legitimate criticisms of other Rangers. To the contrary, they are an affirmation of Utley's contention that prior to the creation of the Department of Public Safety, the quality of Rangers in service at any given time was directly related to the quality of the person sitting in the governor's chair. Utley was referring to the fact that the early-twentieth-century Rangers experienced frequent and often extensive turnover because of the politicization of their ranks that increased exponentially beginning in the 1910s—the awarding of commissions based on political patronage instead of ability and experience. The capricious appointment process for Rangers during this period greatly diminished the reputation of the storied organization and the value of those commissions. Their fall from grace was so acute that a Depression-era Texas journalist once quipped, "A Ranger commission and a nickel will get [you] a cup of coffee anywhere in Texas." A cup of coffee cost a nickel at that time.[24]

San Augustine was just one of many Texas communities where unscrupulous men with unsavory pasts obtained special Ranger commissions from the Fergusons and abused the authority that came with them. The San Augustine troubles and resulting cleanup in the 1930s thus exemplify Utley's point that the quality of the governor determined the quality of the Rangers in service and illuminate how that quality could vary from one administration to the next. Surviving citizens of Depression-era San Augustine corroborate that assertion. Black and white San Augustinians who recall those events, as well as those who had the stories passed down to them through the generations, are precise in their distinction between "Ferguson Rangers" and "Allred Rangers." They mince no words in holding the former in contempt and the latter in the highest regard for their part in bringing about long overdue justice to that community.

— 1 —

SAN AUGUSTINE

"Behind the Pine Curtain"

San Augustine County is largely covered by a dense pine forest and surrounded by waterways, including the Sabine River to the east, the Attoyac River to the west, and the Sam Rayburn Reservoir to the south. The climate is warm and moist, and close to a third of the area is considered prime farmland, which benefits from a growing season that averages 238 days. Logging and agriculture have long been the area's primary economic resources, though ranching and natural gas production developed there in the late twentieth century. All in all, it is a region that has attracted settlers for several centuries but never really prospered after Reconstruction and has remained somewhat isolated. This has contributed to internal and external conflicts, a sense of legal independence, and prolific criminal activities.[1]

The area encompassing the city and county of San Augustine is one of the longest continuously settled regions of Texas, and its geological distinction as "the Redlands" has long been entwined with its identity (in the late 1830s and 1840s the local newspaper was the *Red-lander*). For generations, San Augustinians have asserted that their community is one of Texas's oldest cities. That claim rests on intermittent Spanish and Indian settlements—the latter of which date back to the prehistoric era—in the area where the Anglo-founded town of San Augustine came to be located." There were no institutional or cultural connections between the Anglo founders of San Augustine and previous peoples that had occupied

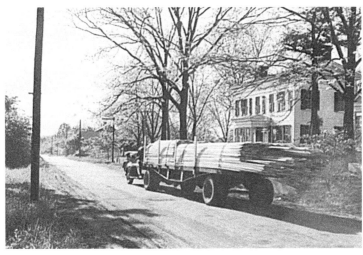

Truckload of lumber from San Augustine sawmill. *Photo by John Vachon. Library of Congress, LC-USW3-024884-D.*

the area, yet locals emphasize the existence of pre-Columbian settlements and short-lived Spanish missions in the area in order to promote the community's claim to be one of the oldest in the state. Some assert that it is the oldest *Anglo-American* community in the Lone Star State, but such claims again are based on informal and unauthorized occupation of the surrounding area by immigrants who arrived well before the legally sanctioned Anglo-Texan communities founded during the early Mexican colonial period.[2]

Though little is known of the relations between the various Indian peoples that occupied the region along the Ayish Bayou between the Sabine and Neches Rivers prior to European arrival in the Americas, the earliest known people to inhabit the immediate area of what would become the city of San Augustine, the Ais Indians, were apparently not well liked by their Caddoan neighbors. The Ais people were either an independent and less-sophisticated band that had broken off from the Caddoan Confederacy or descended from a more ancient culture. Whatever their origins, the main Caddoan bands disparaged and distrusted them. The reputation of the area's inhabitants did not improve with the arrival of Europeans, as both French and Spanish authorities sought influence in the region throughout the eighteenth century. Once French and Spanish settlers moved into the area, they too developed a reputation of being untrustworthy and defiant. The region's position on the northern frontier of New Spain (Mexico) and the

western frontier of the United States, far from the centers of power in early Texas,
isolated its inhabitants from mainstream cultures from which they came. Such
isolation resulted in an independent population with disdain for government
intrusion from afar. Left to their own devices for decades, residents developed a
culture of self-reliance and vigilante justice that persisted even after formal legal
institutions were established in the area.[3]

Anglo-Texans and Tejanos (Texans of Spanish or mixed Spanish-Indian ances-
try), including some from the San Augustine area, played a significant role in the
eleven-year-long war for Mexican independence from Spain. During this time,
the Ayish Bayou region was largely devoid of Hispanic and Indian inhabitants,
leaving it wide open for settlement by newcomers from the United States. It was
during this time, beginning about 1815, that the first Anglo-Celtic immigrants from
the southern states began to move into the area around what would eventually
become the city and county of San Augustine. Otherwise beleaguered Spanish
officials generally ignored their presence as long as they kept out of politics (which
they did, for a while). It was left to settlers to resolve their own disputes, whether
of a civil or criminal nature, and once accustomed to that system they were not
inclined to relinquish power to government institutions.[4]

After Mexican independence in 1821, the dynamic between the Mexican government and the settlers of the Ayish Bayou region was likewise essentially one of
willful neglect. Thus began a local tradition among residents of this remote and
region: avoidance of governmental intrusion.[5]

The town and surrounding community was located within approximately
seventy miles of the Sabine River, an area officially off-limits to Anglo-Texan
settlement under the Mexican colonization law of 1824, which stipulated no
settlement within twenty leagues of the river. In 1834, Mexican authorities finally
conferred the status of *ayuntamiento* (legal municipality) on the town, thereby
giving it separate authority from Nacogdoches for the administration of laws,
local militia, and dissemination of land titles, among other duties. Given that
the town founders were primarily Anglo-Celtic immigrants from the Old South,
San Augustine may have been the first town in Texas not laid out according to
Spanish traditions. Many of the founders were also slaveholders, making African
Americans the second most populous ethnic group in the area. Over the next
several years, San Augustine served as a main entry point into Texas and attracted
many notable residents who would play vital roles in the coming revolt against
Mexico. It also provided substantial political, military, and financial support to
the looming revolt that would eventually lead to Texas's independence, thereby

San Augustinian with three horse- or mule-drawn farm implements, a middle-buster, planter, and cultivator. *Photo by Russell Lee. Library of Congress, LC-DIG-fsa-8a25980.*

Farmers gathered outside the Farmers Exchange in San Augustine. *Photo by Russell Lee. Library of Congress, LC-USF34-032998-D.*

reinforcing the local culture of anti-government sentiment and the willingness to rebel against institutionalized authority.[6]

After its founding, San Augustine was briefly home to some of the most prominent leaders of the Texas revolt. Most significantly, Tennessean Sam Houston opened a law office there in 1835 and used it as a staging ground for pursuing his agenda. Throughout his time in Texas, Houston continued to rely on the town as a base of political support, a location for meeting and strategizing with supporters, and for personal respite. He also built a home there, though he never took up permanent residence on that property. The fact that numerous fellow Tennesseans—including close Houston friends Phil Sublett, William Kimbro, Alexander Horton, James Bullock, and town founder Elisha Roberts—had settled in San Augustine made it a "congenial place" to for Houston to reside. Although Houston had been the sixth governor of Tennessee, from his arrival in Texas he was viewed by the locals as one who would lead them in resisting what they viewed as the increasing tyranny and oppression of the Mexican government, thus bolstering the culture of anti-government sentiment.[7]

Ayish Bayou residents had long disdained what they considered to be oppressive Mexican rule, and the ascendancy of General Antonio López de Santa Anna exacerbated that sentiment. Though Santa Anna had risen to the presidency of Mexico on the back of the federalist movement, he soon decided to rule the country he had conquered more directly and without the interference of constitutional or statutory limitations. San Augustinians were then active in the revolt against Santa Anna that erupted in 1835. Community members supplied political, financial, and military capital toward the war effort; participated in the Consultation and Permanent Council in 1835 (the provisional government of Mexican Texas) and the Convention of 1836 (which wrote the Texas Declaration of Independence and Constitution of the Republic of Texas); and served in the legislative, judicial, and executive branches of the Republic.[8]

Numerous San Augustine residents, including Houston, J. Pinckney Henderson, and John Salmon "Rip" Ford, eventually rose to the highest levels of government service for the Republic of Texas. But before that happened, the revolt against Santa Anna's autocratic regime turned into a war for independence, and San Augustine suffered mightily under the weight of those events. The local economy stagnated as husbands, sons, and fathers joined local militia units and the Texas forces commanded by Houston. Those left behind and unprotected soon joined the mass exodus into Louisiana known as the Runaway Scrape. It was not until well after news of the Texans' victory over Santa Anna's forces at the San

Jacinto that life returned to relatively normal in the Redlands. Normality in this area included opposition to perceived government oppression and interference, as already noted, as well as occasional violent clashes among the locals. With a favorite son at the helm of the new Republic, many Ayish Bayou area residents were content to support the fledgling national government, even when its policies seemed otherwise at odds with local attitudes. As a result, while San Augustine became the arena of numerous intrigues and conflicts, it also enjoyed a period as a bustling commercial and political center.[9]

Despite their support of anti-Mexico efforts on the behalf of the Republic of Texas, Redlanders did not easily forsake their independence and longstanding attitudes and practices regarding the carrying out of justice—which to them sometimes meant retribution. The most famous Republic-era clash involving San Augustine became known as the Regulator-Moderator War. The bloody feud that stretched over more than five years and resulted in countless deaths in neighboring Shelby and Harrison Counties. In August 1844, President Houston called out the militia from San Augustine and three other counties, placed them under the command of General Travis Broocks, and ordered them to arrest the leaders of each side and bring them before him. The combatants were brought for safekeeping to San Augustine, and a company of the San Augustine militia remained in Shelbyville for a time to keep order. Broocks and his fellow San Augustinians were instrumental in the peaceful resolution of this deadly affair. Despite Broocks's role as a force for law and order in the region, some of his descendants would not follow the same path. Having been thoroughly inculcated into the culture that preferred individuals over institutions when it came to delivering justice, they would take matters into their own hands when they perceived having been wronged. They would do so even when the conflicts in question arose after they themselves had broken the law or gone against local customs.[10]

In the period between the creation of the Republic of Texas and the outbreak of the Civil War, San Augustine flourished as a center for trade goods coming from the United States and locally produced cotton. The town grew as land was bought and sold, stores sold all types of wares, and all variety of businesses were opened. Some of the earliest secondary and postsecondary schools in Texas were also founded during this time in the area. The community also faced some hardships, particularly in trying to get its substantial cotton crops to market in New Orleans. The road system was so poor and the terrain so rugged, especially due to the frequent heavy rains, that half of the local mule population was worked to death in 1838.

During this period, San Augustine was one of the busiest towns in the Texas Republic—commercially, politically, and judicially. The town was such an active and significant center of legal activity that it was said, by historian George L. Crockett, that nowhere else in Texas "could a young man find better . . . acquaintance with the elite of the legal profession." Furthermore, San Augustine became the cradle of organized religion in Texas, as the state's earliest congregations were founded in the vicinity. San Augustine was also home to one of the earliest permanent Masonic lodges in Texas, one of three lodges that came together to found the Grand Lodge of Texas in 1837. Overall, San Augustinians were productive and active citizens who contributed significantly to the growth and development of their newly independent Texas Republic. San Augustine continued to grow along with Texas throughout the antebellum period and often led other communities—for example, through the creation of some of the earliest schools and other civic, social, and religious institutions in the republic and state.[11]

Such positive aspects of San Augustinian society notwithstanding, the community did have one significant flaw. Black San Augustinians were slaves and therefore vulnerable to the whims and abuses of whites. After the Civil War and Emancipation, whites' "Lost Cause" mentality, exacerbated by the changing economic and social structures of Reconstruction, widened the gap between the races in the Redlands. During that era, San Augustine was bypassed by railroads, which limited its economic expansion and urbanization. It declined into a sleepy farming community with a shifting economy that provided little opportunity. In that environment, the lives of good people were often interrupted by violence, as feuds erupted and some less scrupulous people engaged in criminal activities. And the slavery essential to the town's success in the antebellum era had led to a marginalized black population vulnerable to victimization where the local institutions of justice lacked the public support to maintain order. [12]

The relationship between blacks and whites in San Augustine was not markedly different from elsewhere in the Old South, and racial tension remained after the war. A company of federal soldiers was stationed in San Augustine but apparently did little to protect the newly freed slaves there. Local white residents resented both the presence of the troops and the newly enfranchised blacks those troops were supposed to defend. They regarded efforts to encourage black citizens to vote as "incendiary propaganda" and those who asserted their newly acquired rights as "turbulent negroes whose minds had been inflamed by Yankee emissaries," according to East Texas historian, George L. Crockett. As with communities throughout the South, white citizens enacted laws to restrict black participation in public life and openly carried out acts of violence intended to convince them not to exercise their newly acquired rights, thereby creating the segregationist cultural dynamic known as Jim Crow. However, white San Augustinians did not wait for the end of Reconstruction to reassert white supremacy in their community.[13]

Attempts by "Radical Republicans"—who controlled Reconstruction policy—to intervene on behalf of the former slaves attempting to assert and defend their rights were met with death threats and violence. In 1867, many black San Augustinians established a fortified community known as the Pre-emption, near the plantation of Colonel F. B. Sexton, and formed a militia to defend themselves. The militia was led by Milton Garrett's apparently educated former slaves, Harry and Dan Garrett, who allegedly communicated certain demands and "threat[s]" in a letter to prosperous local planters I. L. and Reece Mathews. More than two hundred local white men of all ages responded by forming a local chapter of the Ku Klux Klan under the leadership of I. D. Thomas Jr. Thomas dispatched secret squads to roust local blacks said to be disorderly or otherwise "dangerous to society." Those "ghostly riders of the night" dragged unsuspecting black residents out of their homes and beat them until they promised to "reform."[14]

Once the covert squads had sufficiently undermined the local black community's will to fight, the Klan members of San Augustine threw off their "spectral armor" of white masks, caps, and robes and directly attacked the fortified main house at Pre-emption. They chased Harry and Dan Garrett out of the county and rounded up the rest of the black leaders, who they sufficiently intimidated to ensure that there would be no further efforts to subvert white supremacy in San Augustine. Local black citizens were so effectively subdued that the local KKK chapter is said to have been disbanded once federal troops left. Afterward, there would be no organized resistance to unchecked white supremacy in San Augustine for generations.[15]

Once black citizens were no longer chattel property, they became independent members of an oppressed minority. Most former slaves in Texas and their descendants were sharecroppers or tenant farmers because they did not own or have the opportunity to acquire land. Tenants and sharecroppers paid for the land they farmed with portions of the crops they produced. They also typically had to provide their own seed, livestock, and equipment or pay a higher percentage of their crop. To purchase supplies or other necessities, they had to establish a line of credit from local merchants before planting, which they would pay off after harvesting and selling their crops. Goods purchased this way often cost more than those paid for with cash, so tenant farmers rarely turned a profit and became trapped in a cycle of debt.[16]

Constrained to perpetual poverty and marginalized by the social and legal limitations of the Jim Crow South, black San Augustinians relied on the goodwill of their landlords and other white community leaders for protection from those inclined to take advantage of them. If their white patrons were unable or unwilling to protect them from external exploitation, the disenfranchised black residents typically had no form of recourse through white-controlled institutions.

Reconstruction in Texas interrupted the economic growth of the Redlands, and, as happened across the South, poor whites in San Augustine frequently chose to vent their frustrations at that predicament by lashing out at local black citizens, especially those perceived to have achieved some measure of economic success after being freed. The Civil Rights Act of 1875 and other federal and state legislation made equal rights for blacks explicit in matters as such public accommodations and transportation, but the US Supreme Court in 1883 ruled part of the act unconstitutional. Jim Crow then began in full force and, for a time, black Americans rarely attempted to buck its restrictions.[17]

Besides slavery, Anglo immigrants to the Redlands from the Old South brought with them practices of lethal feuding and vigilante justice beginning in the Republic period. When local officials and courts were too incompetent or otherwise disinclined to provide justice or enforce order, "pioneer elite[s]," in the words of historian Robert M. Utley, would organize efforts to protect their own lives and property "by the most direct means," sometimes by rope or bullet. Vigilantes also used their unchecked power to exact vengeance for perceived wrongs and often exploited it to enhance their personal fortunes. Texas Rangers of the late nineteenth and early twentieth centuries arrested countless feudists and vigilantes, but they could rarely get local officials and juries to see the charges through to conviction.[18]

Whenever legitimate law enforcers attempted to restore order and exact institutional justice, Redlanders used the dense pine forests and their skills as expert woodsmen and hunters to evade and resist such authority, often to deadly effect. Beginning in the 1890s and spilling over into the first few years of the new century, San Augustine was plagued by a feud between two factions, the Broocks-Border clan and the Wall clan. The origins of the feud are disputed. Some say it originated in unresolved childhood disagreements and was later fed by political antagonism: the Broocks-Border clan was made up of staunch, old-time Democrats, and the

Walls were involved in the growing Populist movement. Others insist that Curg Border, a key figure from the Broocks-Border faction, robbed and extorted black sharecroppers in a manner that presaged his descendants' actions decades later. In any event, even local historian Joe Combs acknowledged that virtually the entire black community there was "deathly afraid" of Curg Border and that he was well known to have been "overbearing when dealing with Negroes. . . . when he was a collector for the John Lynch Mercantile establishment." Whatever the feud's origins, many members of both factions died violent deaths, leading to multigenerational grudges within the community. Later another generation of the Broocks-Border clan and their associates would again defy local law and order by wreaking havoc on the black citizens of San Augustine and terrorizing any white citizens who dared challenge them.[19]

As the twentieth century advanced, San Augustine County fell further into its traditional disregard for institutional justice in favor of individual measures, marked by an ineffectual local system paralyzed by fear and corruption. One example of how far some local citizens were willing to go to protect against government intrusion into their lives was in July 1918, when two Texas Rangers sent into the area to arrest a fugitive were allegedly ambushed and one was killed. The exact circumstances of why the Rangers were there, just where and when the confrontation occurred, what actually occurred, and even the later disposition of the defendants' court cases are hotly debated, and little formal research has been conducted on the matter. Most of the available information appears to derive from the shooters' descendants and extended family, and little matches up between their accounts.

What is commonly accepted is that at least two Texas Rangers, including John Dudley White and Walter Rowe, were sent into San Augustine County to arrest locals Sam Williams and Daniel Evans—for draft-dodging or deserting during World War I or for hog theft. Williams and Evans had hidden deep in the pine forests on family land, aided by relatives. The Rangers eventually came into direct contact with them and a shoot-out took place, during which one Ranger was wounded and White was killed. Some accounts say that both Williams and Evans were prosecuted and sentenced to death, while others claim that Williams was killed during that shoot-out or in another one a short time later. Most accounts mention that their sentences were later commuted, and many claim that they were pardoned, an assertion that leads some descendants to speculate that the Texas Rangers' accounts of the event were not credible. All accounts are vague, at best, on a great many matters of fact, and none reference any primary sources to support their claims. Regardless of the disparities and ambiguities, there appears to be little debate that a confrontation between Texas Rangers and two local men occurred at that approximate date and time in San Augustine County, that the men resisted arrest through the use of firearms, and that one Ranger, Dudley White, was killed. As the community entered the twentieth century, at least some Redlanders retained the attitude that government interference in their personal affairs was an affront that they would counter with deadly force. Indeed, deadly force was the only law to which some white San Augustinians would ever yield.[20]

While white San Augustinians frequently engaged in violent defiance of local and state authorities with relative impunity, the few black citizens who dared to break the law were subjected to swift and merciless punishment, particularly when they came into conflict with local whites. Perhaps the most stark example of this double standard was the case of a local black man named John Dodd Price, who allegedly murdered a white neighbor, John Kennedy, with whom he'd had a dispute. Kennedy was found shot dead in his home in the early morning of March 19, 1920, and Price was arrested on March 22. He was indicted, tried, found guilty, and hanged in front of a large crowd on the courthouse square, all on March 23. The only solace local African Americans could take from Price's swift public execution, the last known to have occurred in the county, was that it quelled the anger of the local white community and thereby prevented broader extralegal hanging (lynching) or other retaliation against the black community.[21]

By the early 1930s, as the Depression brought another low point in the history of the area (and that of Texas), the diminishing fortunes of white residents further strained relations with local black citizens. As throughout much of the Jim Crow South, African American San Augustinians often became defenseless victims for unscrupulous whites bent on improving their own fortunes by taking whatever they saw fit from those who had no legal or practical recourse against them. Many of these whites had gained positions of power through political patronage and corruption. Local criminals victimized black inhabitants with impunity, which eventually led to confrontations with the few white residents willing to engage them. Such bloody altercations ended in the deaths of several respected local citizens and at least one accused oppressor.

Those events took place during the apex of the Jim Crow era in East Texas, in which black citizens found themselves on the lowest rung of a race-based caste system. Lynching and all manner of violent intimidation of black citizens who did not "keep in their place" were common. In fact, the last Jim Crow–era lynching in Texas occurred in the same year as the San Augustine cleanup. Black residents were

Execution of John Dodd Price, March 23, 1920, the last known hanging in San Augustine County. *Courtesy of Nelsyn Wade family.*

stereotyped as ignorant, childlike, and prone to drunkenness and violence—the last being ironic considering whites' violent methods of racial control. By law they were treated as undeserving of basic human rights, much less due process or other civil rights enjoyed by most members of white society. Besides being forced to use different facilities from white citizens—separate and second-class bathrooms, water fountains, waiting rooms, seating in public transportation, et cetera—black citizens were also denied the same rights as whites in the criminal justice system. Alleged offenses committed by black defendants against white victims typically resulted in far harsher penalties than the reverse. Black victims of white crime meanwhile usually had no recourse within the established criminal justice system of the time.[22]

As has often been the case through the history of the United States, it took the deaths of whites to bring attention to the plight of black citizens. The little town that simmered behind the Pine Curtain again attracted outside notice as a source of trouble and gained the attention of state law enforcement by way of a newly elected governor with a close associate from San Augustine. For generations, the resistance to institutionalized justice had relied on sheer will, which the Redlanders had but outside authorities did not. That changed in January 1935 when, to paraphrase legendary Texas Ranger captain William J. McDonald, a few Rangers who were in the right came to town and kept on a-comin'—and together with black and white San Augustinians broke the dominion of the McClanahan-Burleson gang once and for all.[23]

2

THE TROUBLES

Black sharecroppers and tenant farmers were the chief targets of the McClanahan-Burleson gang. Gang members would frequently rob local black farmers on their way home from selling their crops—when they had significant cash, much of which was owed to their landlords and local merchants. If the gangsters failed to catch black sharecroppers on the road, they would show up at their homes later and extort payment for some pretended debt or fine or point to what they wanted and say, "Thanks for taking care of my [hog, horse, tools, et cetera] for me." In the latter case they would then make off with sharecroppers' personal property. Most quietly acquiesced to the gang's tactics, knowing that resistance would result in severe injury or death. Jim Crow customs did not allow black citizens to testify against whites, usually even on behalf of white victims of crime, much less the right to file their own criminal complaints against a white suspect. Therefore, there was no one to whom black San Augustinians could meaningfully report those crimes, nor was there any expectation that meaningful action would follow if such a report were to be made. More likely than not, reporting would lead to violent retaliation.[1]

In addition to benefiting from the limitations on black civil rights during the Jim Crow era, the gangsters were also emboldened by their increasing control over local law enforcement. The perceived leader of the gang was Charles Curtis "Charlie" McClanahan. With his older brother Wade as his right hand and his nephew Wade Jr. also close by, Charles controlled the San Augustine community through fear. There were multiple witnesses to his commission of murders and assaults perpetrated in public over the years, but none dared come forth, and some left town prior to the arrival of the Rangers sent by Allred.

Although there were earlier efforts to bring leading members of the gang to justice, those efforts had failed because most locals were too afraid to serve as jurors in criminal cases against Charlie McClanahan or his associates, much less to testify against them. In the early 1930s, Wade and Wade Jr. became the town marshals, and all three McClanahans and their close associate Joe Burleson had secured unpaid state law enforcement special Ranger commissions, further entrenching their power. Ties to these commissioned officers of the law aided two of the most prolific oppressors of the local black community, Joe Burleson's brothers Thomas R. and Charles Lycurgus Burleson, known as Curg.

Tom was notorious for illegally carrying a pistol, which he had no qualms about using. (State law then did not permit civilians to carry pistols in public.) Some of his own family regarded him as a violent sociopath and steered clear of him as best they could in such a small and close-knit community. Another Burleson brother, Jim, was never implicated in any murders, but he participated with his brothers and the McClanahans in numerous other felonies, such as extortion and assault, including assault of a federal agent. The Burlesons and their associates typically carried out their extortion and robbery during the post-harvest season, when they knew the sharecroppers would temporarily possess large amounts of cash. As that money was in part owed to landlords and local merchants and the remainder would typically have to last farmers for a year, the gangsters were effectively bankrupting their victims.[2]

The earliest thoroughly documented criminal case relating to this scheme involved a young African American San Augustinian named Edward Clark. Unlike his locally born and raised Anglo-Texan namesake Edward Aubrey Clark, Governor Allred's personal secretary and future Texas secretary of state, who would go on to become US ambassador to Australia and a central figure in Lyndon Baines Johnson's rise to the presidency, Ed Clark was a twenty-six-year-old tenant farmer who rented his field and home from Frank Blount. During the Allred Rangers' cleanup, Clark accused Curg Burleson of having extorted money from him. The accusation was not reported until sometime after the Allred Rangers' arrival in January 1935, although the crime had occurred in early October 1934. Clark grew cotton and owned "plow tools, a few hogs, four mules, and one horse" about a mile down the road from where Curg lived with his wife at her parents' home. At the time of the crime, Clark had gathered seven bales and sold them at market, using proceeds in part to pay off a loan to "the government" that he had taken with a lien against his crop. Clark had also paid off his store account with those proceeds, after which he had fifty-four dollars left to last him until his next crop came in, many months later.[3]

After clearing his accounts, Clark had returned home. Within a few days, Curg had arrived on Clark's doorstep unannounced one late afternoon, accusing him of having stolen money and demanding repayment. Clark and Burleson had never spoken or even met before. Curg (who did not know Clark by sight, as indicated by the fact that he had to inquire as to whether he was at the right house) initially alleged that Clark had stolen $30.25 from Curg at a "colored frolic" west of Chireno in Nacogdoches County. What made the claim improbable was that it was apparently well known that the only white person present at that gathering had been a local law enforcement officer. Curg would be arrested, prosecuted, and tried for extortion in 1935, and during his trial, the allegation that Clark had stolen Curg's money was soon abandoned in favor of a story contending that Curg had loaned the money to Clark, which was arguably even more implausible.[4]

As Clark related in the trial, when Curg Burleson had come to his door and demanded payment, Clark protested and mentioned speaking to his landlord, John F. "Frank" Blount, about the matter. Curg said that he "didn't want anyone to know about it" and told Clark not to tell Blount because Curg didn't want to have to "whip or kill" Clark's landlord. Curg then told Clark that he would kill Clark if he did not give him the money. Out of fear for his life (and that of his landlord), Clark paid Curg a total of sixty dollars over the next several weeks. Clark, as ordered, delivered the first installment, fifteen dollars, to Curg in the front yard of the home of J. Henry and Sarah G. Steptoe, Curg's in-laws, and was refused a receipt from Curg when he requested it. He had paid the remaining three installments at the same location over the next few weeks and then kept quiet about the matter (other than telling his brother, who he cautioned not to tell anyone else). Once Clark paid Curg, he had no problems or interaction with him until December, when Curg and Tom Burleson came to Clark's home. The brothers accused Clark of stealing a pistol, and "[they] pulled me out into the yard," Clark testified. Once again, Curg had extorted payments from Clark, who again acquiesced since there was no one he could turn to for protection. Knowing the extent of the McClanahan-Burleson gang's local power, Clark had again made no immediate report of the crime. It was not until the Allred Rangers had arrested or run the Burlesons and McClanahans out town and then sought out Clark during their subsequent investigations that Clark finally told authorities what Curg and Tom had done to him. With Clark's formal accusation in hand, the Allred Rangers were then able to file formal charges and arrest Curg for the offenses against Clark.[5]

Clark was not the first to experience the greed of the McClanahan-Burleson gang, and he would not be the last. On September 1, 1934, about a month before Clark's first encounter with Curg Burleson, a middle-aged African American woman was the victim. Curg, with two accomplices, showed up at the home of Ella F. Curl and hauled off her livestock, a sow and two barrows (male hogs). Curl was living with her husband, Lamar, and her youngest son, Raymond Washington, on a rented farm belonging to Lee Matthews. The Matthews farm was located several miles outside of the town of San Augustine, near the end of a road called Blount Lane.[6]

To reach Blount Lane, one would have had to travel out of town along the highway until reaching the cotton gin just below Ben Allen's farm. Ella's place was about a mile off the highway, between which were three houses belonging to Tom Davis, Tony Matthews, and Felix Clifton, respectively. At approximately 1:00 P.M. on September 1, 1934, Curg Burleson, along with Vandy V. and Calvin Steptoe (his brothers-in-law), drove a team of two mules pulling a wagon to the last house on Blount Lane and inquired, "Is that Ella's house?" "Yes," Ella replied. With no further discussion, the three white men backed their wagon up to Ella's hog pen, loaded the two barrows and one sow that were in the pen into their wagon, and drove away.[7]

Only Ella and her son Raymond were at the house at the time. Both were sitting on the porch, having just finished their lunch and preparing to return to the fields. Neither of them moved or said anything to the men as they stole the hogs, because, as Raymond would explain during cross-examination at a trial that would be held August 10, 1935, they were afraid. And they had good reason to be afraid. The Curls never reported the robbery to law enforcement, and, just as with Ed Clark's experience, the case would only be investigated and prosecuted due to the Allred Rangers' 1935 cleanup of San Augustine.

In addition to outright theft, Tom Burleson and some members of the McClanahan family also frequently ran another scam on black sharecroppers. After convincing those living on outlying farms that they needed protection, a gang associate would give or sell sharecroppers a pistol. A short time later, either Joe Burleson or one of the McClanahans (who held special Ranger commissions and appointments as city marshals) would show up and arrest the victims for unlawfully possessing a handgun and coerce payment of a fine, under threat of jailing. The pistol was then "confiscated" by the accomplice officer and used to repeat the process on another victim. African American San Augustinians were well aware that leading members of the McClanahan-Burleson gang held local law enforcement posts, thereby giving their associates impunity and endangering the safety of those who sought recourse against them. They also knew that it wasn't just the lower-level gang members who committed these crimes. In July 1934, the de facto leaders of the gang, Charlie McClanahan, his brother Wade, and his nephew Wade Jr., along with then-sheriff W. C. Gary, assaulted a black woman named Della Cook and robbed her at gunpoint of a check worth over $300.[8]

Henry "Dudley" Clay was an African American citizen of San Augustine County who operated a still at his home in the woods far outside and to the east of town, where he produced bootleg whiskey. In 1933, the Twenty-First Amendment to the US Constitution repealed federal Prohibition laws, but the state Prohibition amendment—which had been passed in 1919—remained in effect until 1935. By the mid-1920s, state politics on the matter had shifted so that there was little political will for enforcement on the state level, leaving such matters primarily to local authorities. As the McClanahan-Burleson gang had effectively usurped that power by the early 1930s at the latest, all local producers of liquor were in a precarious position. The gang could exploit them with impunity, controlling all local trade in the officially prohibited but widely demanded product.[9]

Dudley Clay, however, did not submit to this exploitation. In late January or very early February 1934, leaders of the McClanahan-Burleson gang sent an associate named Tommy Davis to Clay's house, allegedly to try to make him sell his whiskey directly to them and at a price that they had determined without Clay's approval. Clay declined the offer, and, when Davis persisted, Clay allegedly chased Davis off his property at gunpoint.[10]

Shortly thereafter, on February 3, 1934, Joe Burleson, Vandy Steptoe, and a black man named Jeff Duffield approached the back of Clay's home at about four in the morning. Clay was in bed at the time, but his wife, Ida, their nephew Young Ruth, and a man named Frank Hart were awake and in the kitchen. Burleson, Steptoe, and Duffield stormed into the house out of the dark, after which Ida ran to the bedroom to wake her husband. When Clay groggily emerged from his room unarmed, Burleson, Steptoe, and Duffield shot him. Once Clay was dead, Burleson and his accomplices left the scene without taking any of the steps that a legitimate law enforcement operation would have taken under those circumstances. No other officers were called out to investigate, the local justice of the peace—Lannie

Smith—was not brought in to perform an inquest, as was customary, and no other local officials were notified or took any additional steps in the matter. Relatives were left to bury Clay in the family cemetery several miles west of San Augustine shortly after the murder.[11]

While the McClanahan-Burleson gang's criminal efforts were most often directed at black San Augustinians, they also had no compunction about inflicting violence against white citizens who dared to intervene on behalf of black victims or otherwise interfered in their illegal endeavors. Whenever local white citizens protested any of the gang's activities, their objections were met with threats, followed swiftly by physical violence if the complainant persisted. Several such people met untimely deaths between 1930 and 1934, and it was this bloodshed that first drew the attention of local leaders and eventually that of Governor Allred and his Texas Rangers. This violence was not random. Rather, it was almost entirely for the tactical purpose of protecting the gang's criminal enterprise by eliminating challengers and solidifying their control over the community.

The McClanahan-Burleson gang's reign of terror was not countered by law enforcement for years, since local law enforcement positions had been infiltrated and co-opted by members and associates of the gang. Its leaders had managed to gain authority through the acquisition of public offices, particularly commissions from Governor Ma Ferguson as special Rangers. As the local newspaper later characterized the situation, "Officials had completely 'layed-down' on the job and misdirected authority had prevailed until conditions had grown well nigh intolerable." This unequivocal statement came from a local editor known for his judicious and reserved treatment of local events generally, and who had totally avoided covering McClanahan-Burleson violence prior to the arrival of the Allred Rangers out of fear of retaliation from the gang.[12]

While the details of only a few criminal cases against the gang after the arrival of the Allred Rangers have been preserved in the court system, those cases emblematize the long-standing and wide-scale operations of the crime ring. The earliest officially documented "troubles" case to be prosecuted was the murder of a fifty-three year-old former manager of the San Augustine Chamber of Commerce, Edward Boone Brackett Sr., by Charlie McClanahan. Brackett was a popular local leader of the farming community who had moved into San Augustine County relatively recently, having come from Angelina County, where he had served as the federal agricultural agent. On October 14, 1930, he was driving into town in the vicinity of the Ayish Bayou Bridge when the forty-year-old McClanahan shot him twice with buckshot.[13]

McClanahan's motives for shooting Brackett are not clear. The tension between Brackett and McClanahan that had been building for at least two years as a result of several run-ins between them were well known throughout the community and beyond. The first may have arisen as the result of a report in the fall of 1928 by Brackett to the US postmaster general that McClanahan, a rural mail carrier at the time, was mishandling the delivery of mail from his assigned route. In addition McClanahan apparently had some sort of mail delivery–related confrontation with a black man named Jack Garrett and shortly thereafter, on November 10, 1928, shot Garrett to death with a pistol inside the Clark-Downs hardware store, claiming Garrett had insulted his wife. Despite being acquitted of murder, McClanahan lost his job as a postal carrier, which he apparently blamed on Brackett and J. W. McKnight, owner of the McKnight Bottling Company, for having reported the mishandling of mail. Sometime later, Charlie pistol-whipped McKnight at a gas station as his brother Wade pointed a gun at the victim to keep him from fleeing. Charlie told McKnight that he would kill him and Brackett too if they did not leave San Augustine County. At that, McKnight abandoned everything he owned, fled to Raymondville in South Texas, and then was said to have attempted to hire two assassins to kill Charlie, Wade, and three of their associates.[14]

Another confrontation between Brackett and McClanahan was of a more personal nature. When the Great Depression hit East Texas, the Brackett family was no more immune than any other. Edward Brackett Sr. had invested in cotton futures in early 1929, prior to the Black Friday stock market crash that ushered in the Great Depression. The financial success he had achieved was wiped out in one fell swoop, leaving the family deep in debt. Brackett did not believe in bankruptcy, so he worked diligently to manage his income from his farm judiciously and sought alternative but fair methods to compensate anyone he happened to owe. Sometime after the crash, Brackett paid one of his sharecroppers—a black man whose name is lost to history—with a set of mules trained for plowing. The arrangement involved an allowance for Brackett's continued access to the mules when needed. When Brackett sought access to the mules, per the agreement, the sharecropper was at first evasive when explaining that he no longer had the mules, which he eventually confessed had been stolen by Charlie McClanahan.[15]

Brackett was infuriated by McClanahan's theft of the mules and took them back at gunpoint, as was alleged later by McClanahan and his wife, but it would prove to be a short-lived victory. It was apparently then that McClanahan and his cohorts threatened Brackett's life, warning him never to show his face in town again. Brackett was apparently unfazed by the threats, however, and continued about his business in the community. But from that day forward, his wife insisted that either she or his daughter, Vivian, accompany him when going to town, assuming that McClanahan would not risk a confrontation in which a woman might be harmed. Brackett and McClanahan nearly came to blows in a local drugstore in July 1930, but Brackett's daughter apparently intervened.[16]

On October 14, 1930, Mrs. Brackett was canning vegetables and ran out of a staple ingredient, so she requested that Brackett go to town to pick up what she needed to complete the process. Since the confrontation and threats over the mules, Mrs. Brackett had typically insisted on accompanying Brackett whenever he went to town, but in this instance she could not leave, with the canning process well underway, so she instructed Brackett to take Vivian instead. Later Associated Press reports, printed in newspapers across the state, erroneously claimed that Brackett "had been to the country and was returning to town," but in fact he lived outside of town on his farm and was heading into town that day.[17]

Vivian accompanied her father part of the way but then asked him to let her out before town so she could meet up with some friends, which he did. Subsequently, about a quarter of a mile west of town, as he drove past the Fussell Cotton Gin, near the bridge crossing the Ayish Bayou, a shotgun blast pumped eighteen slugs of buckshot into the left side of his body, killing him almost instantly. Brackett's lifeless body slumped over in his car, which continued along the road a short distance before going into a ditch and coming to a halt. McClanahan had lain in wait on the side of the road in his own vehicle for Brackett to drive into his sights. After he fired from his seated position, McClanahan lowered the smoking shotgun and drove away.[18]

Numerous workers at the Fussell Cotton Gin had witnessed the ambush, and authorities promptly arrived on the scene, as did A. D. Clark, local mortician and brother of Allred aide Edward A. Clark. Brackett's car was towed to the Clark-Downs mortuary with Brackett's body still inside. Once there, Justice of the Peace J. W. Haygood ordered an inquest, which was conducted by Sheriff H. J. "Judge" Wilkinson, a member of a well-known, longstanding San Augustine family. During the examination of Brackett's body, not only were shotgun wounds found, but so too was a .45 automatic pistol, which Brackett carried under his coveralls. The pistol had a loaded magazine, but no round was chambered, which indicated that Brackett had not considered danger imminent and had not otherwise been planning to use the weapon on short notice. Details regarding the gun found on Brackett's body were omitted from the inquest report but were reported in the *San Augustine Tribune*. The pistol and its location, tucked away under Brackett's clothing, would prove to be an important piece of evidence in the prosecution, used to refute a defense claim that the shooting had been carried out in self-defense.[19]

Charlie McClanahan was the only suspect from the start. In addition to the numerous witnesses—virtually all of the employees of the cotton gin next to where the shooting occurred saw the murder—his history of conflict with Brackett was common knowledge. Local citizens John D. Clark (brother of Edward A. Clark) and Frank Blount both eventually testified to having witnessed McClanahan assault Brackett in the days or weeks just prior to the shooting and said that the attack was directly related to Brackett's opposition to McClanahan in the latter's race for sheriff.[20]

McClanahan was arrested the same day as the shooting and was quickly indicted, and the case was set for trial. The Brackett family engaged private attorney E. J. Mantooth to investigate and prosecute the case, but by the time of trial Mantooth had suffered severe health problems that prevented him from acting as prosecutor. This meant that Roy Blake, then district attorney, had to assume that responsibility despite being completely unfamiliar with the facts, witnesses, and all other aspects of the case. As soon as the trial commenced, Blake learned that few if any of the witnesses who remained in San Augustine had been successfully subpoenaed. It was evident to Blake that some of his key witnesses were not going to show and that a jury was unlikely to convict McClanahan, fearing retaliation. One witness, Ben Adams, committed suicide on the morning the trial began. Bud Hardin and F. K. Parker had also moved out of the county and the state, respectively, shortly after having witnessed the crime. This prompted the prosecutor to move for a mistrial rather than proceed, thus avoiding a not-guilty verdict and the risk of double jeopardy precluding prosecution if witnesses eventually decided to come forth. This wise tactic preserved the case for future prosecution. That chance would eventually come, but it would take five years and the support and protection of the Allred Rangers to create an environment where locals finally felt safe enough to take on McClanahan and his cohorts directly.[21]

Less than two years before murdering Brackett, McClanahan, as noted above, had shot a black man, Jack Garrett, after which he was tried for murder and acquitted. Due to the secret nature of jury proceedings, the reasoning behind the jury's verdict is unknown, but the jury in that trial—led by foreman H. C. Downs—included Sidney Lister Sr., a local citizen. Lister's son, Sidney Lister Jr., would be an eyewitness to a deadly McClanahan-Burleson gang showdown on the courthouse square in December 1934. When Lister Jr. told his father what he had seen, Lister Sr. related his experiences on the Garrett murder jury and advised his son not to speak of what he had witnessed, not to tell to anyone else, out of concern for his safety. By then it was no secret in San Augustine that McClanahan and his associates were to be feared.[22]

As a juror in the Garrett case, Lister Sr. had heard the statements of several witnesses whose testimony had led to McClanahan's indictment for murder, including Bill Mitchell, John Davis, Gladys Womack, and Mrs. A. Jones. Unfortunately, no record of their testimony has survived, but it comes as no surprise that local citizens including the Listers were hesitant to convict a man who appeared immune to prosecution and violently vindictive toward anyone who dared challenge that immunity. The situation caused the Lister family to adjust their lives. For example, Lister Sr. refused to go to town on weekends and holidays when crowds were largest and the likelihood of confrontations and violence were at their highest, preferring to make the trip on Wednesdays when it was typically the quietest, and even then he would not linger.[23]

Brackett was buried on October 30, 1930, in Timpson, about forty miles north of San Augustine, after a funeral was held at the family home near San Augustine. The services were well attended by locals and prominent citizens from surrounding communities, as well as Brackett's six siblings from Atlanta. In addition to Brackett's four brothers, H. R. Weaver from Merryville, Louisiana, and E. J. McElroy of Center, Texas, were pallbearers. Nine prominent citizens of San Augustine served as honorary pallbearers, including M. A. Johnson, W. R. "Dick" Thomas, Lamar Blount, C. W. Hurst, Knight Parker, Felix Lewis, W. F. Hays (editor of the San Augustine Tribune), W. H. Washington, and Edward A. Clark (then an assistant attorney general for Governor Allred). Brackett was eulogized as "a good, devout Christian man [who] was always interested in the welfare of all in every business relation, [and who] was the soul of honor, in every contact with his fellow man he was an exemplar of courtesy and refinement." It was evident that Brackett's family, friends, colleagues, and community would all sorely miss him. Brackett's murder inflicted wounds on the community and his family that would never fully heal and would continue to shape their lives for generations.[24]

In addition to the trauma of Brackett's murder, the delay in institutional justice would have a lasting effect on his family, most particularly for Edward Boone Brackett Jr., his son. Caught in a time and place of transition from culturally accepted vigilante justice to institutional justice, allowing "the system" to determine guilt and appropriate punishment, Brackett Jr. felt that his deeply ingrained sense of honor was at odds with his rational acceptance of law and order. At one point, frustration with the impotent local system of justice drove

Edward Boone Brackett Sr., Carrie Weaver "Non" Brackett,
and Edward Boone Brackett Jr. *Brackett family collection, courtesy
of E. B. Brackett III.*

him to consider taking his own revenge on McClanahan. Sometime shortly after
his father's murder, he sought out the one other man in San Augustine who was
well-known for not being afraid of the McClanahan-Burleson cabal, J. Elbert
Thomas, who, according to an unpublished memoir, agreed to assist Brackett Jr.
in a plan to settle the score with Charlie McClanahan, an effort they rationalized
as "an eye for an eye."[25]

Brackett Jr. and Thomas tracked McClanahan, learning his daily routines and
routes. They choose a location along one of those routes, where Thomas could
serve as the lookout and surreptitiously alert Brackett Jr. when McClanahan
was in sight. The plan was for Thomas to wait at a particular location and, when

McClanahan approached, play a particular song to let Brackett Jr. know he was near. At that point, Brackett Jr. would ambush the unsuspecting McClanahan as he came around the corner. But when the time came to execute the plan and avenge his father's murder, Brackett Jr. could not do it, he says: thoughts of his wife and children, combined with his religious beliefs, stopped him from becoming like the man whose life he had intended to take. Brackett Jr. then moved his family out of San Augustine and spent the next five years seeking justice through the courts, despite receiving no indication during most of that time that justice would be forthcoming. He also assumed the burden of his murdered father's stock market debts. It would take him nearly two decades, keeping his family in abject poverty despite earning a substantial income for the time, to retire those debts.[26]

Many locals shared Brackett Jr.'s disdain for the McClanahan-Burleson gang and frustration with the impotence of the local criminal justice system, though, as noted, most were too afraid to do anything about it. There were at least a few local young men who apparently had both the inclination and courage to speak out and act against the gang's depredations, but they did so at their own peril, and their fates further entrenched local fear and the McClanahan-Burleson gang's growing power. The murder of John Gann is one such case in point.

Despite his murderous disposition, Charlie McClanahan was not the only or most bloodthirsty member of the gang. Their most prolific killer turned out to be Tom Burleson, the youngest of the Burleson brothers, just twenty-one years old in the summer of 1933. Described, even by his own close friends and relatives who professed strong affinity for him, as a violent, unstable sociopath, Burleson was locally infamous for his insecurity, his violent temper, and for the fact that he always carried a pistol in the waistband of his pants—despite the fact that he had no legal authority to do so. It was a volatile combination. Tom was arguably the most unstable and feared person involved in the troubles, and his predilection for violence kept black and white San Augustinians alike on edge. His murder of an unarmed and unsuspecting schoolteacher, John Gann, in broad daylight on the town square cemented his reputation among San Augustinians as a cold-blooded killer and helped to tighten the grip of the McClanahan-Burleson gang.

John Gann was a twenty-three-year old white male, a respected local schoolteacher who was originally from the nearby town of Nacogdoches, the largest city in that part of East Texas. Gann was married and a new father, and he was, by all accounts, an up-and-coming member of the community, with his life before him. According to witness testimony, Gann interfered in Burleson's attempted relationship with a high school student named Almeta Steptoe. Some

Local men gathered outside Mathews store, adjacent to Clark-Downs store. *Photo by Russell Lee. Library of Congress, LC-DIG-fsa-8a25909.*

accounts indicate that Tom had initiated a fight with a competing suitor on the local high school campus where Gann taught. Gann is said to have stepped in to defend the unidentified student and bested Burleson, who swore revenge as he skulked away with his pride more damaged than his body.[27]

Unfortunately for Gann and his new family, sometime before noon on Saturday, August 5, 1933, Tom proved true to his word. Gann was standing on the sidewalk near the west entrance of the Clark-Downs store, apparently doing some shopping while his wife remained at home caring for their infant daughter. Clark-Downs was located in a building facing south on the north side of the courthouse square. It was a single structure partitioned into a dry goods department ("ladies and gents ready to wear") that comprised the eastern half of the building, with its own doorway, and a hardware department on the western side, also with its own entry. Each door was inset, with showcase windows protruding out on either side, along the sidewalk. Clark-Downs was adjacent to (and east of) Mathews and Company grocery, with a concrete walkway in front connecting the buildings, though the walkway in front of Mathews and Company was two to three feet lower than the portion in front of Clark-Downs. West of the grocery was the Café Texan, then a saddle shop, and then Green's Café. The distance between the grocery entry and the Clark-Downs' hardware entry was approximately twenty-five feet, with steps connecting the vertically offset concrete walkway about halfway in between. The Commercial Bank was down at the eastern corner of the block and adjacent to Clark-Downs, with its entrance also opening southward toward the courthouse.[28]

Gann had gone to Clark-Downs to make a purchase and was standing in front of the store after finishing his shopping. He was facing south toward the courthouse and had his arms crossed and his back to the showcase window, at the eastern corner next to the doorway for the hardware department. Suddenly, four men approached him from across the street after parking directly across from Gann. The four men were Tom Burleson, Eron Harris, Sandy Thacker, and Sandy's cousin Noah Thacker.[29]

The four men had been riding around town in Tom's Model A Ford roadster, the type with a rumble seat in the back, drinking liquor and horsing around. Tom, Sandy, and Eron picked up Noah at Tom Smith's store, which was about three to four blocks west of Clark-Downs, on the same side of the same street, around 11:30 A.M. They first drove west, away from town, but by noon they were headed back east straight into town. On the way, they stopped off at J. W. Stewart's grocery store, which was near the railroad tracks and about two blocks from Clark-Downs. They went inside the store to buy a pack of cigarettes, and there they were overheard daring an unknown member of the group, "I bet you a dollar you will" and "I bet you a dollar you won't." Shortly afterward, they returned to the car and drove away toward town. Minutes later, Gann was dead.[30]

Burleson, Harris, and the Thackers were traveling eastbound in Tom's Ford when they stopped and parked across from Clark-Downs. It was Tom's car, and he was the driver, though accounts differ as to who sat in the front passenger seat and who was in the rumble seat, Harris or Sandy Thacker. There was a parking lot adjacent to the courthouse where they stopped, but they left the vehicle parked on the street. When they exited the vehicle, they paused a moment to talk and for Tom to adjust something in his waistband, and then they hurried across the street, walking basically abreast and directly up to Gann. They went straight toward him as a group and jumped up nearly three feet onto the sidewalk together right in front of him instead of diverting a short distance to take either of two sets of stairs up to the sidewalk.[31]

Oblivious to his fate, Gann appeared to be smiling as they approached and began talking to him. Burleson, Harris, and the Thackers took up positions effectively surrounding Gann, who shook each of the four men's hands in turn,

Clark-Downs storefront, site of the murder of local teacher John Gann. *Photo by Russell Lee. Library of Congress, LC-USW3-025299-D.*

Harris last. Noah Thacker said, "Yes, look him in the eye and tell him and shake his hand," and then Harris said, "You Goddamned son of a bitch, I said shake hands with him, and look him in the eye," just before he "shoved Gann or hit him." As soon as Harris released his grip on Gann's hand, he suddenly struck Gann on the left side of the head with his right fist, knocking Gann back three to four feet, past the showcase window and into the doorway. Harris stepped back away from Gann after striking him and said, "Shoot him, Tom," at which point Burleson pulled out pistol and began firing at Gann, who turned and fled into the store as fast as he could in an attempt to escape. Expressing no surprise at this turn of events, the Thackers calmly backed up and moved out of Burleson's way.[32]

Burleson followed the fleeing Gann into the store and continuing to fire at him. One of the shots either missed or passed through Gann and grazed the right arm of sixty-year-old farmer Reece Mathews, a bystander in the store. Gann took ten to fifteen steps inside the store and then collapsed onto the floor and bled to death. Burleson began cursing at Gann, threatening to kill him, although he had shot Gann at least four times and Gann was dead. According to a statement by a witness, as quoted in later trial transcripts, he hollered, "Any

God Dam son-of-a-bitch that jumps on any of my brothers or my brother-in-law [presumably a reference to Harris], I will kill him." Burleson also repeatedly called for the already-deceased Gann to "come on out [of the store] and shoot it out." Noah Thacker walked around the store looking over the counters in an apparent attempt to locate Gann, then left the scene quickly with Sandy Thacker, Harris, and Burleson in tow. Immediately after the shooting, Burleson's oldest brother, Joe—who had been waiting down at the corner near the bank—ran up quickly and "[took] hold of Tom" and removed him across the street and then from the scene to an unknown location.[33]

Gann took his last breaths in the arms of E. L. "Buddy" Mitchell, who had witnessed the shooting and followed Gann into the store in a futile attempt to render aid. Mitchell later provided a description to the court:

> I went on into the store where Gann was. I went up to Gann . . . reached down and raised Gann up and pulled him out from under the counter he fell under and raised him up. Gann breathed I reckon maybe two or three times after I raised him up . . . seemed like blood gushed out . . . just above his hip . . . blood was coming out his mouth and nose.
> John Gann died; he quit breathing and I laid him down.[34]

After the scene cleared, Gann's body was eventually taken to the home of Collis Sowell, which was about fifteen miles south of town. There, Dr. C. H. Huff examined the body and determined the cause of death. Huff had been practicing medicine in San Augustine for about twenty-three years, having moved there in 1912. Huff found multiple bullet wounds in Gann's torso, "midway between the right shoulder and right breast," including one exit wound and another where the bullet had already been removed with a knife. He located another bullet wound "just about the right hip bone in the back" that had "[come] out just under the belt at his watch pocket." Huff found that Gann had a watch in that pocket at the time of his death, and that "the bullet was embedded in the watch; this bullet evidently hit the hip bone and glanced out." Huff also noted contusions on Gann's face, consistent with the later testimony of numerous witnesses who saw Harris punch Gann in the face right before Tom shot him. It was Huff's opinion that the bullet that caused Gann's death was the one "that entered the right breast and came out the lower part of the left shoulder." He concluded by noting that with such a wound, death could have occurred anywhere from instantaneously to thirty to forty minutes later.[35]

Like Brackett's murder, the killing of Gann was senseless, cruel, and demonstrative of the degree to which the McClanahan-Burleson gang was willing to use violence against anyone who dared challenge them or otherwise attempt to interfere with their criminal activities. Those activities ran the gamut of typical early-twentieth-century organized crime, including gambling, robbery, extortion, theft, and counterfeiting. They were also involved in small-scale racketeering, exemplified by their attempts to control local bootleggers. While none of the McClanahans or Burlesons were found to have been manufacturing bootleg liquor during this time, many of their associates did so, and they attempted to control others who wished to remain independent. However, the McClanahan-Burleson gang leaders did not suffer resistance gladly, instead responding with the same brutality that they had visited upon Brackett and Gann.

—3—
NO HONOR AMONG THIEVES

Not all of the white victims of the McClanahan-Burleson gang were people who had resisted or otherwise interfered with the gang's operations. Some had attempted to work with them. One of the gang's crimes, which led to jury trial convictions of two leading members, was the armed robbery of a small-time criminal who came to town looking to do illicit business with them. However, just as gang members saw blacks as easy prey due to their marginalized status, they also recognized the vulnerability of poor whites whose activities as petty criminals compromised them and effectively excommunicated them from mainstream society and its legal protections. When small-time outsiders showed up hoping to do illicit business with the gang, they sometimes found themselves victimized. The San Augustine County gangsters exemplify the proverb "there's no honor among thieves."

A nineteen-year-old Nacogdoches area man named Curtis Butler learned of the McClanahan-Burleson counterfeiting operations and attempted to purchase some counterfeit bills from Jim Burleson, only to find himself a victim of an armed robbery at the hands of Jim and his associate and brother-in-law, Lee "Red" Jordan. An associate who knew Jim Burleson had informed Butler that there was counterfeit money to be had in San Augustine. On July 2, 1934, Butler and three accomplices (Frank Wells, I. J. Stone, and John Minifield) drove into San Augustine together, expecting to purchase some of the fraudulent currency.[1]

Wells introduced Butler to Jim downtown, near the courthouse, and Butler met Jim again later, alone at a nearby café. Jim told Butler that he would not be able to deliver any counterfeit bills to him until late in the evening, after an accomplice "came in off the farm." Jim told Butler that he would not meet him in the daytime and that Butler would have to stay in San Augustine overnight and wait for Jim's associate to contact him if he wanted to buy any counterfeit bills from them. Butler then rented a room at a local boardinghouse at approximately 6:00 P.M. that evening, went to a movie, and then returned to his room around nine-thirty to wait, as he had been instructed to do by Jim.[2]

Approximately thirty minutes later, Jim appeared at the door of Butler's room, though Butler had never told Jim where he would be staying. According to later trial transcripts, Jim told Butler "that [a] fellow called 'Red'" would come to see him and "settle off" the transaction for the counterfeit bills. Jim then left the room, and about a minute later Red Jordan entered the room and pointed a large pistol (of unknown caliber) at Butler and demanded his money. Fearing for his life, Butler turned over sixty-five dollars from his billfold, though he managed to retain approximately five dollars in change that was concealed in his watch pocket. Jim was standing just outside the door watching the robbery as it occurred. Jordan then left the room, left the boardinghouse, and got into a car with Jim, who drove away to the west.[3]

The aspiring criminal discovered how desperate the situation was when he tried to report the robbery. Immediately after Jordan and Jim left, Butler went to the local fire station to find out how to contact local law enforcement so that he could report the robbery. He was given the name of an Officer McClanahan and a phone number, but McClanahan did not respond. Butler went to Wade McClanahan Sr.'s office early next morning and reported to McClanahan and an unidentified officer, who was likely Wade Jr., that he had been robbed at gunpoint and could identify the parties involved. The San Augustine officers refused to record or investigate Butler's complaint but instead advised him to get out of town before he got killed.[4]

Butler took the advice seriously and caught a bus back home to Douglass, Texas, in Nacogdoches County, as quickly as possible, but he did not let the matter drop. After returning home, Butler reported the robbery to the local sheriff, who said he lacked the authority to take action regarding crimes that occurred outside his own jurisdiction. Butler then told his father and a few friends (including Wells and Stone, who had accompanied him to San Augustine) what had happened. Having exhausted all known avenues for reporting the crime and fearing that any continued efforts to get the matter resolved in San Augustine would result in his demise, Butler finally dropped the matter, having learned that justice was not to be found as long as the McClanahan-Burleson regime remained in power.[5]

While murder was the ultimate crime through which the gang enforced its illegitimate rule and gained notoriety locally and beyond, it did not represent their daily criminal activities or how they obtained and maintained day-to-day local control. Key members were commonly engaged in various schemes that they believed would provide them a cloak of legitimacy. Although many of the gang members and associates had managed to obtain special Ranger commissions from Ma Ferguson for their political loyalty, such commissions did not come with salaries and were less effective for their illicit purposes than locally elected or appointed law enforcement positions. Usurpation of local public offices, particularly key law enforcement positions such as county sheriff, constable, and city marshal, was a crucial component of the McClanahan-Burleson gang's rise and preservation of control over the community. They preferred county offices over municipal ones because county offices gave them wider geographical control and came with taxpayer-funded salaries. There are also indications that the gang's special Ranger commission holders or the local sheriff, Warren C. Gary, deputized some of the Burlesons during the last few years of their reign.

It was thus that Wade McClanahan Sr. ran for constable in the election held in July 1934. Wade Sr. chose not to leave the outcome to chance. He and Wade Jr. stole a ballot box from the district clerk's office in an apparent attempt to rig the results. Nevertheless, Sublett Sharp defeated Wade Sr., who was livid and shot out the windows of several stores when he found out their owners had not voted for him. No local law enforcement officers took action.

Shortly after Tom and Curg Burleson and their associates extorted and robbed African American farmers Ed Clark and Ella Curl (see chapter 2), they joined their brothers Joe and Jim Burleson, Charlie McClanahan and his brother and nephew Wade Sr. and Wade Jr., and Sheriff Gary in what was arguably their most brazen crime: attacking a federal officer who had come to town to investigate one of their many alleged illicit activities. The assault took place in broad daylight and in full view of hundreds of people.[6]

On October 6, 1934, Secret Service agent E. C. Cleveland, who was in Beaumont to investigate counterfeit notes and forged checks that had recently been passed in that town, received a telegram from his superior at the regional headquarters in San Antonio with information regarding a possible counterfeiting ring operating out of San Augustine. The telegram instructed Cleveland to meet with Chief of Police Lucien B. Maddox of Beaumont, who would provide additional information. This instruction to Cleveland reveals the federal government's ignorance of the extent of the corruption in San Augustine. Chief Maddox advised Cleveland that a man named W. S. Smith had direct knowledge of the San Augustine counterfeiting ring but was currently in his hometown of Vidor. Cleveland went to Vidor to speak with Smith directly, only to learn that he had departed for Galveston and left no forwarding address. Cleveland then returned to Beaumont, where Maddox assured Cleveland that he would be able to "obtain authentic information" in regard to counterfeiting in San Augustine, including the exact location where the notes were being made.[7]

On October 9, Cleveland telegraphed his boss, saying that he was going to San Augustine "unless otherwise directed," to proceed with further investigation. The "operative-in-charge" of the Secret Service field office in San Antonio, which exercised jurisdiction over San Augustine during the mid-1930s and to which Cleveland was assigned, was Edward Tyrrell. As operative-in-charge of a regional office, Tyrrell reported directly to the chief of the US Secret Service, at that time William H. Moran. The day before, Cleveland had waited more than two hours for W. S. Smith, who had failed to show up for a scheduled meeting Maddox had arranged with him at the Beaumont Police Station. Since Tyrrell had provided him with the name of an additional potential informant who was supposed to be located in San Augustine, Cleveland proceeded directly there to investigate.[8]

Cleveland did not know that the counterfeiters he was seeking in San Augustine were actually corrupt local officials who controlled the town, enabled in part by Ferguson special Ranger commissions. Upon his arrival in San Augustine on the morning of October 11, Cleveland telegraphed Tyrrell to advise him that there was no hotel in town and therefore Tyrrell would have to contact him via the local US Post office. Secret Service operatives had been authorized to carry firearms since the agency's inception, but Cleveland did not indicate whether or not he was armed when he set off for San Augustine.[9]

Cleveland drove to the farm of the informant that Tyrrell had told him about, a local man named Robert L. Ellis, who was sharecropping a farm belonging to the Burlesons. Ellis was not there when Cleveland first arrived, and according to Secret Service records "a negro" informed him that the San Augustine County Fair was going on and that Ellis would be returning home from there at about one that afternoon. Cleveland returned to the room he had rented in town waited until one, and then returned to Ellis's farm. Finding Ellis, Cleveland did not immediately identify himself as an officer. Ellis said that he believed his landlords

US Secret Service chief William H. Moran (*left*), retiring in 1936 after fifty-four years of service, with his successor Frank J. Wilson (*center*) and Secretary of the Treasury Henry Morgenthau Jr. (*right*). *Photo by Russell Lee. Library of Congress, LC-DIG-hec-21921.*

were manufacturing counterfeit notes in cooperation with the McClanahans and said they had cheated Ellis out of several hundred pounds of cotton (which may explain his willingness to talk despite the risk to his safety).[10]

Ellis described the McClanahans and Burlesons as "great crooks and bad men," who had all "killed one or two men each." But Ellis insisted that they trusted him enough that he would be able to obtain more extensive details on their counterfeiting operation. When Cleveland finally told Ellis that he was a Secret Service agent, Ellis indicated unequivocally that he was willing to assist Cleveland but expressed great concern over being found out, fearing for his life. Ellis suggested that they remain at his farm until dark and then head to the fairgrounds, by which time all of the suspects would be there. Cleveland agreed, and they left together for the

Entrance to San Augustine County Fairgrounds, site of the assault on a US Secret Service operative by leaders of the McClanahan-Burleson gang. *Photo by Russell Lee. Library of Congress, LC-DIG-fsa-8a25897.*

fairgrounds at approximately 7:30 P.M., at which point they split up after agreeing on a time to meet back at Cleveland's car later in the evening.[11]

Unbeknown to Cleveland, members of the McClanahan-Burleson gang—Wade McClanahan Jr. (a special Ranger and deputy city marshal) and Burleson brothers Joe (who was also a special Ranger), Jim, Tom, Curg, and Edward Jr.—along with Sheriff Gary, Deputy Sheriff Walter Sheffield, and Hillis Smith had become aware of his presence at the fairgrounds and began coordinating to gather and confront him. Sheffield, Joe Burleson, and Smith then went into town to find Charlie and Wade McClanahan Sr., who returned to the fairgrounds with them in search of Cleveland. At approximately 8:30 P.M., those eleven men approached Cleveland, "all wearing belts and pistols," the record would later state, and introduced themselves as McClanahans and Burlesons.[12]

Although Cleveland was ostensibly undercover, wearing nondescript street clothes and possibly unarmed, the gangsters told him that as "State Rangers" and the local sheriff, "they had heard [he] was a Federal" and "that they did not allow federal men" in San Augustine, adding that they thought it would be a good idea to kill him. Cleveland showed them his Secret Service credentials, but they suggested that he had found them and again threatened to kill him. Suddenly one of them struck him in the head from behind, and then the others joined in, beating, kicking, and pistol-whipping him. As described by a witness, "Several men flashed guns on [Cleveland] and someone hit [him] from behind. [He] was knocked down and manhandled." Tom struck Cleveland with brass knuckles, which he "always carried on the side," the record would state. In what almost resulted in the cold-blooded murder of a federal agent, in broad daylight and in front of hundreds of people, Tom attempted to shoot Cleveland. Fortunately Deputy Sheffield "grabbed [Tom's] gun and did not allow him to do so." Charlie and Wade McClanahan Sr. and Sheffield then took Cleveland outside of the fairgrounds, where they examined his credentials under a flashlight, again threatened to kill him, and finally let him go.[13]

The assault on Cleveland left him with two head lacerations and a black eye. He managed to get away from his attackers and reached his car around 9:30 P.M., only to discover that his two front tires had been slashed. Cleveland changed the tires and tried to find a local garage to store his car overnight, to prevent any further vandalism, but no one would allow him to do that, fearing reprisal. Cleveland was forced to drive to Nacogdoches that night, arriving around midnight, after which he sent a telegram to Tyrrell. The next morning he drove to Beaumont, but his car broke down en route because someone had put sand in the engine. Shortly after finally arriving in Beaumont, Cleveland stopped by the police station, where Chief Maddox gave him a letter from W. S. Smith, the informant from Vidor who was supposed to have information regarding the counterfeiting operation. Smith advised in the letter that he was working on a road gang six miles south of Nacogdoches. The available documents do not show whether Cleveland or his fellow operatives made any further effort to contact Smith. Rather, their attention became focused on the assault from that point forward.[14]

Tyrrell had not received any communications from Cleveland since the day before he went to San Augustine, until a telegram sent from the Redland Hotel in Nacogdoches late on October 11, 1935, arrived on the morning of the following day with the terse update, "FINISHED VICINITY SAN AUGUSTINE PLEASE WIRE INSTRUCTIONS CARE REDLAND HOTEL HERE." The next two telegrams from Cleveland only stated, "IN BEAUMONT EDSON HOTEL STOP REPORTS SUBMITTED TO DATE" and "NOTHING HERE NEEDING ATTENTION PLEASE WIRE INSTRUCTIONS." Tyrrell had no reason to suspect that Cleveland might be in danger, although he did express concern that Cleveland's daily reports had not yet arrived. Operatives had been required to file detailed daily reports of their activities since the agency's founding, so their absence indicated that something might be amiss.[15]

Cleveland's reports did not arrive until the evening of October 12, after Tyrrell had gone home. Upon learning the next morning that Cleveland had been "ganged" and "badly beaten" by eleven men in San Augustine, "including the Sheriff," Tyrrell advised Cleveland to immediately notify the US attorney for the Eastern District of Texas in Beaumont, S. D. Bennett, and then report Bennett's response. Tyrrell also reminded Cleveland to refer Bennett to the "new act against the assault of federal officers in the discharge of their duties," an apparent reference to a statute included in the Crime Control Acts of 1934. Tyrrell ordered also Cleveland to send him a comprehensive written report of the entire affair. Chief Moran concurred and advised Tyrrell to "adopt every possible measure . . . to prosecute persons responsible for the attack on Operative Cleveland." Tyrrell also ordered his other operatives back to their headquarters in San Antonio at the same time as Cleveland, presumably to advise them of the assault and engage them in the investigation.[16]

On Saturday, October 13, 1934, Cleveland met with Bennett, who directed him to file a complaint against all of the men he could identify from San Augustine and to try to obtain some witnesses to the assault. Cleveland called to relay those instructions to Tyrrell, who then instructed Cleveland to go back to Bennett and advise him that Tyrrell was under subpoena in both Houston and San Antonio on Monday and therefore would be unable begin that process until the following week. Tyrrell also asked Bennett to use his own judgment as to whether or not to have the US marshal for his district serve a warrant on his own or wait until Tyrrell and some of his men would be available to assist with the warrant and begin the investigation. Tyrrell noted that it would behoove them to conduct those witness interviews while the accused assailants were out of town being arraigned.[17]

After meeting with Bennett and submitting a complete report as instructed, Cleveland returned to San Antonio and reported to Tyrrell in person on Sunday morning, the next day. After interviewing Cleveland about the incident and observing his injuries, Tyrrell sent the agent home to rest and recover. Tyrrell then assigned Luis M. Benavides—believed to have been the first Latino Secret Service agent—to assist him in investigating the assault on Cleveland. The two of them moved quickly to locate and interview witnesses. In the process they uncovered not only witnesses but also widespread fear of testifying against the McClanahan-Burleson gang.[18]

At Chief Moran's suggestion, Tyrrell called Bennett directly to discuss "the Burleson-McClanahan gang in San Augustine." Bennett told him that "he believed that a case could be made against all parties involved in violation of 454-B, Title 18, U.S.C.A." and that he was open to suggestions from the Secret Service command as to handling of the case. Charges were filed that same day against the seven assailants who could be identified by Cleveland at that time. Charges were also filed against the informant Robert Ellis, as Cleveland believed that he must have set him up for the assault. On Monday, October 15, Tyrrell received a collect call from a "Mr. York," manager of the Burns Detective Agency in Houston, informing Tyrrell that Ellis was with him and had not only witnessed Cleveland's beating in San Augustine but had himself been beaten up by the same men shortly thereafter. Tyrrell arranged for York and Ellis to contact Benavides, who was already in Houston under subpoena to testify in a federal court hearing. Tyrrell then contacted Benavides, who arranged to meet with York and Ellis that evening.[19]

Tyrrell left for Houston early the next morning and soon arrived at the Milby Hotel. There he met with Benavides before Cleveland arrived around noon, a day earlier than originally expected. They met with York that afternoon, arranged a follow-up meeting with Ellis, and then went to see him at the home of a relative "on the outskirts of Houston." Tyrrell noted that he observed extensive injuries to Ellis, including extensive bruising on his face, indicating that he had indeed been badly beaten up.[20]

Ellis related the events that had followed after he and Cleveland had split up at the San Augustine Fairgrounds on the evening of October 11. Not only had he witnessed the beating of Cleveland and could name each of the attackers, he also related the details of his own attack. He claimed that, the following evening, the gang members confronted him about Cleveland, at which point he admitted that Cleveland was a "government agent" and that Cleveland had questioned Ellis about them. Ellis said that Wade McClanahan Sr. "met him on the road" and struck him several times about the head and face with a "six-shooter." Ellis further related that McClanahan had informed him that they knew Cleveland was a federal agent and that he had questioned Ellis about them. McClanahan then ended the conversation by ordering Ellis "to leave that section of the country," which Ellis promptly did. He went to stay with relatives in Houston, where York had brought Tyrrell for the interview. Ellis's injuries and eagerness to cooperate with the Secret Service by identifying and testifying against the McClanahans and Burlesons demonstrated to Tyrrell that Ellis had not betrayed Cleveland and would be a "handy" informant and witness in the case. The charges against Ellis were dropped, and Tyrrell assigned Cleveland to work some cases in the Rio Grande Valley.[21]

In further investigation of the San Augustine assault, Tyrrell and Benavides headed to Beaumont on Wednesday, October 17, after calling ahead to Bennett to request a joint meeting with him and the US marshal to discuss the San Augustine case. After Tyrrell and Benavides arrived in Beaumont, Bennett picked them up at their hotel and drove them to the home of Deputy Marshal Abernathy. Tyrrell said that he and Benavides could accompany Abernathy into San Augustine to serve the warrants, but Abernathy declined their assistance and insisted that he would go alone. Abernathy apparently cut the meeting short, indicating that he had just arrived back in town and had not received the warrants or any other information on the case and requesting that Tyrrell and Bennett meet him at his office the next morning. Tyrrell stopped by the marshal's office in the morning, at which point Abernathy told Tyrrell to call US Marshal John B. Ponder (Abernathy's boss) in Tyler to discuss the San Augustine case. When Tyrrell offered again to accompany Abernathy into San Augustine to serve the warrants, Abernathy claimed that he "was under a doctor's care" and would not be able to make the trip.[22]

Tyrrell was skeptical of Abernathy's claim, believing that Abernathy had become frightened once he learned of the extent of the McClanahan-Burleson gang's violence. Tyrrell wrote in his daily report, "[Abernathy] evidently was scared hearing the reports of the out-lawed bunch in that county." During a subsequent phone call, Tyrrell related to Ponder's chief deputy his concerns regarding Abernathy's unwillingness to act on the warrants, and this person, the chief deputy, requested that Tyrrell discuss the matter with Bennett and have him phone the marshal. Bennett then suggested that Tyrrell call US district judge Randolph Bryant in San Augustine and have him arrange for all of the accused to turn themselves in, thereby avoiding embarrassing the deputy marshal or worse in case of a showdown. When Bennett finally reached Marshal Ponder in Tyler, Judge Bryant got on the phone and also counseled them to proceed with caution. Tyrrell acquiesced, and Bennett called San Augustine County Attorney C. Smith Ramsey, who said that he would call back that afternoon with an answer as to whether the McClanahans, Burlesons, and others accused in the assault on Cleveland would voluntarily turn themselves in to federal authorities in Beaumont.[23]

Ramsey called back later that day to say that the sheriff would produce all the men named in the warrant—that they would appear the next day at the federal courthouse in Beaumont. This commitment was not particularly reassuring to Tyrrell, since the sheriff, Warren Gary, was one of those involved in the assault. Upon receiving this news, Bennett requested that Tyrrell remain in town to see whether the men would actually appear and, if they did, what their initial response to the charges would be. Despite his many other obligations across the state, Tyrrell made arrangements to stay in Beaumont with Cleveland and Benavides. He also had subpoenas issued for Robert Ellis and his wife in case their testimony was needed to substantiate the government's charges.[24]

The next morning, Friday, October 19, Tyrrell, Benavides, and Cleveland met at length with Bennett at his office to prepare for the hearing later that morning. Bennett had received word earlier that morning that the suspects were in town and would appear as promised. The hearing was presided over by a US commissioner (federal magistrate judge) named Morris and got underway at 11:00 A.M. Upon hearing presentation of the government's evidence as well as the defendants' claims and denials, Commissioner Morris ruled that there was sufficient evidence to hold the suspects under bond in anticipation of federal grand jury proceedings that would take place the following Monday. After negotiations between Bennett and defense counsel Steve M. King, Commissioner Morris approved bonds in the amount of $1,000 for each defendant. The defendants were allowed to return to San Augustine to prepare their bonds and instructed to return to Beaumont on Monday with the required documents. That afternoon, Tyrrell and Benavides departed for Houston, leaving Cleveland in Beaumont to prepare additional reports and otherwise assist Bennett in preparing to present the case to a federal grand jury.[25]

By the time Tyrrell arrived in Houston, Cleveland had already sent him a telegram saying that Bennett would not present the case to the federal grand jury on Monday and that Bennett insisted instead that Tyrrell conduct a more thorough investigation of the matter. Bennett specifically requested that Tyrrell go into San Augustine and seek more witnesses to the assault. Tyrrell expressed frustration at the delay, and his dissatisfaction was compounded by the fact that the assailants' only defense, as articulated by defense counsel King at the preliminary hearing, consisted of a simple denial and the claim that Cleveland had been intoxicated, which he considered to be ridiculous.[26]

Tyrrell believed that such a delay would merely serve the defendants' interests and that the combination of Cleveland's and the Ellises' testimony was more than sufficient for an indictment. But since Bennett was the federal prosecutor with discretion over which cases to present and when, his request for supplemental investigation had to be fulfilled. Pursuant to Bennett's instructions, Tyrrell and Benavides spent the next several months going to San Augustine and seeking witnesses to the assault on Cleveland. While they found many who corroborated Cleveland's claims and debunked the intoxication defense, few were willing to risk testifying in open court, fearing reprisal by the McClanahans and Burlesons. Tyrrell began by interviewing the city manager, G. C. Mitchell, who explained at length that the McClanahans and Burlesons were both corrupt and deadly and that everyone in town knew it, and no locals were likely to testify, fearing for their lives. Locals were so fearful that they would not even serve as jurors against them, he said, adding, "The Sheriff and the rest of the bunch would frame Cleveland if they could."[27]

It was becoming clear to the Secret Service that it would be difficult to obtain willing witnesses. Two who agreed were "Mrs. Athenian Wade, postmistress," and her husband, William M. Wade, proprietor of the City Café, who both stated that Cleveland was sober. William Wade added that any suggestion otherwise was "a pure frame up" on the part of the defendants, just as Mitchell had said. Mrs. U. D. Lynch, who ran the boardinghouse where Cleveland first tried to get a room, volunteered to testify on his behalf. Mrs. Fred Rike, proprietor of the Uptown Inn where Cleveland stayed, also agreed to testify to his sobriety and professional demeanor.[28]

Other locals identified as witnesses, including "garage man" P. B. Bickley, either denied to Tyrrell and his men having seen anything or refused to speak to them at all, fearing retaliation. Bickley referred Tyrrell's agents to a "Mr. Stewart," a grocery store butcher, but he made it clear to them that Stewart would back up the McClanahans' story. A former local law enforcement officer named Watkins and another man, who refused to provide his name, both stated that they had seen the entire event and that Cleveland "did nothing in any way to justify the attack." Watkins was apparently willing to testify, but the anonymous man was unwilling, although he stated that a former sheriff, Henry J. Wilkinson, had also witnessed the attack and was willing to testify. But Wilkinson was out of town, and Tyrrell would not get the opportunity to meet with him until months later. A Mr. Roberts at Commercial State Bank referred Tyrrell to Lula Graham, who acknowledged that she had seen the Burlesons "jump on [Cleveland] without cause" and said that Cleveland was "sober and in his right mind." Graham expressed reluctance to testify, though. The Secret Service records note: "[She] lives alone and they would not hesitate to kill her."[29]

Once they had exhausted their leads in San Augustine, Tyrrell and his men began to look farther afield. Mitchell, the city manager, suggested talking to the fair operators (Roy Gray and his wife, owners of Big State Shows) because he knew them to have been witnesses along with some of their crew. He theorized that since they did not live in the community, they might be less reticent about testifying. The Grays acknowledged witnessing the assault, stating that they saw a group of men surrounding Cleveland with their guns pointed at him and that he did not appear to be intoxicated or otherwise impaired. Unfortunately, the Grays were equally aware of the McClanahans' and Burlesons' reputations for violence, and therefore they were just as fearful of testifying.[30]

The Grays referred Tyrrell to a couple of their crewmen, Lee Vernon and his son, Mearle. Lee told them that he had arrived at the scene of the attack at the very end and seen a hatless, blonde young man about five foot eight, weighing about 155 pounds, "attempt to pull a gun from inside his shirt to shoot at Cleveland," but then "some woman took this man on with her." Tyrrell noted that the description fit "the youngest McClanahan," presumably Wade McClanahan Jr. Vernon told Tyrrell that he and his son could both "swear that Cleveland was perfectly sober and in his right mind at all times during the affair" and that they would be "glad to make sworn affidavits to these statements," but that they preferred "not to appear in court personally" because they planned to work in San Augustine again the following year.[31]

Cleveland, Tyrrell, and their fellow Secret Service operatives may have been the first government authorities from outside of San Augustine County to encounter the violence of the McClanahan-Burleson gang, the realization of which intimidated both their colleagues in the US Marshals Service and the prosecutors at the regional Department of Justice office. For many local citizens, this fear was becoming desperation and resentment of the oppression and violence. On December 22, 1934, events were set in motion that would shift the community's course away from a culture of unregulated justice and toward legitimate institutional justice.

Tom Burleson was well known as a violent and vindictive enforcer for the McClanahan-Burleson gang, but not everyone in San Augustine was afraid to confront him. One local man, J. Elbert Thomas, had directly challenged Tom regarding his mistreatment of the Thomas family's black tenant farmers more than once. Elbert was the son of prominent local farmer and businessman Murry B. Thomas and the nephew of local hardware store proprietor William R. "Dick" Thomas. Tom is said to have extorted more than one of the Thomases' sharecroppers and attempted to murder another, a young black man named Felix Maxey. Given that the local justice system had repeatedly failed to hold members of the McClanahan-Burleson gang accountable for their crimes, Elbert was willing to take matters into his own hands in pursuit of individual justice. As noted in chapter 2, several years earlier he had plotted with Edward Boone Brackett Jr., it seems, to avenge the murder of Brackett's father.[32]

Thomas Brothers Hardware storefront, site of the December 1934 shoot-out that resulted in four deaths and led to the stationing of the Allred Rangers in San Augustine. *Photo by Russell Lee. Library of Congress, LC-USF34-032995-D.*

On December 22, 1934, Elbert was working in his uncle's hardware store on the town square, just across the street from the county courthouse, along with other members of his family due to the holiday rush, when Tom Burleson came up the sidewalk. Right after Tom walked past the store, Elbert took him by surprise and assaulted him. Elbert initially had the upper hand in the fight, striking Tom repeatedly and taking his pistol away, placing it on a toy wagon in the store. The fistfight culminated with Tom lying prone and Elbert holding Tom's ears and smashing Tom's head into the pavement repeatedly. Elbert's father (Murry) and uncle (Dick Thomas) quickly realized that Elbert was out of control and that Tom might not survive if they did not act, so they pulled Elbert off to stop the fight and save Tom's life.[33]

Tom then retrieved his pistol from the toy wagon and opened fire on both his assailant and his rescuers. His first victim was the unarmed Murry Thomas, who begged the man whose life he had just saved to spare his own, to no avail. Tom shot Murry in the gut as he pressed forward after Elbert. Next Tom shot the fleeing Elbert in the back and then turned to engage Elbert's cousin, Maurice A. "Flick"

Thomas, son of Dick. Maurice had found a .25 caliber pistol in a hardware store showcase and was trying to load it as Tom continuing firing. Around the same time, several onlookers (who had just seen Tom shoot Murry) opened fire on Tom. The crossfire struck bystanders, and the crowd of men, women, and children who were in town socializing and doing their Christmas shopping fled in terror.[34]

When the dust settled, Elbert lay dying, his father and his cousin lay dead, and a bystander named Plato Elliott was wounded in the face. Tom had also been shot, but it was unclear whether the bullets that had struck him had come from Maurice, onlookers, or both. One thing is certain: none of the Thomases other than Maurice had wielded a gun. Tom fled the state to Louisiana, where he succumbed to blood poisoning in early January 1935. Weeks after the shoot-out, young Wade McClanahan III brought some pistol slugs to school to show his friends and claimed that they were the ones that had killed Tom, although it seems that no one other than family members ever saw Tom or his remains after the evening of the shoot-out. His body was secretly transported back to San Augustine and buried in an unmarked grave in a family cemetery, out of fear that the grave might otherwise be vandalized in retaliation for the deaths of the Thomases.[35]

The uncontrolled violence that had been gripping San Augustine for several years deeply affected the townspeople, and the December 1934 shoot-out on the town square was the pivotal event that finally convinced local leaders to reclaim control over their community. Many people began to travel miles out of their way to trade in other communities to avoid the volatile environment, and this quickly took a severe toll on local business owners. One San Augustinian—a young child at the time—recalls to me that her parents and other adults even whispered in their own homes when discussing the "troubles," even though they lived well outside of town. Another woman, already a young married adult at the time, recalls to me how those in town "pulled the shades and never let them up at night, it was so scary." Threats were also reportedly made between members of the Thomas and Burleson families after the shoot-out.[36]

After the December 1934 hardware store shoot-out, law-abiding citizens decided to seek outside help. A group of them met with the district judge in Jasper, Texas, about forty-five miles south of San Augustine, too afraid to hold such a gathering at home. The district judge requested assistance from the governor, asking that Texas Rangers be stationed in San Augustine, but Ma Ferguson was still in office, and it was her special Ranger commissions that the McClanahans had wielded against their neighbors. Some accounts indicate that the gang received word of that meeting before it was over and later lined up their cars along the highway just outside of town and shined their headlights on the participants as they returned home in the middle of the night in a show of intimidation.[37]

Newly elected sheriff Virgil Worsham—who had just defeated McClanahan-Burleson associate Warren Gary—sent a similar request to the governor shortly after being sworn in on January 1, 1935. He advised the governor that the situation was so desperate that he could not find any men willing to work for him as deputies. In response to these pleas, Governor Ferguson sent Captain George Johnson and two other Texas Rangers, Sharp Young and Joe Branom, who arrived in San Augustine on January 5, 1935. After their arrival, Worsham told newspaper reporters that he and the Ferguson Rangers had decommissioned some of the local special Rangers thought to be at the root of the troubles, although he did not provide any names, making verification of his claim impossible. Regardless, Worsham and the Ferguson Rangers made no effort to disarm or arrest any of the McClanahans or Burlesons.[38]

Far from bringing order to a town that had reached out for their aid in desperation, the newly arrived Ferguson Rangers only emboldened the McClanahan-Burleson gang. The Ferguson Rangers treated some local special Rangers (the McClanahans and Joe Burleson) as colleagues rather than suspects. Further, there is reason to believe that the Ferguson Rangers may have given the McClanahans the names of those who had requested help from the state, since the complainants suffered retaliation from the McClanahans shortly thereafter, including threats, harassment, and bricks through windows.[39]

The presence of the Ferguson Rangers also did nothing to deter the ongoing victimization of black San Augustinians. While the Rangers were putting on a show of kicking in a door to arrest three out-of-towners alleged to be involved in selling counterfeit bills, two gunmen robbed six black men on the road just outside of town. Adding insult to injury, the robbers took not only the victims' money but all of their clothes as well, forcing them to run back into town in the nude—which led to their being seen in such a state and a resultant newspaper report. The two Ferguson Rangers also claimed that they had been in a shoot-out with unidentified passengers in an allegedly suspicious car they claimed to have had followed, a car they said had no license plate, yet refused assistance offered by their chief, Dennis Estill Hamer (estranged older brother of legendary Texas Ranger Frank Hamer). Although things continued to look bleak for San Augustinians after the arrival of the Ferguson Rangers, they would soon get the help they needed.[40]

— 4 —

BRINGING ORDER TO CHAOS

The Allred Rangers Arrive

The local citizens who had risked their lives to reach out to Governor Ferguson for deliverance from the McClanahan-Burleson gang soon realized that she and her Rangers were less committed to bringing the local outlaws to justice than they had hoped. But this realization was tempered by the fact that her term as governor was coming to an end and a new administration beginning, that of newly elected Governor James V. Allred. That turn of events resulted in the immediate dispatch of freshly commissioned Allred Rangers, including James W. McCormick, Fred L. McDaniel, Daniel J. Hines, Leo Bishop, Sid Kelso, Manuel "Lone Wolf" Gonzaullus, and possibly others in the days following Allred's inauguration on January 18, 1935.[1]

Depoliticization, modernization, and professionalization of state law enforcement were key components of Allred's gubernatorial campaign, and once in office he began overhauling the Texas Rangers. He expelled all but three of the Ferguson Rangers and revoked the commissions of every single special Ranger in the state, estimated to have been as many as five thousand during Ma Ferguson's final term. Allred then appointed only experienced and trusted lawmen to fill the Ranger ranks.

Although it would take some weeks after Allred's inauguration and considerable deliberation to complete the process, his new command staff was filled with some of the most respected names in Texas law enforcement at that time.

Long-time Texas Ranger commander Tom Hickman, who was on Allred's campaign advisory committee for state law enforcement reform, was appointed captain of Headquarters Company in Austin. Under the Adjutant General's Department, the headquarters captain traditionally functioned as the chief executive officer of the Texas Rangers and, as such, was informally referred to as the "senior captain" throughout the Ranger Force period, 1901–35. Those interchangeable yet unofficial titles were formalized by statute later that year when Allred and the Forty-Fourth Texas Legislature combined the Rangers with the Highway Patrol to create a new state police agency.[2]

Roy Aldrich and Sid Kelso were the only two command-level holdovers from the Ferguson era. They had been the only longstanding and generally respected Rangers that Ma Ferguson had kept, because they carefully avoided political entanglements no matter who occupied the governorship. Aldrich retained his post as quartermaster, and Kelso was given the rank of sergeant and put in command of Company A in Houston. James McCormick had been picked by Allred to lead the San Augustine cleanup and was therefore placed in command of Company C in East Texas, while Captain Fred McDaniel was given command of Company B, headquartered in McCormick's hometown, Wichita Falls.[3]

Captain Will McMurrey was given command of Company D, in the Rio Grande Valley, where many of the worst abuses by Ferguson Rangers had often occurred, dating back to Pa Ferguson's first term as governor, beginning in 1915. Allred also brought back two former long-time rangers who were highly respected in the Rio Grande Valley, William L. Wright and Edgar T. Neal. Both in their mid-to late sixties in 1935, Wright and Neal accepted commissions as privates in Company D and saw active service throughout Allred's two terms as governor. Despite Wright's extensive previous experience as a ranger captain, he gave no indication that he was in any way unhappy with his appointment as a private. Wright served actively and efficiently as ever, often as the senior Ranger paired with new recruits for training, indicating that his appointment at that level may well have been of his own design.[4]

At the core of Allred's reform platform had been a plan to upgrade the Rangers by combining them with the Highway Patrol, and the new state agency incorporating both was the Department of Public Safety (DPS). The San Augustine troubles and the Allred's Rangers' success in cleaning up the community would later be pointed to as proof of the need for, and success of, that reform. Fortunately for San Augustine, a favorite son took a prominent position within the new administration. San Augustine native and former county attorney Edward A. Clark had recently served as a special prosecutor in the East Texas oilfields under Allred during Allred's tenure as attorney general. Upon his inauguration, Allred appointed Clark first to the position of personal secretary to the governor and shortly thereafter appointed him secretary of state.[5]

Clark took advantage of his access to the chief executive and promptly arranged to send Texas Rangers to return control of his hometown to legitimate authorities. Clark informed Allred that conditions in San Augustine had deteriorated to such an extent that the local criminal justice system had ceased to function. Numerous deadly shoot-outs had occurred in broad daylight, in full view of the public. Even leading citizens of the community had become too frightened to hold those responsible accountable under the law, because some who had dared to stand up had been killed. In short order, the Rangers' cleanup of San Augustine became a massive, more than yearlong investigation. It is unclear whether Clark and Allred knew of the gang's depredations against the black community and therefore whether that influenced their decision to send the Rangers, but local blacks consequently found themselves playing unprecedented roles in Jim Crow Texas.

Allred had a prosecutorial history of defying Jim Crow and taking on the Ku Klux Klan, in pursuit of justice on behalf of black victims. As a twenty-five-year-old district attorney in Wichita Falls, Allred had prosecuted a railroad policeman (and former Texas Ranger) named Elmer B. McClure, who had shot and killed a black man and then claimed it was an accident. Despite his previous Ranger service, McClure had a controversial history in law enforcement and had "figured in several questionable shooting scrapes," historian John Boessenecker says. In 1925, Allred secured a murder conviction against McClure, one of the few such prosecutions of the Jim Crow era (in which a white person was convicted in the killing of a black person). However, McClure was pardoned two years later by Ma Ferguson, at the request of railroad officials and Ranger captain Frank Hamer. Hamer had attacked Allred mercilessly in the press for his successful prosecution of McClure, who had served with him on the border several years earlier. After decades of service and his successful effort to end the killing spree of the infamous Bonnie Parker and Clyde Barrow in 1934, Hamer seemed to many the obvious choice to head the Rangers again. However, Allred had neither forgotten nor forgiven Hamer, who would never again serve as a Texas Ranger.[6]

McCormick, Hines, and Bishop all had prior service that connected them to Allred or Clark or both. McCormick was a Ranger and sheriff in Wichita County (where Allred had served as district attorney). The son of a Cherokee mother and an Irish father, McCormick suffered from racial discrimination for much of his life and was uniquely suited to lead state efforts to uncover and end the McClanahan-Burleson gang's mistreatment of black San Augustinians. Hines had served on a "special detail" as an undercover officer in the East Texas oilfields under Hamer from 1931 to 1933, when Allred was attorney general and Clark was his special prosecutor there. Bishop had served previously as a Ranger, also working the oilfields during that same time along with famed Ranger Manuel "Lone Wolf" Gonzaullus. These were experienced lawmen accustomed to confronting violent crime and enforcing the law in complex, high-pressure situations.[7]

The ensuing operation consisted of three distinct yet sometimes overlapping phases. Allred's Rangers recognized that the only way to convince long-silent victims and witnesses to come forward and testify was to remove the source of their fears. Therefore, the first phase was driving out or arresting the lead gang members. That was essential to winning the confidence and trust of the long-suffering community, especially African Americans—who were least likely to trust unknown white lawmen. The second phase was investigating the extent of the gang's activities over the years, which required not only finding out about specific crimes committed but also convincing victims and witnesses to share their stories and then be willing to testify in court so that the offenders could be formally charged and prosecuted. The third phase of the cleanup was seeing many of the hundreds of charges through to trial by securing indictments and protecting victims and witnesses from retaliation.

The Allred Rangers promptly took control of the situation after arriving in San Augustine on January 18, 1935. In a deliberate show of force, they each sported dual pistols displayed openly on their belts and carried .30-.30 rifles at all times. They quickly confronted all of the Ferguson Rangers, regular and special, and demanded that they surrender their commissions, which had been revoked by the new governor. Using profanity and bravado as weapons, they publicly berated leading members of the Burleson-McClanahan crew in an effort to run them out of town. This show of force was also intended to demonstrate to those who had been living in fear that they could now come forward and file their complaints with confidence that they would be protected and their grievances finally addressed.[8]

The Allred Rangers found the circumstances to be every bit as dire as they had been warned. Captain McCormick, a peace officer with decades of experience in some of the most violent boomtowns of early-twentieth-century Texas, later described the state of affairs in San Augustine as "the worst situation . . . that I have ever been in," saying that "a gang of criminals, backed by officers and others . . . were in complete control." He noted that at first the Rangers "were unable to get witnesses to inform against members of the gang . . . as the good people were afraid." Allred Ranger Hines, who had also served as an undercover special Ranger in oil boomtowns, reported that the information locals provided about the "depredations of the gang that has operated here for the past several years" was "almost unbelievable."[9]

One of the most commonly repeated and relatively consistent stories recalling the Allred Rangers' arrival in San Augustine is an anecdote about Hines verbally excoriating Wade McClanahan Jr. after he approached Hines on the courthouse square wearing a pistol and carrying his special Ranger commission from Ferguson. Hines confiscated the commission, warned Wade Jr. to leave his pistol at home, and possibly intimated that McClanahan and his associates should get out of town. In keeping with their show of force, the Allred Rangers frequently practiced their marksmanship in public, shooting bottle caps thrown into the air or mounted on tree trunks and empty cans on the side of the road from moving cars. They were also careful to watch each others' backs and often kept their own backs covered by leaning against a wall with their rifles at hand, so that the gangsters would have no opportunity to sneak up on them from behind.[10]

Another anecdote showing how the Allred Rangers attempted to intimidate members of the Burleson-McClanahan gang describes an encounter in William M. Wade's City Café. Wade had been one of the people who met in Jasper and requested state assistance from Governor Ferguson after the December 1934 shoot-out on the square, and he had witnessed the assault on Secret Service operative E. C. Cleveland at the local fairgrounds. As the story goes, McCormick, Hines, and Bishop were sitting and visiting with William Wade. Wade McClanahan Sr. walked through the door, and the proprietor alerted the three Rangers. McClanahan approached them and stated that he had come to give himself up. McCormick replied, "Well, it's about time, seeing as how you've been mistreating these people for so long." McCormick then instructed that either Hines or Bishop take McClanahan to the jail, in response to which the two Rangers began arguing playfully between themselves. Each admonished the other, "You better take him, 'cause I'll probably just shoot him on the way." While the account may be apocryphal, it reflects the Allred Rangers' use of intimidation through threats of deadly force to convince both the local criminals and law-abiding citizens that they would not be deterred in their mission to bring order to San Augustine. While the details of such anecdotes vary, there is no debate that the Allred Rangers intended to take control of the town—and by brute force if necessary.[11]

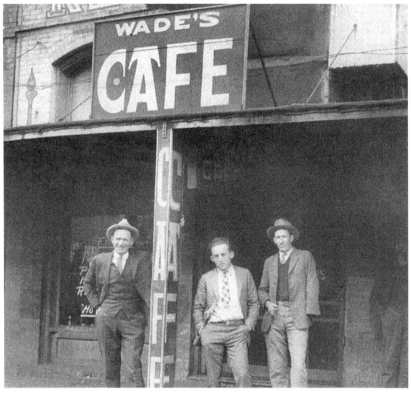

Unnamed local men standing outside Wade's Cafe, formerly City Café, unofficial early local headquarters of the Allred Rangers. *Courtesy of Nelsyn Wade family.*

McCormick regaled the press in explaining why he preferred to carry a single-action pistol, so that he could use it as a club, by "slap[ping a man] below [his cheekbone]"—"that'll smash his cheekbone, but it won't kill him." In a time many decades before pepper spray and Tasers, such a tactic was advocated as a nonlethal means of taking violent men like the McClanahans and Burlesons into custody. As to his methods in initiating the San Augustine cleanup, McCormick would later boast, "The first thing we did . . . was to get a line on one of the killers [and] . . . we kicked him across the street to the jail. Then we went roughshod after the rest of them." The Allred Rangers' frequent and colorful public statements of their willingness to use violence generally appear to have rendered the actual application of such violence unnecessary. However, the Allred Rangers weren't bluffing, a fact the gangsters quickly realized.[12]

The Allred Rangers' intimidation tactics quickly achieved the desired effect, and the Burlesons, McClanahans, and many of their associates left town. Some of them complained to the press and the courts, acknowledging that fear of the Allred Rangers had driven them out of the community. Shortly afterward, victims and witnesses began cooperating and coming forward in droves to file complaints for virtually every sort of crime, including theft, assault, moonshining, "highway robbery," "white slavery," counterfeiting, election fraud, and murder. The Rangers also actively pursued victims whose names they learned from witnesses and informants, particularly African American tenant farmers who were uniquely vulnerable to the schemes and violence of the McClanahans and Burlesons. Several of these victims eventually testified that their day in court had been made possible through the Allred Rangers' efforts. The Rangers' investigations that year involved a multitude of crimes and more than fifty suspects and defendants, but it was several previously unprosecuted murder cases that formed the core of the Rangers' inquiries. Within two months of the Allred Rangers' arrival, San Augustine's reign of terror was over.[13]

Allred Rangers investigated each lead and sought out victims and witnesses to learn as much as they could about what had transpired in the years preceding their arrival. They sought justice on behalf of black victims, poor white victims, and those with checkered pasts. Although it remains unconfirmed, the Allred Rangers likely had the aid of a member of the African American community. Many members of that community who recall those events insist that their friends and relatives would have been reticent to speak openly with unknown white lawmen and thus that the Allred Rangers would have needed a liaison from their community to persuade victims and witnesses to cooperate.[14]

The most concrete evidence that Allred's Rangers had an active working relationship with a member of the black community in San Augustine is a set of photographs of Dan Hines and Leo Bishop that can be found in both Rangers' personal papers. The photos depict the two Rangers with a young black man and give the appearance of a relationship that was friendly but also professional. In the photos, the Rangers are smiling when they are facing the camera or looking at the young man, who is wearing and carrying firearms alongside the Rangers, sometimes posed in a firing position. Bishop's copy of one of the images, which shows the young man with Hines, has a handwritten label at the bottom that reads "Two Rangers." It was likely that such a unique relationship for that time and place enabled the community of San Augustine to buck an otherwise intractable Jim Crow culture and bring the McClanahan-Burleson gang to justice. Local blacks

Inside the City Café, June 1, 1920. *Courtesy of Nelsyn Wade family.*

and whites joined with the Allred Rangers to defeat the local mobsters who had terrorized them for years. The conviction of white gang members and associates by white juries based on the testimony of black victims and witnesses at the height of the Jim Crow era was the product of trust established first between black San Augustinians and the Rangers. That trust was reciprocated by white jurors who refused to tolerate the gang's depredations any longer and chose to defy Jim Crow norms in order to restore law and order.[15]

The Allred Rangers also effected the removal of several public officials who, though they appeared to be cooperative at first, proved to be corrupt and associated with some of the illegal activities involved in the gang's crime wave. And no one was happier about that than the throngs of San Augustinians who came out to several events that year held in appreciation of Governor Allred and his Rangers. The tide had turned in San Augustine, and the McClanahan-Burleson gang that once oppressed its citizens with impunity was now facing justice, thanks to the efforts of the Allred Rangers. Leading members of the community—and the population at large—demonstrated their gratitude.[16]

Once the cycle of subjugation through intimidation was broken, San Augustinians wasted no time seizing and securing the peace through law and order that

Dan Hines (*right*) and unidentified young man. Prints of this photograph were located in the family papers of both Hines and Leo Bishop; this one comes from Bishop's papers. *Photo probably by Leo Bishop, courtesy of John and Betty Oglesbee.*

had been denied them for so long. One by one, they stepped forward to once again serve on juries and testify against the men who had intimidated them. While dozens of investigations and trials would continue for nearly a year and a half, local business owners and community leaders immediately recognized that the continued presence of the Allred Rangers was the key to shoring up public confidence, which in turn was essential to the revitalization of the local criminal justice system. Hundreds of San Augustinians wrote expressions of appreciation and support to Governor Allred for his Rangers' presence and work in their community. A consistent theme among those letters, as well as many local and regional newspaper articles and commercial advertisements, was that the overwhelming majority of local citizens, typically quantified as 90–95 percent, appreciated the actions taken to restore law and order, and they welcomed the stationing of the Allred Rangers in their community.[17]

On January 18, 1935, the day after the Allred Rangers arrived in San Augustine, local merchant John Burrows, president of the San Augustine Grocery Company, wrote to Governor Allred "to express our appreciation of your sending Rangers to our assistance to subdue lawlessness in our town." Burrows commended the governor's choice of men sent to do the job, including the leadership of Captain McCormick. Burrows made particular reference to the positive effect that the Allred Rangers' presence was already having on the local economy after just a day: "It is quite noticeable the number of people on our streets . . . back to trade, who have not been here for months." He also noted that the Allred Rangers were "courteous in every way and yet efficient," and he assured the governor that the local citizens would "give them our very best cooperation." Burrows was only the first of many local business and community leaders to express such sentiments.[18]

On February 12, 1935, San Augustine County Clerk Fred T. Fisher wrote to Governor Allred to express his "appreciation for what you have done for this town and County by sending Rangers here to enforce the law as it should be." Fisher wrote that "95% of the citizens of this County greatly appreciate you sending them here and hope that they continue to stay as long as they are needed, as everything is beginning to get back to normal again." He explained that although there had been "several individuals who have been running things in an out-law manner . . . everything is looking quite a bit different now, due to the presence of the Rangers." On the same day, local jeweler and optometrist G. Z. Moore also wrote to the governor to express his gratitude for the presence of the Allred Rangers and note that "a large majority of the citizenship of the county" was equally appreciative. Moore also mentioned the "high class, fearless type of men sent" by the governor and said that he hoped that Allred would "see fit to leave them here until they have completed the clean-up campaign that they have well under way."[19]

Another letter posted that same day was from William M. Wade, owner of the local movie theater and the City Café, which the Allred Rangers made their unofficial headquarters. Wade expressed his "sincere thanks and appreciation" to the governor for having assigned the Allred Rangers to San Augustine indefinitely. Like Burrows, Wade noted that "the streets are full of people now who have smiles on their faces because they know they are protected," and he further commented, "Before the [Allred] Rangers came the streets were practically clear of people." Wade assured the governor that his Rangers were "doing a good work" and said that he hoped that the governor would "continue leaving them" there.[20]

Less than a week after Burrows, Moore, and Wade posted their letters, Matt Johnson, owner of M. A. Johnson Groceries, also wrote to the governor. In addition to communicating his approval and appreciation for the Allred Rangers' presence and actions since their arrival, Johnson also insisted, "We do not hear any expressions other than commendation of the action of yourself and your Rangers that are now here. The people of both country and town appreciate the protection they now have. All opinions I have heard expressed are favorable toward having the Rangers here as long as there is any need, whatever, in bringing the lawless element to justice and completely under control." Johnson claimed that those locals who had not voted for Allred had since changed their minds as a result of his having sent in his Texas Rangers and the success they had so quickly achieved. He insisted that those citizens were now "for Jimmie Allred forever" and expressed support for the governor's overall platform, not just his law enforcement policy. Johnson said he was proud to have supported Allred for governor in 1934 and declared, "[Many] next door business neighbors with whom I had many arguments during the last campaign tell me that I was right and that they are glad that my man won."[21]

Within two months of their arrival, the Allred Rangers had so effectively reversed the tide in San Augustine that locals held the first of what would be several public events to honor the Rangers' accomplishments. At a time when many local communities expressed reticence or outright opposition to Texas Rangers in their midst, San Augustine embraced the Allred Rangers. The March 22, 1935, issue of the *Dallas Morning News* reported: "In striking contrast to other cities whose peace officers have resented the intrusion of Texas Rangers on their illicit home-town industries, San Augustine will show the State officers true East Texas hospitality Friday night. A street dance will be given in honor of the rangers, who have been stationed here since January." The March 22, 1935, Beaumont *Enterprise* included an article on the same event under the headline "Street Dance Tonight Will Be Given in Honor of Texas Rangers." The paper reported that San Augustine's streets were roped off in anticipation of a large crowd and that music was to be provided by the Stephen F. Austin College Orchestra from Nacogdoches. Considering that just two months earlier most area residents were avoiding the town center altogether, widespread participation in such an event demonstrates the community's dramatic turnaround.[22]

That out-of-town newspapers took such an interest in what would typically have been regarded as a local affair demonstrates the larger significance of the dance. But it is the March 28, 1935, *San Augustine Tribune*, published less than a week after the celebration, that best reveals the extent of the changes accomplished by the Allred Rangers and the level of community support. A bold banner on the front page stated "NEW ERA," under which a headline spanned the width of paper: "APPROVE RULE OF RANGERS." A subheading elaborated, "4,000 People

Butts-Hurst Chevrolet dealership on the San Augustine town square. *Photo by Russell Lee. Library of Congress, LC-USF34-032992-D.*

San Augustinians gathered at Rushings' Drug Store soda counter, some perhaps enjoying a locally popular "grapefruit hi-ball." *Photo by Russell Lee. Library of Congress, LC-USW3-025103-D.*

Gather for Big Street Dance Celebrating General Clean-Up." Even the newspaper's ads referenced the cleanup: "We Have CONFIDENCE In San Augustine" (Rushing's Drug Store); "WE HAVE GREAT CONFIDENCE IN THE FUTURE OF SAN AUGUSTINE" (local Chevrolet dealer); "With New Confidence Restored in San Augustine, Many thanks to Captain McCormick, Leo Bishop, Dan Hines, and all law enforcement officers" (local Ford dealer).[23]

Included above the fold of the front page of that issue of the *San Augustine Tribune* was a telegram from Governor Allred to the editor-in-chief, Webster F. Hays, omitting only the "stop" between sentences for clarity:

Telegram From Governor Allred
Austin, Texas, March 25
W.F. Hays
San Augustine Tribune
San Augustine, Texas

The fine spirit of good citizenship which the people of San Augustine County have shown in approving the action of the Texas Rangers is gratifying, indeed, to the Governor of your state. Your street dance celebration honoring the Rangers is indicative of a healthy public sentiment which will not tolerate vicious, violent lawlessness. With the powerful force of public approval behind them local officers cannot fail in their efforts to enforce the laws. As Governor of Texas I heartily commend your action and promise you my continued efforts to rid the State of lawlessness.

JAMES V. ALLRED,
Governor of Texas[24]

Also on the front page were these words from Ranger captain McCormick:

To the Citizenship of San Augustine County:

With a feeling of pride in your approval we greet you. The expression of confidence accorded us last Friday evening warms our heart with gratitude and we are glad, indeed, to be here to serve a people who respond so readily to leadership.

In this connection we desire to say that when our final report has been made to the Governor on conditions in San Augustine

San Augustine Tribune editor-in-chief W. F. Hays at his desk. *Photo by Russell Lee. Library of Congress, LC-USF34-033001-D.*

County we unhesitatingly assure you that it will be complete in every detail and that law and order will prevail here as it should. We will be pleased to have the co-operation of the general public and again thank you for the splendid demonstration and honor in our behalf upon this occasion.

Respectfully,
CAPT. J. W. McCORMICK[25]

Offices of the *San Augustine Tribune*. *Photo by John Vachon. Library of Congress, LC-USW3-025298-D.*

Reinvigorating the local criminal justice system was a key goal of the Allred Rangers' in San Augustine, and one of their early actions was providing supplemental investigation and courtroom security for a trial for the double murder of two young hunters by a local bootlegger (a crime that took place near the Sardis Cemetery). Although the Eighteenth Amendment to the US Constitution was repealed in 1933, marking the end of Prohibition on the federal level, Prohibition laws still existed in Texas until August 1935, and it remained illegal to distill unlicensed whiskey. Prohibitionists and religious groups that viewed alcohol and gambling as vices detrimental to Texas society at large undergirded Governor Allred's political base, and he had campaigned in 1934 on a platform of strong law enforcement.[26]

The defendant in the murder trial, thirty-year-old Lee Parrish, was described in press accounts of the time as a "typical mountaineer" who was part of a reclusive backwoods subculture in northwestern San Augustine County that resisted outside influence and interference. As an example of that community's resistance to the authority of governmental institutions, Parrish's compatriots in northwestern San Augustine County burned two schoolhouses and a church in 1933 "as a protest against . . . civilized intrusions upon their hillbilly privacy." These outcasts were prolific bootleggers and skilled marksmen, and the combination of these two had led to the murders of Lonnie Hooper, "a barefoot boy of sixteen," and his twenty-year-old cousin Ewell Hooper, on October 11, 1934. The victims had accidentally ventured too close to the source of the bootleggers' livelihood.[27]

Despite the initial arrest of several of his relatives too, Parrish was the only person charged with the murders. San Augustine County Attorney C. Smith Ramsey brought the initial charges against Parrish just a few days after the Hoopers were killed. Parrish was brought to trial on January 28, 1935 in San Augustine, with Allred Rangers stationed strategically and conspicuously around the courthouse to prevent interference or disruption. Judge F. Pat Adams of neighboring Jasper County presided over the proceedings, with District Attorney Hollis M. Kinard of Orange representing the state and attorneys Joseph R. Bogard of San Augustine and J. R. Anderson of Center, Texas, serving as counsel for the defense. A mistrial would ensue even though Parrish was convicted, as jurors differed on length of sentence, with some favoring not more than twenty-five years and others insisting on thirty years to life. In this circumstance, Texas law then required that a mistrial be declared and a new trial eventually convened. The murder of the Hooper cousins did not appear to have any connection to the McClanahan-Burleson gang's crime wave, but it was the first felony case to go to trial in San Augustine in several years and the first after the arrival of the Allred Rangers. As such, it kicked off the reinvigorated local court system, which quickly manifested in the investigation, indictment, and trials of the various principals and associates of the McClanahan-Burleson gang.[28]

The same week that the Parrish trial was held in San Augustine, the first case to be originally investigated and filed by the Allred Rangers was set for trial. This case was against Ocie Carroll, who was found guilty on three counts of forgery and sentenced to two years in state prison. Willis Murphy was also brought to trial that week for a deadly assault on V. W. Barge that allegedly had occurred in 1932, but the disposition of that case is unknown. The Allred Rangers were just beginning what would be more than a year of work to not only restore peace to the community and but also to exact justice for past crimes, at least from the perspective of most law-abiding San Augustinians. The Allred Rangers and local prosecutors had their sights firmly set on members and close associates of the McClanahan-Burleson gang as well as anyone who took advantage of the lawless atmosphere they promoted to participate in illegal activities, and one by one they began taking them down.

The Allred Rangers not only aided in the reinvigoration of the local criminal justice system, they also assisted in the federal investigation into the beating of

E. C. Cleveland. Pursuant to US Attorney S. D. Bennett's instructions, Edward Tyrrell and Luis Benavides had spent several months traveling to San Augustine and seeking witnesses to the assault. While many earlier had corroborated Cleveland's claims and debunked any notion of his having been intoxicated, prior to the arrival of the Allred Rangers few had been willing to risk testifying in open court, fearing reprisal by the McClanahans and Burlesons.[29]

After the Allred Rangers restored peace and a sense of security among the local citizens, Tyrrell and his men were eventually able to secure a sufficient number of witnesses to satisfy Bennett, who finally took the case to the federal grand jury in March 1935, almost five months after the attack occurred and more than a month after the Allred Rangers had wrested control of the town from the McClanahan-Burleson gang. On March 4, 1935, twenty federal grand jurors, led by foreman W. Wahrmund, indicted all seven suspects on three counts, alleging that all of them had "unlawfully, knowingly, willfully, feloniously, and forcibly" (1) "assault[ed]," (2) "use[d] certain dangerous and deadly weapons, to wit: pistols, knives, and revolvers," and (3) "resist[ed], oppose[d], impede[d], intimidate[d], and interfere[d]" with Cleveland while he was "engaged in the performance of his official duties." Those findings appear to have been the first indictment in the nation for a violation of the provision against assaulting a federal officer, which had been passed less than a year before as part of the Crime Control Act of 1934.[30]

Tyrrell's daily report noted that US District Judge Randolph Bryant, who was assigned as the presiding magistrate for the case, gave indications during court proceedings that day that revealed that he was "very interested in the prosecution of these officers for their attack on Operative Cleveland" and that they would likely be "forced to trial immediately." Tyrrell and Cleveland then attended a post–grand jury conference with Bennett to prepare the case for that possibility. Judge Bryant did call for hearing on the case the very next day, though the case was discontinued until 9:30 A.M. the day after that, March 6, 1935. In the meantime, Tyrrell made arrangements to gather the witnesses in the case for that hearing. Upon receiving a telegram from the new sheriff of San Augustine, Virgil B. Worsham, identifying W. T. Parmer as a witness in the case, Tyrrell called Captain McCormick to ensure the witness's presence in federal court.[31]

Tyrrell noted in his report, "State Rangers are now in San Augustine and have run all of the defendants out of the county," and he noted that there was a state warrant for murder out for Charlie McClanahan. Tyrrell had established a strong rapport with the Allred Rangers after they arrived in San Augustine and kept apprised of the local situation. He reported that the Allred Rangers had quickly and effectively displaced the McClanahan-Burleson gang as the base of power in that community, a development that Tyrrell shared with Bennett in an attempt to encourage him to take the case to a federal grand jury. Unfortunately, Worsham's witness, Parmer turned out to be a plant meant to aid the defendants. He claimed that Sheriff Gary and Hillis Smith had not been present during the attack on Cleveland, and he blamed the entire incident on Tom Burleson, who had since died of blood poisoning from wounds he received during the December 1934 hardware store shoot-out. This would not be the last time that members of the McClanahan-Burleson gang would try to lay all the blame on the late Tom Burleson for their illegal acts in the hope of avoiding criminal convictions. After Tyrrell released Parmer from his subpoena and told him he could return home, he was seen associating with the defendants around the courthouse, thereby confirming Tyrrell's suspicions that the witness and Sheriff Worsham were aligned with the defense.[32]

—— 5 ——

PROSECUTIONS AND POLITICS

All of the defendants appeared in court as required except Charlie McClanahan. His bond was forfeited, a warrant was issued for his arrest, and he was declared a federal fugitive from justice. As a result of Charlie's absence, his defense attorney, Steve King of Beaumont, requested a continuance until the next term of court, which would be some months later. Judge Bryant refused, and King responded by requesting that the case be transferred to another court, which Bryant also refused. Instead he reset the court date for the following Monday morning. Judge Bryant instructed counsel, both Bennett and King, not to tell their witnesses about the agreed-upon delay but to keep them in town and ready to appear at a moment's notice. Tyrrell noted that Judge Bryant expressed sincere concern regarding the fact that state and local law enforcement officers had attacked a federal officer and insisted on having the case adjudicated as expeditiously as possible.[1]

Tyrrell decided, in part on Judge Bryant's recommendation, to use the delay to go to San Augustine in search of more witnesses to buttress the government's case. Tyrrell and Cleveland met with Allred Rangers McCormick and Hines on Thursday, March 7, 1935, and were immediately encouraged by the good news Hines had for them. He had convinced Walter Sheffield, one of the defendants in the case, to confess his and the others' roles in the assault and to testify on behalf of the government. Sheffield was a twenty-five-year-old distant relative of the McClanahans who had been employed that night as a "Special Deputy" at the fairgrounds on the night of the assault on E. C. Cleveland. Sheffield provided both verbal and written statements to Hines, in which he explained that Joe Burleson and Hillis Smith had come and gotten him and informed him of Cleveland's presence in town. The three of them had located and stopped Cleveland on the fairgrounds to question him. They wanted to know whether he was a "government officer" and whether he was looking for Joe's brother Tom. Sheffield said that Cleveland acknowledged that he was a federal operative but that he "could not make known the nature of his business."[2]

The Allred Rangers promised Tyrrell that they would locate another witness and produce him in court in Beaumont the following Monday if he could testify as had been claimed. Tyrrell and Cleveland then left San Augustine, taking Sheffield with them to meet with Bennett in Beaumont. It was in that meeting that Tyrrell began to doubt Bennett's commitment to prosecuting the case. Tyrrell reported that Bennett tried repeatedly to get Sheffield to change his statement in regard to several key points, most notably that Bennett kept insisting that Cleveland had not identified himself as a government officer, even as Sheffield stood firm in stating that Cleveland had indeed identified himself as such, repeatedly, before and after the attack. Tyrrell interpreted this interaction as an effort by Bennett to eliminate a key element of the cause of action (that the defendants knew Cleveland was a federal officer), thereby allowing him to dismiss the case. Tyrrell further noted that Bennett had been pushing him to agree to dismiss the case for many months, although it was obvious (to Tyrrell, at least) that Judge Bryant and others were very interested in seeing the McClanahan-Burleson gang prosecuted in federal court. In his daily reports Tyrrell expressed substantial frustration with Bennett in regard to this matter and suggested that Bennett's motivations were politically influenced.[3]

Tyrrell was unable to locate the US marshal in Beaumont after his meeting with Bennett, so he personally remanded Sheffield to the custody of the Jefferson County sheriff and then drove to Houston to look for Charlie McClanahan since he had learned that McClanahan had relatives there. Tyrrell noted that McClanahan had "sent word to all the officers" that he did "not intend to be taken alive" and that he was "going to shoot it out on sight with any officer attempting to arrest him." Tyrrell further reported that McClanahan had been spotted the day before on the Beaumont Highway, "heavily armed." Tyrrell and his men had no luck locating McClanahan over the weekend. Cleveland spent Saturday looking for potential counterfeit notes at local banks, print shops, and photo supply houses in Houston and then all day Sunday staking out the house of a McClanahan relative at 2322

Everett Street in the same city. However, he did not see anything that indicated McClanahan was hiding there. He also was unable to find Robert Ellis, who had accompanied Cleveland to the San Augustine fairgrounds and had himself been beaten, to ensure that he would be appearing in court the next day.[4]

On Monday, Tyrrell returned to Beaumont for court as ordered by Judge Bryant. Cleveland also returned as ordered, having located Ellis early that morning. When Tyrrell met with Bennett in his office, Bennett told him that Judge Bryant had called from Sherman, Texas, to inform them that he would not be able to hold court that day but would reconvene the case on Tuesday. Bennett then insisted to Tyrrell that "the best thing to do" would be to continue the case until the next term of court some months away, arguing that Charlie McClanahan's absence would hurt the government's case. Tyrrell disagreed with that assessment and opposed any continuance.[5]

After a meeting with defense attorney King, Bennett returned with a defense petition that requested that the federal government pay the expenses to bring in eight or ten witnesses on the defendants' behalf, claiming that the defense had "no means" to bring in the witnesses themselves. The petition also alleged that those witnesses would testify that both Cleveland and Ellis had been drinking alcohol throughout the day and had even offered the gang liquor, claims that Tyrrell considered to be preposterous and therefore unworthy of Bennett's concern. Tyrrell ordered Cleveland to return to San Augustine with the Allred Rangers, who had come to Beaumont for the hearing, and further investigate the list of witnesses so that they could be located and interviewed by the three law enforcement officers to determine whether they were willing to offer such testimony under oath and whether they had been threatened in an effort to keep them from doing so.[6]

Tyrrell continued to refuse to agree to Bennett's incessant pressure to postpone the case; instead he proceeded with supplemental investigation, including a trip to the city jail in Beaumont. At about noon that Monday, Bennett called and said that King was now claiming that Gary, the former sheriff, was ill, thereby necessitating a continuance. Tyrrell considered that claim to be dubious, and he called Captain McCormick in San Augustine and requested that he contact the local doctor to verify Gary's condition.[7]

At approximately 6:40 P.M., Cleveland called from San Augustine to report that he and Captain McCormick had located three of the witnesses on the defense list: Elbert Taylor, Vandy V. Steptoe, and Rupert Edwards. Each of those disavowed the claim that Cleveland and Ellis had been intoxicated as asserted in defense affidavits and affirmed that they had been forced to sign them. Additionally, the local doctor reported that Gary was not ill and that there was no reason that he should not go to trial that day. Cleveland and Captain McCormick also located several more eyewitnesses to the attack on Cleveland: Sam Ware, Sidney Bodine (a Ferguson special whose commission was signed by Sheriff Gary), and A. P. McCrasky. All three testified that they saw Joe and Jim Burleson, Charlie and Wade McClanahan Sr., and Hillis Smith with their pistols drawn on Cleveland, and that Sheriff Gary was also present during the attack.[8]

Cleveland also reported that King had called San Augustine and claimed that Bennett had agreed to postpone the case but that Tyrrell was interfering with that agreement. Tyrrell angrily remarked that Bennett was a "holdover" from the previous presidential administration who would soon be leaving his post and was therefore "[doing] everything to upset our case." Tyrrell also reported that he believed that since Judge Bryant was sympathetic to the case, Bennett had "not dared to defy me so far." Tyrrell complained that Bennett's actions were unnecessarily complicating matters and that his (Tyrrell's) continued presence at court in Beaumont was essential to preventing Bennett from derailing the case altogether.[9]

Tuesday, March 12, 1935, did not bring much of a change for Tyrrell and the federal assault case. At their pre-hearing meeting, Bennett continued to press Tyrrell to agree to a continuance. Tyrrell stood firm in defiance of Bennett's aims, informing him that the witnesses listed in the defense petition admitted that the supporting affidavits contained statements that had been coerced and were utterly false. Further, Tyrrell notified Bennett that several of those witnesses had prepared new affidavits affirming that the ones the defense had presented contained statements that had been obtained under threat of death. Tyrrell also informed Bennett, the federal prosecutor, that King's claims that Gary was ill were false and that he (Tyrrell) wished to be allowed to make a statement to the judge before any decision regarding a continuance was made. Bennett agreed to do so. However, according to Tyrrell, the judge "rushed" into the courtroom when the hearing began and, without giving Tyrrell a chance to speak and without any comment or objection from Bennett, reported that he was rescheduling the case to the October 1935 term. Tyrrell was livid.[10]

Tyrrell, his operatives, and the Allred Rangers had all gone to great lengths to ensure that a large number of good witnesses were present so that the federal government's case would be proven conclusively that day. In his daily report Tyrrell lamented that the continuance led all of those witnesses to fear that "they would meet with violence or [have] their homes burned down by this

[McClanahan-Burleson] gang." He was convinced that this turn of events was a result of collusion between Bennett and King, opposing counsel. Despite his open and direct criticism of both the US attorney and the defense counsel, Tyrrell gave no indication in his report as to his thoughts on Judge Bryant's role in resetting the case or the manner in which he had done so.[11]

Tyrrell did not end his criticism of King with the issue of the continuance. He opined that King should have himself been jailed for filing fraudulent affidavits and petitions. In his daily reports he referenced not only the coerced witness statements but also King's claims regarding his clients' financial status. Tyrrell noted that King had reported to the court that his clients had all been unable to pay him, but Tyrrell found records proving that they had given him a retainer of $2,500—a substantial sum in the midst of the Depression. Further, their claims of indigence when the defense requested that the court cover the costs of bringing in their witnesses were fabrications, as Tyrrell learned that "every one of them owns a new car and property in San Augustine." Cleveland had learned from Ben T. Wilson, manager of the Chevrolet Motor Sales Company in Nacogdoches, that both Charlie and Wade McClanahan Sr. had purchased brand-new 1935 Chevrolet sedans that spring. They had paid for the vehicles in full, with cash. Cleveland also obtained certified copies of the property tax records for Sheriff Gary, the Burlesons, and the McClanahans from the San Augustine tax collector, Paul Whitton. The defendants were far from destitute, contrary to the contentions in their petition. Unfortunately, there is no record as to whether any of this evidence was ever presented to a federal judge or jury.[12]

On Saturday, March 16, four days after the federal assault case was continued over into the fall term of court, Charlie McClanahan surrendered to Jefferson County sheriff W. W. "Bill" Richardson and was placed back into federal custody in Beaumont. McClanahan had been a federal fugitive for two weeks prior to his surrender, having forfeited his bond by failing to appear in court as ordered after the indictment in the federal assault case, and therefore he was kept in custody pending trial. However, he was released to Ranger Hines on March 19, to be tried in state district court for the murder of Edward Boone Brackett Sr.[13]

The death of the senior Brackett had continued to haunt his family long after they buried him. Brackett Jr. and his wife had moved forward with raising their family, but the death of his father and his inability to exact vengeance plagued him for the rest of his life. He became a man for whom all aspects of life were black or white as well as a strict taskmaster to both his children and himself. Brackett Jr. found it difficult to forgive himself or others for slight infractions or perceived moral weaknesses, and this narrow and inflexible outlook strained his personal relationships. He packed up his family and moved to Abilene and thus moved them away from San Augustine forever, though he did not leave behind the burden of his father's death. Brackett Sr. had leveraged the family farm in cotton futures in 1929, the value of which collapsed along with the entire stock market and national economy in October that year. Brackett Jr. "did not believe in bankruptcy" or any other means of "shirking" one's financial obligations, which he regarded as a "post hoc lie." So despite the fact that the debts were not his and that the person, his father, who had incurred them, had been murdered, he spent twenty years paying off his father's debts at great personal sacrifice. He, his wife, and their children spent most of their lives near or below the poverty line, despite producing a regular and often substantial income. To this day, the family still holds the title to the land that Brackett Sr. originally purchased and then mortgaged nearly eighty-five years ago, although they have no intention of ever returning to live in the community because of the trauma their family endured there so many years ago.[14]

Leaving San Augustine was arguably the best thing Brackett Jr. could have done, for himself, his family, and the community. The McClanahan-Burleson gang threatened him with death, and the tensions between his family and the associates of his father's killer must have been intolerable. Brackett Jr. was not the only one haunted for life by his father's death. His sister Vivian, the teenager who rode to town with their father and left his company just before the shooting to meet her friends, harbored guilt for decades over the timing of the shooting.[15]

As soon as the Allred Rangers had learned about the murder of Brackett Sr., they had recognized its prosecutorial potential and notified Governor Allred. As a former prosecutor, Allred also immediately recognized the case's significance and potential, both legally and symbolically, for the community. He demonstrated his resolve in the matter by seeking out and funding special counsel to aid the already overburdened local prosecutors in investigating and adjudicating the Brackett murder case. He engaged the services of former Shelby County district judge S. H. "Spot" Sanders, who was at that time working in private practice in the town of Center (the seat of Shelby County, north of San Augustine). The Rangers had not been in San Augustine much more than a month, and possibly less, when Allred sent Sanders to work directly with McCormick and Hines on the Brackett murder case.[16]

This case thus became one of the matters granted priority status by the governor, sometimes to the exclusion of other criminal cases in the same region. When Sanders mentioned to Governor Allred that the Rangers had asked him about

Cullen House—the San Augustine, Texas, residence of Judge "Spot" Sanders—during the period of the cleanup and the trial of Charles McClanahan. *Photo by Russell Lee. Library of Congress, HABS TEX,203-SUAG,3-*.

"assisting them in ferreting out the officers who were taking 'rake-offs' [payoffs] from the operators of [illegal] slot machines and receiving fines and costs without the cases going through the proper channels of the courts," he further noted that he had advised the Rangers that they would have to handle such cases on their own, because he "did not feel that [the governor] wanted [him] to be employed in this particular [matter] but only in the killings that have occurred in San Augustine which the rangers are now investigating."[17]

Sanders commented on the professionalism and courtesy of the Allred Rangers and the fact that "the good citizenship of San Augustine are deeply grateful that they can now go about the streets freely and know they will not be molested." He also noted, however, that one family had already left the area out of fear, perhaps referring to the Bracketts, and added that another was preparing to go. While Sanders went wherever he deemed necessary to interview witnesses and collect evidence, the Rangers confined their investigation to San Augustine County, in order to maintain a constant presence that would reassure the locals that they would continue to be safe from potential retaliatory violence at the hands of the McClanahan-Burleson gang.[18]

Sanders wrote to Governor Allred on February 22, 1935, to report on his progress. He indicated that he had been working on the case for some time prior to that date, likely a week or more. He advised the governor that, based on the witness affidavits he and the Allred Rangers had recently obtained, it was apparent that McClanahan was indeed the only suspect in the murder of Brackett Sr. Sanders further told Allred that the witnesses at that stage were still understandably reticent to "emphatically" testify that McClanahan had fired the shots, though they acknowledged without equivocation that he was the only person there and was holding the murder weapon immediately after the shots were fired. Nevertheless, he assured Allred that he already felt confident not only in regard to the potential for securing an indictment but also in a successful conviction in the case. Sanders closed by saying that he would soon send a report detailing the evidence.[19]

Less than a week later, on March 1, Sanders wrote to the governor again, reporting that, since his last letter, his and the Allred Rangers' investigative efforts in the Brackett murder case had produced substantial additional evidence that he believed were cumulatively so compelling that "any grand jury will indict and a jury will convict, we believe, that person." Sanders noted that they had obtained affidavits from witnesses in Jasper County and Harris County, with the aid of additional investigators in those areas. Sanders insisted that the evidence they had collected clearly demonstrated that they had "a case of cold-blooded assassination" and that the witnesses were by then "talking very freely since they know they have ample protection [from the Allred Rangers]." Sanders again commented on the Rangers' efficiency and professionalism, and he asked that they continue in their activities in San Augustine County.[20]

Sanders then discussed the arrangements for his appointment to actually prosecute the Brackett case, which at that point had not been confirmed. He outlined proposed terms and compensation for his employment. He agreed to accept a flat fee of $1,000, plus payment of "actual expenses," in exchange for "prosecut[ing] the case to its final termination." Sanders also noted that he was open to suggestions from the governor in regard to such details but that, in any event, it was necessary to take immediate action in order to ensure successful prosecution. Sanders was concerned that delay could undermine public confidence, particularly that of the witnesses, and play into the hands of the defendant.[21]

Allred agreed to the amount proposed by Sanders but he preferred to pay it on a monthly basis. He noted that Sanders would be obligated to see the case to its conclusion, no matter how much longer than the three months (over which the fee would be paid) that might take. Allred also advised that he expected Sanders to be active on the prosecution immediately, including making preparations for submitting the case to a grand jury. Sanders replied that those terms were completely acceptable and said he "appreciate[d] the confidence . . . placed in [him] by reason of such employment . . . more than [he did] the fee."[22]

Allred, as a former district attorney and former attorney general of Texas, also offered strategic legal advice for prosecuting the case. He did not think that it would be in the state's best interest to hold a pre-indictment examining trial, because that would make the defense aware of at least some of the state's witnesses. Under the circumstances, this might have put their witnesses at risk or have prevented them from testifying out of fear that the defendants would retaliate were they were able to get out on bail pending the trial. He also reminded Sanders that although he was duly empowered to lead the prosecution of the Brackett murder case and could present evidence directly to the grand jury, he was not legally authorized to remain in the grand jury room during deliberations. Only the actual county or district attorney could be present in the room during that process. Clearly Allred was concerned that all legal matters be conducted properly and in a manner that would preclude a successful appeal. Other than making those two points, Allred told Sanders that he could "proceed in such a manner as [he] deem[ed fit]," thereby indicating confidence in Sanders's legal knowledge, abilities, and judgment.[23]

Sanders then put forth his own ideas as to prosecution strategy. Of particular note was his insistence that there needed to be a change of venue, that the case needed to be tried in a county other than San Augustine. Sanders was obviously concerned, once again, that local citizens might still be too fearful to serve on a jury and return a guilty verdict. He also mentioned that he anticipated a vigorous defense and asserted that it would likely require "considerable expense and time" to prosecute the case.[24]

Sanders also mentioned to Allred having been "interviewed" by the defense counsel, who claimed that when former district attorney Roy Blake had dismissed the original murder case back in 1930, he had made an agreement "that no other indictment would be returned." Sanders disputed the existence of any legal basis for such an agreement but wanted Governor Allred to be aware that defense planned to make that argument in court "should an indictment be returned." The fact that the issue was neither addressed during the trial nor raised on appeal casts doubts on the claims of McClanahan's attorney in the matter.[25]

Sanders wrote to Allred again on March 19, 1935, to report that while he and the Rangers were making good progress overall with the investigation, they had hit a procedural snag. As he had previously noted, Sanders did not want a murder complaint filed against McClanahan in a justice of the peace court because that might require them to hold an examining trial, which neither Sanders nor Allred believed was necessary or advantageous to the prosecution. However, it turned out that Captain McCormick had already filed such an instrument in a justice court, prior to Sanders's official involvement in the case. Sanders then suggested that they could still avoid an examining trial if they could convince the state district judge, F. Pat Adams, to call a special term of the district court to hear the matter, and noted to Allred that he had already written to the judge with that request.[26]

Sanders also mentioned that he had not been able to make contact with the district attorney who held prosecutorial jurisdiction in the county, Hollis Kinard. He wanted to inform Kinard that the governor had retained him (Sanders) to assist in prosecuting the Brackett murder case. This concerned Sanders regarding his legal legitimacy, though he expressed the resolve to carry on as long as it was the governor's desire that he do so.[27]

Allred appreciated Sanders's concern regarding confirming his role in the case with the district attorney, and he promptly wrote to Kinard to let him know that Sanders's involvement was at his (the governor's) request. Kinard, as it happened, had not been ignoring Sanders but was in Nacogdoches actively engaged in the prosecution of the first murder case to be tried following the arrival of the Allred Rangers in San Augustine, that of Lee Parrish for the killing of Ewell Hooper in October 1934.[28]

Kinard called Sanders the day he received the letter from Allred and requested that they meet in Nacogdoches to discuss the case and Sanders's role in the prosecution. Kinard not only welcomed Sanders's assistance, he asked him to take charge of the case. This alleviated Sanders's concerns and reinforced his resolve to see the case through. Sanders's news for Allred that day was not all good. He had met with the defense counsel, Steve M. King of Nacogdoches and W. T. Davis, who were requesting an examining trial, just as Sanders had feared. Sanders advised King and Davis that some of his witnesses were not available due to illness and convinced them that an examining trial would not be of benefit to either party at that point.[29]

The defense counsel agreed because by that time McClanahan was in custody under federal charges for his participation in the beating of E. C. Cleveland and under a failure-to-appear warrant, for which he allegedly could not afford to post a new bond. Judge Bryant in Beaumont signed an order releasing McClanahan to Allred Ranger Hines, who brought McClanahan before Judge Adams in San Augustine for arraignment. Sanders was relieved that the defense had agreed to forgo an examining trial because he had not wanted to "expose [the prosecutors'] hand," which they would have been forced to do by introducing witness testimony in order to have the defendant bound over for trial while awaiting a grand jury indictment. Since Judge Bryant had made it clear that he would allow the Allred Rangers to transfer McClanahan back to San Augustine whenever necessary to face the state charges, as long as he was in federal custody, both sides were free to take the time necessary to prepare their respective cases.[30]

On the same day that Hines brought McClanahan back from Beaumont, Constable Sublett Sharp arrested the second son of Sheriff Worsham, Tandy, for bootlegging. Along with Earl Moench and R. E. "Dick" Reeves, Tandy was illegally manufacturing liquor just blocks from the San Augustine town square. In mid-February Sharp had arrested Worsham's other son, Waymon, for possession of illegal liquor with the intent to sell. Apparently unable to make bond, Tandy would remain in jail for months. The Worsham boys learned the hard way that the arrival of the Allred Rangers meant an end to local corruption in law enforcement, so that now even the sons of the sheriff would be held accountable for their crimes.[31]

The Allred Rangers had wasted no time wresting control of San Augustine from the McClanahan-Burleson gang, and, as noted earlier, every move they made in those first days and weeks had had a dual purpose. First, they had sought to effectively frighten the gang members so that they left the area and could no longer intimidate and control the local citizenry, and, second, they had aimed to instill in the law-abiding citizens of the community a sense of security so that they would finally be able to come forward and report on the crimes committed by the McClanahan-Burleson gang and its associates over most of the past decade. San Augustinians had been so thoroughly demoralized by the gang's viciousness and impunity over time that a substantial show of force was crucial to restoring their faith in the local criminal justice system, which had all but collapsed. Fortunately, the Allred Rangers' strategy had worked as planned, and citizens came forward to report all manner of crimes perpetrated by the gang, including theft, robbery, extortion, counterfeiting, assault, racketeering, and murder. Now that the community was under official governmental control and the grip of the McClanahan-Burleson gang had been broken, the Allred Rangers could get down to the business of fully investigating those crimes and working with prosecutors to prepare them for trials. A reckoning had finally come to the Redlands.

— 6 —

THE WHEELS OF JUSTICE BEGIN TO TURN

With San Augustinians' fears of the McClanahan-Burleson gang all but eliminated and their faith in the local criminal justice system restored, the Allred Rangers got to work investigating a litany of criminal complaints, many dating back nearly a decade. They worked in cooperation with new local law enforcement officials, judges, prosecutors, and federal agents to secure massive amounts of evidence against the gang's leaders and associates. They documented and investigated complaints reported to them by victims and witnesses who eagerly came forward to provide accounts of crimes suffered at the hands of the gang members, and they also actively sought out those who remained reticent. Through various contacts, informants, and intermediaries, the Allred Rangers were able to find out about and reach out to those who had long given up hope—if they had ever had any—that justice would be served. Allred Rangers James W. McCormick and Dan J. Hines assured those individuals that the Rangers would protect them from retribution or retaliation, see the cases through the entire process of adjudication, and seek the greatest penalties for those who were convicted.

African American victims and witnesses presented a unique challenge. Their initial suspicions of any Anglo law officers were to be expected, not only because so many of their oppressors had carried law enforcement credentials but also due to the racial dynamics of the time. As noted in chapter 4, it is likely that the Allred

Rangers had an emissary in the local black community through whom they were able to reach and gain the trust of black witnesses and victims.[1]

As the Allred Rangers went about the business of investigating and preparing cases for trial, San Augustinians continued their expressions of their gratitude via letters and newspaper commentary. Further, in April 1935 San Augustine city manager G. C. Mitchell presented J. W. McCormick with a Colt pistol "in appreciation of the splendid work being done by Captain McCormick and his Rangers." The community made a concerted effort to ensure that the Allred Rangers felt welcome and would remain in town. After two months spent helping his colleagues restore order in San Augustine, with the gang dispersed and in hiding and witnesses beginning to come forward, Leo Bishop was assigned back to his regular duty station in the Rio Grande Valley in late March 1935. McCormick and Hines would remain fixtures in the community for the next year and a half as they pursued their objectives. Hines lived in San Augustine full-time, and McCormick came through regularly in the course of his duties as captain over the expansive East Texas region, supervising San Augustine operations and participating in court hearings and the like. Other Allred Rangers assisted at times.[2]

Due to the increased stability and sense of security established by the Allred Rangers, Secret Service operative-in-charge Edward Tyrrell and his men were finally able to obtain more effective public assistance for their investigations. They continued to develop their case regarding the assault on E. C. Cleveland while waiting for the next federal court hearing. They also sought evidence of counterfeiting by the McClanahan-Burleson gang in San Augustine by maintaining contact with local banks and businesses, who kept a lookout for counterfeit currency that might be passed to them. They did not have long to wait for some bogus bills to surface. In early April 1935, J. B. Bell of the First National Bank sent them a counterfeit fifty-cent coin. On April 8, Cleveland returned to San Augustine to follow up on the coin and learned that Justice of the Peace Lannie Smith had received it from a candy salesman named W. W. Galloway. Smith had then given it to Bell to verify as counterfeit. For his part, Galloway insisted he could not recall who had passed it to him.[3]

Bell also reported that William M. and Athenian Wade had received several counterfeit coins recently, so Cleveland interviewed both of them. Athenian, the postmaster for San Augustine, said that she had received a counterfeit quarter passed by a unidentified customer at the post office, and that her husband had received a bogus quarter and half-dollar from a unknown patron at the movie theater ticket office. Cleveland took all three coins into evidence and headed out of town to pursue other cases to which he was assigned. Despite such efforts and the presence of counterfeit coins and bills being passed in and around the area, Tyrrell's men apparently never attempted to charge anyone in San Augustine for counterfeiting. This might have been due to a lack of further evidence, or it may have been a practical decision in light of the fact that their primary suspects faced far more serious state charges. As a direct result of the Rangers' investigations, the San Augustine grand jury handed down five indictments for murder in early July 1935, as well as many more for a variety of state felonies against numerous key members and associates of the gang.[4]

Although the majority of law-abiding black and white San Augustinians were fully engaged with the Allred Rangers by this time and aware that their presence had ushered in a complete shift in the local law enforcement, regardless of the race of the victim, no white man in the area had yet been convicted by a jury for crimes against blacks. This apparently left some whites with the mistaken impression that they were still free to victimize blacks with impunity. Such was the case of the robbery of Fred "Snooks" Garrett by Wiley Green and Robert Lee. Garrett was a twenty-six-year-old native-born San Augustinian who lived west of town, worked as a general laborer for Fred Roberts, and played first base for the San Augustine baseball club. Garrett was single at the time and lived with his mother, who he supported with the one to two dollars per week he earned from Roberts and whatever else he could earn from odd jobs, such as chopping wood for Leon Sheffield.[5]

On May 30, 1935, Garrett got off work at about one thirty in the afternoon and then was in town ("down on the lower end") playing dominoes with Charlie Garrett and Jack Johnson until about eleven that evening, when he headed west toward home on foot. Along the road just below the creek bridge, he noticed a black, two-door Ford Model A with a chicken coop on the back and two men inside. About two hundred yards west of the bridge, near Joe Bewley's house, the car pulled alongside of Garrett. The bareheaded driver, Robert Lee—a twenty-three-year-old magazine salesman from Nacogdoches—and the hat-wearing passenger, Wiley Green, had both been drinking heavily that evening at J. L. Prince's café. Garrett was asked where he lived and replied "down the road," after which Green told him to get in the car. Thinking it was someone who knew him, Garrett started to step on the running board and then noticed Green pointing what he recognized as a black-handled .25 automatic pistol at him. Green told Garrett to put his hands up.[6]

Garrett did as he was ordered, and then Green reached through the window and took three dollars out of Garrett's pocket. The money consisted of two one-dollar bills (his weekly pay) and change that Garrett had won playing dominoes. Green then ordered Garrett to get in the car, at which point Lee spoke for the first time, directing Garrett to sit in the middle as Green lowered the gun to open the door. Garrett saw his opportunity to escape and, afraid of what Green and Lee might have in store for him, bolted back toward town, running till he was back across the bridge. Green and Lee didn't follow but instead sped off in the opposite direction.[7]

As would not have been the case before the arrival of the Allred Rangers, Garrett knew he could expect assistance from local officers and went straight to Constable Sublett Sharp, who was known for his close working relationship with the Allred Rangers, to report the crime and give a description of the robbers and their vehicle. After taking Garrett's statement, Sharp set out to investigate the crime and traveled as far as Denning that night, about nine miles west, in an effort to locate Lee and Green. After a fruitless search, Sharp returned to town and interviewed Prince after learning that he'd had a pistol stolen and that two men matching Garnett's descriptions of the robbers and their vehicle had been at his café that evening.[8]

The next morning, Sharp, McCormick, and a Deputy Jones went to Green's mother's home at "the upper edge of the county." Locating Green, Lee, and the suspect vehicle there, they arrested the two men and confiscated two one-dollar bills and seventy-five cents in change they found in their possession. McCormick took custody of Green for the trip back to the San Augustine jail, while Jones took Lee and traveled back separately by way of Camp Worth. Green and Lee learned that African American citizens were no longer fair game in San Augustine.[9]

Green and Lee did not spend long in jail. Two days later they escaped, not on their own but unwittingly. Sheriff Worsham's son Tandy had been in jail since February after his arrest for bootlegging, and it seems the sheriff wanted his son freed. On June 2, 1935, six prisoners, including Tandy Worsham, Green, and Lee, escaped from jail, but the sheriff left his son's name off the list of escapees when talking to the press. The other escapees were Jeff Duffield, an associate of Joe Burleson and accomplice in the murder of Henry Clay; Melvin Walls, a black man "held as a witness in several cases"; and Henry "Lightning" Washington, a black man charged with murder. Sheriff Worsham said they had been "given help from the outside," that a bar had been was pried loose, and that "a prisoner crawled through the hole and obtained the key to the main door. . . . [and] from the vestibule they [had gone] through a hole in the wall to a storage room leading to the outside." Given that Worsham was in charge of the jail and responsible for the inmates, and given that his son Tandy was among the escapees yet the sheriff failed to report this, the Allred Rangers certainly knew he wasn't to be trusted. Worsham already had an unsavory reputation in the community, which the Rangers also undoubtedly knew by this time.[10]

Bootlegging remained a widespread illegal practice in San Augustine County, and the Allred Rangers were responsible for curtailing the activity, which was often connected to racketeering efforts by the McClanahans and Burlesons. None of the gang engaged in the manufacture or direct sale of illegal liquor, but they attempted to control local distribution and take a cut of the proceeds. They also took "rake-offs" (illegitimate fees) from operators of slot machines. On June 12, 1935, Ranger Hines led a raid in the "badlands" of northwestern San Augustine County, an area that had seen two schoolhouses and a church burned and the murders of Lonnie and Ewell Hooper in the preceding two years. Hines's team—including Constable Sharp of San Augustine and Sheriff Jess Sample from Shelby County—seized a large liquor still, one hundred gallons of "mash," and twenty-two gallons of moonshine whiskey. The raid also resulted in the arrests of Watt Parrish (Lee's brother), Tommie Payne, and one A. Adams (reported as being from Waelder, Texas, a town between Houston and San Antonio) although Hollis Fulton and Parrish's seventeen-year-old son Clifton managed to escape.[11]

Later that month Hines led Sharp, Deputy Sheriff Tom Beard, and "Judge" Wilkinson—who was working as a "night officer"—on a raid about thirty miles southwest of San Augustine. This time they arrested Walter Lakey, seized his copper still, and confiscated nine gallons of whiskey. Hines was also tapped to assist in such raids in surrounding counties, such as one led by Ranger Artie Purvis in Port Arthur on June 15. Deputy Sheriff J. H. Allen assisted Rangers Purvis and Hines as they seized an estimated $4,000 worth of liquor and several slot machines from the Brown Derby and Leblanc's. Sensing the law pressing in on them, fugitive gang members began to surrender to authorities.[12]

Jim and Curg Burleson, who had skipped town to avoid arrest shortly after the Allred Rangers arrived in January, turned themselves in to Sheriff Sample in Center in early June, just as prosecutors were preparing to present cases against them for indictment. Both men later failed to appear and had to be rearrested. Curg had absconded to Dickens County in West Texas, where he would be caught in early August. Jim would surrender again in October, to Constable Sharp in San Augustine. The July 1935 term of the San Augustine County grand jury, led by County Attorney John F. McLaurin, was the second to convene since the arrival of the Allred Rangers and the first to consider cases investigated by them once they had established order and convinced the community that it was then safe to make complaints and give testimony against members of the McClanahan-Burleson gang.[13]

This was the grand jury that first indicted numerous white men for all manner of crimes against black San Augustinians and that indicted gang leaders for crimes ranging from robbery and extortion to murder. District Court judge F. P. Adams appointed Albert S. Mathews to serve as foreman for the grand jury and charged jurors to "make diligent investigation into all law violations, high or low, great or small, and where sufficient evidence [is] available to return true bills of indictment." Adams instructed them to be look for evidence of dereliction of duty by local public officials and promised that the court would try any and all such charges for which they found sufficient evidence to indict.[14]

After the grand jury term concluded, Mathews issued a report to Judge Adams that was published in the *San Augustine Tribune*. The report stated that the grand jury's term had lasted twenty-one days, during which time it had heard testimony from more than 450 witnesses regarding approximately 150 criminal cases and returned 66 indictments against dozens of defendants. Mathews noted that some cases had been left open for the next grand jury, because witnesses in those cases were not available to testify during the term. Mathews elaborated on the widespread cooperation the grand jury had received from the "majority of the people of the county" and thanked them for helping to enforce the law in San Augustine. He specifically thanked the district attorney and Rangers McCormick and Hines for their "splendid service." He also commended the sheriff, constable, and judge for their services to the county. Mathews closed with a call for continued public cooperation with law enforcement and a request to be adjourned. The wheels of justice in San Augustine were turning steadily, and the cleanup was producing tangible results. In fact, the volume of cases to be adjudicated was so unusually high that the court had to convene a special term in September to keep from developing a backlog and jeopardizing prosecutions.[15]

Five of those sixty-six indictments were for murder. On July 11, 1935, Joe Burleson became the first gang leader to be indicted for murder as a result of the Allred Rangers' investigations in San Augustine. Due to the intervention of a corrupt local justice of the peace who would later be removed from office—Lannie Smith, who signed a belated search warrant to give Joe cover—and a disgraced former sheriff who was Burleson's codefendant in the federal E. C. Cleveland assault case and indicted locally for assault and extortion, Burleson would also become the only member of the gang to be acquitted of a charge against him. In his trial for the murder of black bootlegger Henry Clay (see chapter 2), Burleson

Rangers. McClanahan went so far as to feign a nervous breakdown in order to get transferred out of the Beaumont City Jail and into a Roman Catholic charitable (and racially integrated) hospital and mental health facility called Hotel Dieu. In response to that news, Sanders requested the governor's prompt assistance in quickly arranging for either Dr. William Thomas of Rusk State Hospital—a mental health facility—or some other "reputable" mental health physician to conduct an examination of McClanahan at the jail in Center.[24]

Sanders was concerned that they would not have sufficient time otherwise to prepare and respond to such a plea. Allred promptly contacted Claude Teer, chairman of the State Board of Control, the agency that oversaw the state mental hospitals at the time, who advised that either Thomas or one of the other qualified physicians at Rusk go to Center to conduct the requested examination. Allred further suggested to Sanders that Rangers McCormick and Hines, as well as other law enforcement officers, might be effective witnesses for refuting McClanahan's claim of insanity. In the end, defense counsel attempted no such plea, instead proffering the original self-defense claim, to no avail.[25]

Sanders and the Allred Rangers spent most of their time in the weeks before the trial on supplemental investigative efforts, securing witness statements and evidence to prepare for whatever direction the defense might take the case. In addition to Sanders, Hollis Kinard (the district attorney for San Augustine) and Wardlow W. Lane (district attorney for Shelby and Panola Counties) were also assisting with the preparations for the case, and they all believed that it was "in most excellent condition for trial," Sanders informed Allred. However, McClanahan also had multiple attorneys working on his defense, and the prosecutors took nothing for granted. While making final preparations for the Brackett murder case to go to trial, the Allred Rangers were also preparing to present another years-old murder case to a San Augustine jury.[26]

claimed to have been acting as an officer of the law at the time of the killing—he had a special Ranger commission issued by Ma Ferguson. He testified that he had gone to Clay's house on official business as a law enforcement officer, that Clay had come out brandishing a rifle, and that he had fired at Clay in self-defense.[16]

Burleson's defense was aided by the testimony of former local sheriff Warren C. Gary and local justice of the peace Lannie Smith. Both testified that Burleson had a warrant to enter Clay's home. However, Ida Clay and Young Ruth both testified that Henry was unarmed when Joe Burleson and his two accomplices shot him in his kitchen in the middle of the night. It also appears that Burleson offered no explanation why, as an unpaid officer with no specific official role in such matters, he would have served an allegedly lawful warrant without a local officer in the lead, in the middle of the night, accompanied by two men without law enforcement credentials or affiliation. Impeding the prosecution was a complete lack of postmortem investigation or medical examination. Unlike the Ella F. Curl and Edward Clark cases, which eventually resulted in convictions of white criminals who victimized blacks, it appears that the all-white jury in Burleson's trial accepted the accounts of Burleson and the corrupt former judge and sheriff and had "reasonable doubt" despite the contradictory testimony of black witnesses. Burleson was acquitted, to the chagrin of the victim's family, prosecutors, and the Allred Rangers. However, he would not prove immune to prosecution for much longer.[17]

Despite the verdict acquitting Burleson in the killing of Henry Clay, the Allred Rangers and the San Augustine criminal justice system had bucked the Jim Crow laws and customs of the time by investigating and indicting two white men (and one black man) for a crime against a black man, for which there were only black witnesses able to testify. As it happened, corruption allegations had not yet surfaced against Lannie Smith, whose testimony was essential to buttress Burleson's claim of having entered the Clay home in the course of a lawful investigation. Burleson's other key witness, Gary, was by this time disgraced and was Burleson's codefendant in the federal assault case, so one wonders whether the jury would likely have returned the same verdict if it had been aware of defense witness Smith's dubious credibility. Being the very first jury to hear a case against such a prominent member of the McClanahan-Burleson gang might have had a chilling effect on their willingness to convict him.[18]

As with the murders of Brackett and Gann, the assassination of Henry Clay characterized how vicious the McClanahan-Burleson gang had become in the pursuit of its illegal enterprises and enforcement of its illegitimate local regime. It also illustrates how it had moved from facing the inconvenience of an indictment or the likes of a failed trial when no witnesses testified to the apparent assumption that local law enforcement officials would not bother to arrest them, regardless of the crime. This may have been particularly true when the victim was black, but whites were targets of the McClanahan-Burleson gang, as well.

Of the surviving records regarding the final disposition of all three cases—those of the murder of Clay, the murder of Brackett, and the murder of Gann (see chapter 7) the files for Vandy Steptoe and Jeff Duffield, Joe Burleson's accomplices in the murder of Clay, are incomplete and therefore somewhat unclear. Duffield escaped from the San Augustine jail on June 2, 1935, along with others held under indictment. Sheriff Worsham's description of the escape suggests that whoever enabled it must have had access to the interior of the jail. The suspicious circumstances did not escape the notice of the Allred Rangers, who had been losing confidence in Worsham almost from the beginning. For the moment, however, they focused their attention on bringing Charlie McClanahan to justice in a cold case, a murder that had been a key event in reinforcing the gang's power.[19]

Special prosecutor S. H. Sanders completed the presentation of his case against McClanahan for the murder of Edward B. Brackett Sr. to the San Augustine County grand jury on July 5, 1935. He had called twenty-two witnesses. Sanders expressed great appreciation for the professionalism of the court, the district attorney, the county attorney, and the grand jurors. He noted that he had been allowed to present his case inside the grand jury room, but he then left immediately so that he would not jeopardize the legality of the indictment. In a letter to Governor Allred, Sanders described portions of his presentation, including how the Allred Rangers had assisted him in addressing McClanahan's anticipated defense, namely the claim of self-defense was based on threats Brackett Sr. was alleged to have made against McClanahan prior to the shooting.[20]

While McClanahan's defense was planning to present several witnesses who, it was supposed, would testify that they had heard such threats from Brackett Sr., similar witnesses had already admitted to the Allred Rangers that no such threats had ever been made in their presence. Plenty more witnesses had come forth to testify that not only had Brackett Sr. never made any threats against McClanahan, he had instead made numerous overtures to bury the hatchet and on at least two occasions had agreed to meet with McClanahan to clear the air. It would eventually be shown that it had been McClanahan who had refused to let the matter go. Sanders concluded his report by asserting that the evidence uncovered indicated that McClanahan's killing of Brackett was a "case of cold-blooded assassination."

He praised Governor Allred "in connection with the good citizenship of S. Augustine" for sending the Allred Rangers there, and he expressed his confiden that the case would receive a change of venue for the trial. Allred thanked Sande for his report and "fine services" in the Brackett case, and he confirmed that had written to both the district judge and the district attorney in support o change of venue.[21]

In the first week of July 1935, the grand jury returned a "true bill" of indictme against McClanahan for the murder of Brackett. Sanders wrote to Allred th he had been assured by the "proper officials" that the venue in the case wou be changed at a hearing that had been scheduled for July 15. He was told it w possible that the case would be sent to his home county of Shelby, immediate north of San Augustine, as it would be "convenient and accessible for the w nesses," but he noted to the governor that there was no guarantee of that and th wherever it was sent would have to be with the agreement of the prosecutio At that hearing for change of venue, Judge F. Pat Adams transferred the ca to Panola County, instead of Shelby, in response to concerns raised by defen counsel Steve King. King argued that "it would be most unfair" to transfer t case to the lead prosecutor's home county, though he also agreed that it wou be equally unfair to transfer it to Nacogdoches, just west of San Augustine, that was King's former hometown. Sanders was satisfied that they could form fair and impartial jury from the citizens of Panola County, where Carthage w the seat of government.[22]

Governor Allred commended Sanders for his diligence and sound judgme in prosecuting the case up to that point and commended Judge Adams for h swift decision on the motion for change of venue. Allred commented that distri judges would often "wait for the thing to be thrashed around on both side before reaching such a decision. McClanahan was initially ordered back int federal custody at the end of the hearing, but it appears that he remained in th San Augustine County Jail until he was transferred to the Shelby County Jail i Center sometime in August and stayed there until he was moved to Carthag for the trial.[23]

Even before his trial, it became more and more apparent—even to McCla nahan—that he was losing his grip on the citizens of San Augustine. By lat August 1935, it was widely rumored that the defense was shifting from a claim o self-defense, which depended on witnesses to testify that Brackett had threatene McClanahan, to a claim of insanity. If true, this shift might have been prompte by the reversal of witnesses, some of whom had already recanted to the Allre

═ 7 ═

JUSTICE DELIVERED, NOT DENIED

Eron Harris, Tom Burleson's brother-in-law and the first defendant in the murder of local teacher John Gann, was finally brought to trial in August 1935 as a direct result of the Allred Rangers' efforts in San Augustine. Like the three Thomas family members after him, the twenty-three-year-old, unarmed Gann had been shot to death by Tom Burleson on San Augustine's courthouse square before a number of witnesses. Gann left behind a wife and small child, and his murder terrorized the community. The McClanahan-Burleson gang held most of the local law enforcement positions, so who would protect witnesses and victims should they speak out about what had occurred? And since juries had already refused to serve in cases involving McClanahan-Burleson gang members, fearing retaliation, what would have been the point of testifying? However, once the Allred Rangers took control, citizens began opening up to the Rangers about countless crimes, including the murder of Gann, and this provided prosecutors with the witnesses they needed to put together their cases.[1]

There were four men directly associated with Gann's death: Tom Burleson, Sandy Thacker, Eron Harris, and Noah Thacker. Burleson and Sandy Thacker both died before they could be brought to trial, Burleson from lead poisoning after the December 1934 shoot-out. Eron Harris and Noah Thacker would be convicted in 1935 and 1936 as accomplices, although the latter's conviction would still later be reversed on appeal, based on a lack of evidence that he had demonstrated any previous knowledge of the plan to shoot Gann or taken any direct action to assist in it.

Harris, who had enabled Burleson to shoot Gann without any risk of retaliation by striking the victim in the head, was the first to be tried as an accomplice to the murder. With the Allred Rangers in attendance, the trial began on August 22, 1935, in the district court of Judge T. O. Davis in Center. The attorneys for the state were Wardlow Lane and Hollis M. Kinard, of Center and Orange, respectively. The law firm of Adams & McAlister of Nacogdoches served as counsel for the defense. Lane and Kinard presented five witnesses during direct testimony for the Harris trial: E. L. "Buddy" Mitchell, Elbert Nichols, Luther Stotts, Virgie Scurlock, and Aubrey Mathews. Mitchell, Nichols, and Stotts would also be the lead witnesses in the case against Noah Thacker, which would begin on January 30, 1936. These three had been standing on the sidewalk about twenty-five to thirty feet west of where the attack on Gann occurred and had all seen the attack. Of the five witnesses, only Nichols knew who Gann was prior to the day he was murdered, and he only knew Gann by sight and was otherwise unacquainted with him.[2]

Scurlock had observed the attack on Gann from a much closer vantage point than the first three witnesses, having "walked right up behind Tom Burleson" from east of the Clark-Downs store just after exiting the Commercial Bank. Scurlock testified that she had heard the men cursing and walked over to see what was going on. She provided specific testimony regarding what each man had said and noted that neither Burleson nor Gann were the ones talking. Scurlock stated that Noah Thacker had said, "Yes, look him in the eye and tell him and shake his hand," and then Harris had said, "You goddamned son of a bitch, I said shake hands with him, and look him in the eye" just before Harris "shoved Gann or hit him." She further testified that Gann had turned to leave and that she had done the same, at which point she heard five or six shots fired. Scurlock also corroborated Mitchell's account that after the shooting, Burleson began cursing at Gann and threatening to kill him, although he had already shot Gann at least four times and Gann had died. Scurlock also noted that, after the shooting, Noah Thacker walked around the store, looking over the counters in an apparent attempt to locate Gann. She said Burleson had also stepped into the store briefly after the shooting, but left quickly as Noah Thacker scanned the premises more thoroughly before they all left the scene.[3]

Witness Virgie Scurlock was the daughter of Virgil Worsham, who had resigned as sheriff in the wake of a sex scandal the day before her testimony. Because he had participated in some investigations and arrests of Burleson family members and claimed to have been acting as an officer of the law at the time of the killing—he had a special Ranger commission issued by Ma Ferguson. He testified that he had gone to Clay's house on official business as a law enforcement officer, that Clay had come out brandishing a rifle, and that he had fired at Clay in self-defense.[16]

Burleson's defense was aided by the testimony of former local sheriff Warren C. Gary and local justice of the peace Lannie Smith. Both testified that Burleson had a warrant to enter Clay's home. However, Ida Clay and Young Ruth both testified that Henry was unarmed when Joe Burleson and his two accomplices shot him in his kitchen in the middle of the night. It also appears that Burleson offered no explanation why, as an unpaid officer with no specific official role in such matters, he would have served an allegedly lawful warrant without a local officer in the lead, in the middle of the night, accompanied by two men without law enforcement credentials or affiliation. Impeding the prosecution was a complete lack of postmortem investigation or medical examination. Unlike the Ella F. Curl and Edward Clark cases, which eventually resulted in convictions of white criminals who victimized blacks, it appears that the all-white jury in Burleson's trial accepted the accounts of Burleson and the corrupt former judge and sheriff and had "reasonable doubt" despite the contradictory testimony of black witnesses. Burleson was acquitted, to the chagrin of the victim's family, prosecutors, and the Allred Rangers. However, he would not prove immune to prosecution for much longer.[17]

Despite the verdict acquitting Burleson in the killing of Henry Clay, the Allred Rangers and the San Augustine criminal justice system had bucked the Jim Crow laws and customs of the time by investigating and indicting two white men (and one black man) for a crime against a black man, for which there were only black witnesses able to testify. As it happened, corruption allegations had not yet surfaced against Lannie Smith, whose testimony was essential to buttress Burleson's claim of having entered the Clay home in the course of a lawful investigation. Burleson's other key witness, Gary, was by this time disgraced and was Burleson's codefendant in the federal assault case, so one wonders whether the jury would likely have returned the same verdict if it had been aware of defense witness Smith's dubious credibility. Being the very first jury to hear a case against such a prominent member of the McClanahan-Burleson gang might have had a chilling effect on their willingness to convict him.[18]

As with the murders of Brackett and Gann, the assassination of Henry Clay characterized how vicious the McClanahan-Burleson gang had become in the pursuit of its illegal enterprises and enforcement of its illegitimate local regime. It also illustrates how it had moved from facing the inconvenience of an indictment or the likes of a failed trial when no witnesses testified to the apparent assumption that local law enforcement officials would not bother to arrest them, regardless of the crime. This may have been particularly true when the victim was black, but whites were targets of the McClanahan-Burleson gang, as well.

Of the surviving records regarding the final disposition of all three cases—those of the murder of Clay, the murder of Brackett, and the murder of Gann (see chapter 7) the files for Vandy Steptoe and Jeff Duffield, Joe Burleson's accomplices in the murder of Clay, are incomplete and therefore somewhat unclear. Duffield escaped from the San Augustine jail on June 2, 1935, along with others held under indictment. Sheriff Worsham's description of the escape suggests that whoever enabled it must have had access to the interior of the jail. The suspicious circumstances did not escape the notice of the Allred Rangers, who had been losing confidence in Worsham almost from the beginning. For the moment, however, they focused their attention on bringing Charlie McClanahan to justice in a cold case, a murder that had been a key event in reinforcing the gang's power.[19]

Special prosecutor S. H. Sanders completed the presentation of his case against McClanahan for the murder of Edward B. Brackett Sr. to the San Augustine County grand jury on July 5, 1935. He had called twenty-two witnesses. Sanders expressed great appreciation for the professionalism of the court, the district attorney, the county attorney, and the grand jurors. He noted that he had been allowed to present his case inside the grand jury room, but he then left immediately so that he would not jeopardize the legality of the indictment. In a letter to Governor Allred, Sanders described portions of his presentation, including how the Allred Rangers had assisted him in addressing McClanahan's anticipated defense, namely the claim of self-defense was based on threats Brackett Sr. was alleged to have made against McClanahan prior to the shooting.[20]

While McClanahan's defense was planning to present several witnesses who, it was supposed, would testify that they had heard such threats from Brackett Sr., similar witnesses had already admitted to the Allred Rangers that no such threats had ever been made in their presence. Plenty more witnesses had come forth to testify that not only had Brackett Sr. never made any threats against McClanahan, he had instead made numerous overtures to bury the hatchet and on at least two occasions had agreed to meet with McClanahan to clear the air. It would eventually be shown that it had been McClanahan who had refused to let the matter go. Sanders concluded his report by asserting that the evidence uncovered indicated that McClanahan's killing of Brackett was a "case of cold-blooded assassination."

He praised Governor Allred "in connection with the good citizenship of San Augustine" for sending the Allred Rangers there, and he expressed his confidence that the case would receive a change of venue for the trial. Allred thanked Sanders for his report and "fine services" in the Brackett case, and he confirmed that he had written to both the district judge and the district attorney in support of a change of venue.[21]

In the first week of July 1935, the grand jury returned a "true bill" of indictment against McClanahan for the murder of Brackett. Sanders wrote to Allred that he had been assured by the "proper officials" that the venue in the case would be changed at a hearing that had been scheduled for July 15. He was told it was possible that the case would be sent to his home county of Shelby, immediately north of San Augustine, as it would be "convenient and accessible for the witnesses," but he noted to the governor that there was no guarantee of that and that wherever it was sent would have to be with the agreement of the prosecution. At that hearing for change of venue, Judge F. Pat Adams transferred the case to Panola County, instead of Shelby, in response to concerns raised by defense counsel Steve King. King argued that "it would be most unfair" to transfer the case to the lead prosecutor's home county, though he also agreed that it would be equally unfair to transfer it to Nacogdoches, just west of San Augustine, as that was King's former hometown. Sanders was satisfied that they could form a fair and impartial jury from the citizens of Panola County, where Carthage was the seat of government.[22]

Governor Allred commended Sanders for his diligence and sound judgment in prosecuting the case up to that point and commended Judge Adams for his swift decision on the motion for change of venue. Allred commented that district judges would often "wait for the thing to be thrashed around on both sides" before reaching such a decision. McClanahan was initially ordered back into federal custody at the end of the hearing, but it appears that he remained in the San Augustine County Jail until he was transferred to the Shelby County Jail in Center sometime in August and stayed there until he was moved to Carthage for the trial.[23]

Even before his trial, it became more and more apparent—even to McClanahan—that he was losing his grip on the citizens of San Augustine. By late August 1935, it was widely rumored that the defense was shifting from a claim of self-defense, which depended on witnesses to testify that Brackett had threatened McClanahan, to a claim of insanity. If true, this shift might have been prompted by the reversal of witnesses, some of whom had already recanted to the Allred

Rangers. McClanahan went so far as to feign a nervous breakdown in order to get transferred out of the Beaumont City Jail and into a Roman Catholic charitable (and racially integrated) hospital and mental health facility called Hotel Dieu. In response to that news, Sanders requested the governor's prompt assistance in quickly arranging for either Dr. William Thomas of Rusk State Hospital—a mental health facility—or some other "reputable" mental health physician to conduct an examination of McClanahan at the jail in Center.[24]

Sanders was concerned that they would not have sufficient time otherwise to prepare and respond to such a plea. Allred promptly contacted Claude Teer, chairman of the State Board of Control, the agency that oversaw the state mental hospitals at the time, who advised that either Thomas or one of the other qualified physicians at Rusk go to Center to conduct the requested examination. Allred further suggested to Sanders that Rangers McCormick and Hines, as well as other law enforcement officers, might be effective witnesses for refuting McClanahan's claim of insanity. In the end, defense counsel attempted no such plea, instead proffering the original self-defense claim, to no avail.[25]

Sanders and the Allred Rangers spent most of their time in the weeks before the trial on supplemental investigative efforts, securing witness statements and evidence to prepare for whatever direction the defense might take the case. In addition to Sanders, Hollis Kinard (the district attorney for San Augustine) and Wardlow W. Lane (district attorney for Shelby and Panola Counties) were also assisting with the preparations for the case, and they all believed that it was "in most excellent condition for trial," Sanders informed Allred. However, McClanahan also had multiple attorneys working on his defense, and the prosecutors took nothing for granted. While making final preparations for the Brackett murder case to go to trial, the Allred Rangers were also preparing to present another years-old murder case to a San Augustine jury.[26]

JUSTICE DELIVERED, NOT DENIED

their associates, they regarded him as an adversary. But his daughter's testimony gave no evidence of bias or dishonesty. Further, she had been estranged from her father since early childhood. The separation was so pronounced that it was revealed under cross-examination that her father, as sheriff, had had to track her down at church on a Sunday to serve her the subpoena compelling her presence and testimony at trial.[4]

The final witness, Mathews, was a Clark-Downs employee. His testimony as to the persons involved in the killing, including their locations and actions, corroborated that of the other witnesses. Mathews had seen both the preliminary events (including when Harris punched Gann) and the shooting, he had seen Gann lying on the floor some six to eight feet inside the store, up against the wall, and he had seen Gann die. He also testified that there was not a case of guns anywhere near where Gann ran in to the store at the time of the murder and that there was no gun found anywhere near Gann's body.[5]

The prosecution's five witnesses, as a whole, offered detailed, compelling, and consistent testimony, even under cross-examination by the defense counsel. All were eyewitnesses to the murder, and the prosecution restricted its presentation strictly to the facts surrounding the events in question. That was the prosecution's case: no other evidence was presented during any portion of the trial. There was no sense that any of the state's witnesses were biased or in any way tied to any factionalism against the defendant, the other suspects in the case, or their families. After the prosecution rested its case against Harris, the defense introduced the testimony of thirty witnesses, including the defendant and Noah Thacker. Nine of the thirty claimed to be eyewitnesses to the Gann shooting. This number included the defendant, Harris, Noah Thacker, and Lee "Red" Jordan, who would subsequently be convicted of armed robberies committed in collusion with Jim Burleson.[6]

The defense's case got off to an inauspicious start. Defense witness H. B. Sparks sought to testify about the diagram of the store that he had created from measurements taken only a few weeks before the trial. But the state objected to this testimony on the grounds that evidence as to the *current* state of the store was irrelevant and would not relate to the state of the store when the shooting had taken place two years prior. The court sustained the state's objection, ruling that Sparks would only be permitted to testify about facts relating to the time of the shooting. Sparks, however, did not have sufficient knowledge to testify about the state of the store in August 1933. His testimony therefore failed to advance the self-defense argument that relied on the existence of a case of guns near the door; the gun case that was near the door when Sparks made his diagram had not been there at the time of the murder. The layout of the store had changed substantially between the time of the murder and the time of the trial.[7]

Another defense witness, J. H. "Henry" Johnson, was supposed to testify about a separate incident (the December 1934 shoot-out at the hardware store), which had resulted in the death of the primary codefendant in the Harris case. That testimony was never heard, as the judge sustained the state's objection based on lack of relevance. It was the correct legal decision, but historical researchers would thus lose the opportunity to read another firsthand account of those events.

Several defense witnesses contradicted each other (and even themselves) during cross-examination. This confusion, which likely did the most damage to the defense's case, may have stemmed from the simultaneous advancement of two completely separate defense arguments: (1) that Gann's killing had been self-defense, not murder (with testimony and questioning seemingly focused on exonerating the deceased shooter, Burleson, rather than the defendant on trial), and (2) that the defendant was a Samaritan who had tried unsuccessfully to stop a deadly brawl, not an accomplice to murder.[8]

In addition to the inconsistencies, some of the defense testimony was demonstrably inaccurate. As noted, a gun case present near the front of the store in 1935 had not been there at the time of the shooting in 1933 (it had been located in the far back corner of the store). But defense counsel argued that Burleson shot Gann in self-defense because he had reasonably believed that Gann was attempting to reach a gun from this case. The validity of this imminent "threat" was also undermined by the reality that it would have taken a long time for Gann to retrieve and load a pistol from the case even if it had been immediately accessible. These facts did not support the defense contention that the killing was justified as self-defense.[9]

The second contention alleged in support of the self-defense argument was that Gann had possessed and threateningly displayed a knife during the conflict. This was evidently introduced during the questioning of the state's witnesses, although only one defense witness testified to having seen Gann with a knife. That witness was Lee Jordan, who would later be convicted of robbery along with Jim Burleson. However, all of the prosecution's witnesses, and all of the defense eyewitnesses, contradicted Jordan's assertions on this matter; even those who had known Jordan at the time of the murder testified to not having seen him at the scene. Jordan claimed not only to have seen Gann produce and wield a knife but also to have picked up the knife after Gann dropped it upon being shot; again, only Jordan noted any such thing. He also claimed to have turned the knife over to then–special Ranger Charlie McClanahan. But McClanahan (who was also soon to be tried for murder) had never produced a knife or testified about one at Tom Burleson's trial in early 1934, and he didn't do it in this case either. As a well-known close associate of the Burleson family, and of Tom in particular, he would have had a vested interest in providing Tom and Harris with exculpatory evidence. That Jordan was unable to provide corroborating evidence for his claims undermined the defense.[10]

During his own trial later for armed robbery, it would be proven that Jordan had instructed a witness to provide false alibi testimony on his behalf. In light of the facts now known, it appears that Jordan's testimony in the Gann murder case was manufactured in an attempt to aid a fellow Burleson associate and also vindicate Tom Burleson in the matter. However, the testimony of the other defense witnesses, which indicated that Tom was a violent sociopath who threatened or killed anyone who crossed him, significantly outweighed Jordan's dubious testimony.[11]

After the self-defense argument floundered, the defense counsel abandoned that approach in favor of asserting the Samaritan story. This transparent change of direction was undermined by the testimony of the defendant himself, who (according to the testimony of all the witnesses) had been closer to the shooter and victim than anyone else. Harris made no mention of a knife during his direct testimony and, upon cross-examination by the state, denied that Gann had possessed or displayed a knife. The defense offered very little to explain the root of the apparent conflict between Gann and Burleson, save for a vague, brief story by Almeta Steptoe claiming that Gann had advised her against dating Tom Burleson because "he wasn't fit for a decent girl to go with" and that she had subsequently relayed that conversation to Tom, who had become angry and fought Gann a few days later. She failed to mention that Tom had apparently lost that fight and afterward vowed to get Gann. (In the 1936 trial of Noah Thacker, testimony by Virgie Scurlock and Buddy Mitchell would suggest that the originating conflict might have been between Gann and Harris rather than between Gann and Tom.) Altogether, most of the defense testimony in Harris's trial raised more questions than it answered, leaving the impression that the witnesses were for the most part biased and either confused or dishonest.[12]

Other than the nine eyewitnesses, the remainder of the defense witnesses can mostly be divided into two groups. The first is that of family members offering testimony regarding events before or after the shooting, the purpose of which remains unclear because much of the testimony consisted of claims about what the victim, shooter, or defendant said before or after the shooting (much of which was hearsay) or merely about peripheral matters that shed no light on the killing, such as the defendant's employment over the previous few years or activities immediately surrounding or altogether unrelated to the murder. Most perplexing is that the majority of these witnesses, mostly relatives of Tom Burleson, seemed more intent on providing excuses for Tom, the deceased and undisputed shooter, than defending the living participant who was on trial.

The second group consisted of character witnesses for the defendant, who all admitted under cross-examination that they had not known or had contact with the defendant for several years. In rebuttal, the prosecutor produced several witnesses who testified to more recent and local knowledge of the defendant's poor reputation for "truth and veracity." All in all, the testimony of the defense witnesses, including the defendant, was not compelling or credible. The testimony of the state's witnesses, which had all been secured through the investigative efforts of the Allred Rangers, convinced the jury that the state's case was an accurate description of how Gann had died and of who was responsible.[13]

Collectively, the testimony presented by the state's witnesses was clear, concise, sufficiently detailed, specific, to the point, and, most of all, consistent. Those witnesses did not recant anything or become confused under cross-examination; they were just as clear and detailed in their responses then as they had been under direct examination. There were no substantive contradictions of fact among them. The defense witnesses, on the other hand, offered no consensus regarding facts and no clarity of argument but presented instead as a loose collection of unrelated, contradictory, and often irrelevant testimony. Defense counsel appeared to be trying every trick in an attempt to raise doubt in the minds of the jurors but had no clear plan guiding their efforts. The jury rejected all the defense arguments, convicted Eron Harris of murder, and imposed a sentence of ten years. The Texas Court of Criminal Appeals later affirmed Harris's conviction and sentence. Further, as a direct result of evidence offered during the Harris trial, Noah Thacker would be indicted, arrested, tried, and convicted of having aided in Gann's murder, although, as noted above, this conviction was later reversed and the final disposition is unknown.[14]

After the San Augustine criminal justice system was reinvigorated thanks to the stability and security provided by the Allred Rangers, preparations were underway there for more trials, which were beginning to take place more frequently. But other matters also demanded the attention of McCormick and Hines. While most of the known gang leaders and associates had left the area or were behind bars, corrupt members of the local community still held positions of power and needed to be removed. One in particular had been apparent to McCormick and Hines from the outset, but they took the time to confirm their suspicions with solid evidence before moving against him.

Sheriff Worsham had won the election in November 1934 to replace Gary, who had been indicted in federal court in October for participating in the beating of Cleveland, the Secret Service agent, along with other members of the Burleson-McClanahan gang. From the outset, the Burleson and McClanahan families regarded Worsham as an antagonist and were frustrated by his involvement in the arrests of their family members and associates.[15]

The Allred Rangers arrested Worsham's adult sons, Waymon and Tandy, for running a bootlegging operation just a few blocks from the San Augustine town square. The Rangers' suspicion of corruption on the part of Worsham was heightened after his son and several others escaped from jail on June 2, 1935. As noted in chapter 6, Worsham failed to mention his son as having been among the escapees and vaguely asserted that the escapees had had "outside help," but the Rangers were aware of this important detail and suspected that the aid escapees received was from inside rather than outside. In light of this knowledge and his interference with their efforts to enforce the law against his associates, they devised a plan to get Worsham removed from office.[16]

Hines and McCormick arranged for an attractive blonde woman from Beaumont to serve as bait and later surprised Worsham in a hotel room in Center with her. In his memoir published nearly twenty years later, Worsham claimed to have known all along that it was a setup and that nothing happened between them, although he offered no explanation as to why he went to the hotel with her if he knew he was being set up. He also claimed contrarily that he never went to the hotel, having instead sent an unnamed friend to survey the scene for him. His strange account of the incident raises far more questions than it answers. While Worsham never names the individual "Allred Rangers" he aggressively disparages in his memoir, he does name Leo Bishop, who had left San Augustine in late March. Worsham insisted, "Leo Bishop would help and advise me, and would not have been a party to such dirty deeds."[17]

Regardless of Worsham's effort much later to argue his innocence, the Allred Rangers' sting operation prompted him to resign his office on August 21, 1935, a move for which he offered no official reason at the time, though he did write a letter to the *San Augustine Tribune*, "To the Citizenship of San Augustine," stating, "I have done no wrong, and have no apologies to offer" (despite the fact he was resigning under threat of being removed for cause, solicitation of prostitution). He concluded the letter by saying, "I am tendering my resignation with a clear conscience." In his book published decades later, Worsham again offered no plausible explanation for having resigned. He contended that he had not been receiving adequate financial support from the commissioners' court, but he waited nearly twenty years to express this in his memoir. This claim is unexplained, undocumented, and otherwise unsubstantiated. If county officials removed his funding as an inducement for him to resign, that fact would support the contention that he was forced out of office. But he offered only vague allusions to professional jealousy and corruption to explain the commissioners' and Rangers' antagonism for him. No other San Augustinian is known to have ever offered any words of support—much less corroborating evidence—in defense of Worsham in these matters.[18]

From a thorough review of all available information, it appears that Worsham was a corrupt and incompetent officer who repeatedly attempted to take sole credit for the cleanup of San Augustine, both in talking with journalists at the time and writing decades later in his memoir. His claim to have had everything under control before the Allred Rangers arrived was an assessment not shared by anyone else in town at the time. A deluge of contemporary news articles and the consensus view of people decades later who remember those events decisively show that it was the efforts of the Allred Rangers that brought the town under control and restored law and order.[19]

Worsham was not the only local official to resign in the wake of the Allred Rangers' cleanup of San Augustine. Justice of the Peace Lannie Smith, who testified that he had issued a search warrant to Joe Burleson the night of the Henry Clay murder, was also forced to resign from office at the same time due to allegations of corruption, allegations that stemmed from the Rangers' investigations. (One wonders whether the jury that heard the Clay murder case would have returned a different verdict if they had been aware of the witness's dubious credibility.) No documentation in regard to the circumstances of Smith's resignation or those of others has been discovered, other than that they were a result of investigations by the Allred Rangers. Constable Sublett Sharp, who had aggressively assisted the Allred Rangers, was endorsed by them and immediately appointed to replace Worsham as sheriff. The San Augustine County commissioners' court also appointed Ranger-endorsed" Deputy Sheriff Erwin Wade to the post of city marshal. Sharp then hired a highly recommended and experienced peace officer, Jim Greer of Nacogdoches, to be his first deputy sheriff. With these changes in place, the Allred Rangers aggressively continued their investigations focused on cleaning up San Augustine, together with strong local law enforcement backing.[20]

The vast majority of San Augustine citizens endorsed the changes in local leadership, as evidenced by their continuing expressions of gratitude for the Allred Rangers. They appointed only men endorsed by McCormick and Hines, wrote letters and newspaper pieces affirming their approval, and held additional widely attended public events at which they again broadcast their esteem for McCormick and Hines. In April 1935, San Augustine held its first Trades Day, which included a variety of entertainment, such as stunts by a performer from Dallas. With Sheriff Worsham and one Wesley Chumley as passengers, R. T. Smith drove a car blindfolded through heavy traffic, complete with turns, ending up at Partin Grocery. There "Daredevil Smith then climbed a ladder to the top of the building and walked the ledge of same to the applause of the large crowd." A contest of some sort was held, for which Ranger Hines was one of the judges along with Constable Sharp and *Tribune* editor Webster Hays, in which Mrs. Jesse Mathews, Homer Whitworth, Mrs. Lister Smith, and W. H. Fussell were awarded first through fourth place, respectively.[21]

The *San Augustine Tribune* reported that thousands of people "from practically all over the trade territory" were in attendance. The paper noted that McCormick, Hines, and their wives led the opening dance, which commenced with an announcement by local attorney Joseph R. Bogard. The dance, Bogard stated, was a "continued celebration of the wonderful change in conditions in San Augustine [and] the stamping out of lawlessness by the Rangers, assisted by local officers." Everyone present, he said, was "shaking hands and commenting favorably upon the new era for San Augustine, that of law enforcement, and all were loud in their praise of Captain McCormick and his assistants, Rangers Dan Hines and Leo Bishop." The event was such a success that the townspeople were soon scheduling their second Trades Day for May 25, just a month later. For San Augustinians in mid-1935, gone were the days of avoiding the town center and cowering in their homes. Instead they were publicly reveling in the freedom and peace they had regained, and they credited the Allred Rangers for instigating that change.[22]

These events indicated the strong public support for the Texas Rangers' accomplishments in San Augustine, and local leaders continued to express their gratitude to Governor Allred too. They invited the governor and his Rangers to be their special guests for "the big East Texas Championship Rodeo" in August at the local fairgrounds, where, less than a year before, the Burlesons and McClanahans had beaten E. C. Cleveland. The event was billed as a celebration of the town's return to law and order. The *San Augustine Tribune*'s August 8 front page covered the two-day event and included a huge picture of Governor Allred. The affair included a parade (led by the governor on horseback), a dance, and such rodeo events as "bull-dogging," wild horse saddling and racing, breakaway and tie-down calf roping, bronco and Brahma bull riding, wild mare milking, a "cowboy boot race," and a bullfighting clown. Just before the parade, five-year-old Jacqualin Cartwright presented a bouquet of flowers to the governor on behalf of the San Augustine History Study Club.[23]

Ranger Hines—an experienced rodeo competitor and organizer whose local popularity was frequently mentioned in local and statewide news reports—was tapped to direct the rodeo, along with G. T. Bell of Beaumont. Hines and Bell brought in other Texas Rangers and cowboys from across Texas, Oklahoma, Louisiana, and from as far away as New York to compete for $1,000 in cash prizes. Hines knew how to give rodeo audiences a great show.[24]

The East Texas Championship Rodeo was a huge success, and Hines was given much credit for this in the *San Augustine Tribune*. Captain McCormick presented the awards to the winners, Hines won the breakaway calf roping competition, and he and Allred received high praise from the crowd. The *Tribune* also reported that Allred had received "continued and universal applause" when, during his speech, he had stated that "San Augustine County citizens need suffer no uneasiness whatsoever about crime conditions here and that ample protection to all good citizens would be extended San Augustine County through the State Ranger force." Allred was responding to numerous inquiries on the matter from local citizens and leaders needing reassurance that the Rangers would not leave and thus create a law enforcement vacuum in which the McClanahan-Burleson gang might reassert itself. Scarred from years of oppression, the community needed the Rangers to remain to ensure closure to that dark period in their history. Allred and his Rangers repeatedly reassured, without hesitation or equivocation, that the Rangers would be stationed in San Augustine as long as Allred held office as governor.[25]

= 8 =

JUSTICE FOR ALL

As Governor Allred and his Rangers basked in the adulation of thousands of appreciative San Augustinians, his legislative triumph, statewide law enforcement reform, went into effect. The Texas Department of Public Safety (DPS) officially came into existence on August 10, 1935, ninety days after the passage of Senate Bill 146 by the Forty-Fourth Texas Legislature. Creation of the new state police agency entailed collaboration between the legislature and governor's office and was based on an in-depth senate committee report on statewide crime, a report from Chicago-based public administration and finance consulting firm Griffenhagen and Associates, a plan submitted by the Sheriffs' Association of Texas, independent studies of new state police agencies around the nation, and even some European models described by Ranger captain Tom Hickman and Dallas attorney Albert Sidney Johnson, who Allred appointed as the first chair of the Public Safety Commission.[1]

The act removed the Texas Rangers from the Adjutant General's Department (the state military arm and National Guard office), combined them with the Highway Patrol (formerly under the Highway Department), and created additional statewide bureaus of intelligence (led by legendary former Ranger captain Manuel Gonzaullus), identification and records, and communications, as well as a law enforcement training academy. A governor-appointed three-person body, the Public Safety Commission, would oversee the DPS, and that commission would select a director to run the entire agency. Allred had promptly delivered on a major progressive campaign promise, and the legislative success was buttressed by his Rangers' accomplishments in San Augustine.[2]

Upon its inception, the three original DPS commissioners—Albert Sidney Johnson (chair), Ernest S. Goens, and George W. Cottingham—convened and addressed the Rangers and Highway Patrol commanders to announce their plans for the new agency. Johnson gave a lengthy speech in which he emphasized the commission's goal to depoliticize Ranger appointments and admonished current Rangers and applicants to avoid the old process of reaching out to politicians to influence hiring decisions. While the legislation creating the Department of Public Safety called for three companies totaling no more than forty commissioned Rangers, the five companies of thirty-four Rangers that were transferred over from the Adjutant General's Department remained intact and continued to function under the new agency. All individual personnel retained their positions, including Tom Hickman as headquarters/senior captain and Roy Aldrich as quartermaster, both in Austin; Sid Kelso commanding Company A in Houston; Fred McDaniel over Company B in Wichita Falls; James McCormick commanding Company C in San Augustine; and Will McMurrey over Company D in Hebbronville. This command structure would remain in place until complete reorganization took effect at the end of the year, which would be brought about by an internal controversy involving Hickman.[3]

In fact, Hickman's reappointment as senior captain by the DPS commissioners was evidence of their commitment to political independence, given that Governor Allred had strongly recommended that they choose someone else, due to his frustrations with Hickman's apparent reluctance to enforce state gambling laws. Further evidence was that they chose to appoint former Ranger captain Manuel "Lone Wolf" Gonzaullus to lead the Bureau of Intelligence. Johnson noted that Gonzaullus had not applied for the job or even known it was going to be offered to him. He also acknowledged that the commissioners knew some politicians would be opposed to Gonzaullus, yet they hired him anyway. The appointment was also at odds with the statute stipulating that the senior Ranger captain would be in command over that bureau. The commissioners' decision to exercise discretion in that instance may have indicated that they did not entirely disregard the governor's concerns about Hickman.[4]

In his address to DPS command staff and the Rangers, DPS chair Johnson also read through the new agency regulations and discussed the importance of measures aimed at enhancing the Rangers' professionalism. He stressed that

The first DPS Texas Rangers badge, after the creation of the Department of Public Safety and about three decades before the now-iconic "wagon wheel" style badge, each crafted from a five-peso coin, came into use. *Courtesy of Tobin & Anne Armstrong Texas Ranger Research Center, Texas Ranger Hall of Fame and Museum, Waco.*

command staff and rank-and-file officers all needed to follow the established chain of command and said that the Rangers and highway patrolmen were equally valued and needed to cooperate rather than compete. Johnson also emphasized the need to reassure local authorities that the new state law enforcement agency was there to assist them in their efforts and not to usurp their authority. He also laid out the new rules for issuing special Ranger commissions, which would only be considered for full-time paid lawmen who would have to pass a background investigation and post a bond. The days of being rewarded for political patronage with a state law enforcement commission regardless of one's qualifications or criminal history were over. Johnson completed his initial comments by discussing plans for the DPS Bureau of Education, which was headed by Highway Patrol captain Homer Garrison Jr., and then introducing former Highway Patrol chief Louis H. Phares as the acting director of the new DPS.[5]

For his part, Phares reiterated the necessity of internal cooperation and loyalty, proclaiming, "We can overlook some of your other faults, if you are loyal," and he reassured the Rangers that their role and traditions would be respected and retained. To further emphasize the goal of depoliticization, he also announced the new rule established in the statute (still in force today) barring DPS employees from attending political gatherings in uniform, running for public office, and openly advocating for particular candidates. Given that they were only months away from the beginning of the Texas centennial and the year-long celebrations being promoted nationwide to help boost the state's Depression-era economy, Phares also instructed all DPS officers to learn Texas history and knowledge of local historical sites, battlefields, and other state heritage sites so that they could assist tourists and promote the new agency. With this transition from the Adjutant General's Department to the Department of Public Safety complete, a new era in Texas Rangers history had begun.[6]

A variety of additional laws also went into effect on August 10, 1935, though not all would burnish Allred's progressive credentials. New regulations on the funeral and transportation industries were certainly in keeping with them, as were permitting the use of German- and Czech-language textbooks in public schools and making attempted burglary of vessels, steamboats, or railroad cars a felony. But other laws going into effect that day were arguably contrary to progressive values: the require-ment for teachers of public schools to make oaths of allegiance to state and local governments, the overriding of local control in the matter of condemning land for highway construction, and, certainly not progressive, requiring buses to provide separate accommodations for black and white passengers. Allred's progressive mantle was therefore relative to the time and place in which he governed, it seems. Nevertheless, while Allred was complicit in expanding segregation in one area, his Rangers and San Augustinians were pushing back against Jim Crow in another.[7]

Arguably the most significant trials resulting from the Allred Rangers' cleanup of San Augustine were not the cases of murder with white victims but cases in which white men had victimized blacks. As noted, during the Jim Crow era, neither Texas nor federal law provided for the rights of blacks to have effective redress against whites in the court system, and social custom prohibited blacks from bringing charges or testifying against whites. The earliest major trials that resulted from the Texas Rangers' efforts in San Augustine during 1935 dealt with murders that stemmed from the unsuccessful attempts of local white residents to contest the power of the McClanahan-Burleson regime. But the gang's core activities were common theft, robbery, and extortion, and their most frequent victims were the African American residents of San Augustine County, most of whom were sharecroppers and tenant farmers surviving on the proceeds of their crops, which came in at regular intervals through the year.

Trial transcripts, including witness testimony, and the records on file in the Court of Criminal Appeals at the Texas State Library and Archives in Austin are practically a verbatim confirmation of this type of crime during the era of the San Augustine troubles. Those records are also a testament to the fact that the Texas Rangers sent by Governor Allred and the white citizens of San Augustine countermanded the social norms and strictures of the Jim Crow era in search of justice. During that time, blacks were segregated from whites in most public venues, including the criminal justice system. Nevertheless, in the two trials of Charles Lycurgus "Curg" Burleson, all-white juries convicted a white man solely on the testimony of black victims and witnesses, based on investigations launched and charges filed by the Allred Rangers, which could be fairly termed unusual for that time.[8]

The black victims and witnesses in these trials testified that they had not reported or otherwise sought official intervention prior to the arrival of the Allred Rangers and that Rangers Dan Hines and James McCormick had been the ones who sought *them* out, recorded their statements as to what crimes had occurred, and arranged for them to attend trial and testify. The Rangers spent much of the summer of 1935 investigating cases involving black crime victims in San Augustine. By the time fall approached that year, the fruits of those labors began to pay off, and Curg Burleson was indicted and tried for the felony charge of "Threats to Extort Money" in the district court of San Augustine County on September 12, 1935. The victim, local black sharecropper Edward Clark, testified that he had not reported any of his troubles with Burleson and his associates to the authorities, fearing for his life, until after the Allred Rangers came to town. "Up until that time I had told nobody but my brother," Clark asserted under cross-examination. "The first officers I talked to about [those troubles] was the rangers, all three of them." Clark further testified that Constable Sublett Sharp had brought him to meet the Allred Rangers at the local tailor shop in early March 1935, in connection with their ongoing investigations of cold cases and other yet-to-be prosecuted crimes. Clark had not reported the crimes previously because Curg's relatives and friends held most of the local law enforcement positions at the time those crimes had occurred.[9]

With the state represented by District Attorney Hollis M. Kinard of Orange, Texas, and the firm of Adams & MacAlister of Nacogdoches representing the defense, Curg Burleson testified that he had loaned ten dollars to Clark just shy of a week before Clark came to his house to "pay [Curg] back." Burleson insisted that Clark had only paid him the one time and that the amount was just ten dollars.

He also insisted that he never threatened Clark in any way, claiming instead that he had always been "very kindly and very friendly" when asking Clark "for my money." The witnesses in the case were Clark and his friend Leroy Garner (a state's rebuttal witness who had accompanied Clark more than once to deliver money to Burleson at the home of his in-laws, J. Henry and Sarah G. Steptoe), and then Burleson and his mother-in-law appeared for the defense.[10]

The case against Burleson came down to conflicting witness testimony. The state alleged that he had demanded thirty dollars from Clark under threats of violence, while the defense claimed that the transaction was the repayment of a ten-dollar loan. An all-white jury accepted the testimony of two black witnesses over that of two whites—a fact of no small significance in 1935 East Texas—and convicted Burleson, and the Court of Criminal Appeals would later affirm the conviction and sentence of six years in a state penitentiary. The appellate court noted that both Curg's defense and appellant argument amounted to no more than a simple denial of the state's case, which the jury had determined to be the truest account of the relevant events. Among other contentions, the defense had argued (incorrectly) that the case involved "only the testimony of one negro against one white man." Kinard, the prosecutor, countered, "Naturally, the appellant complains because the jury accepted the testimony of the witnesses for the State, who were Negroes, as against those for the appellant, who were white people. It was within the province of the jury to pass upon the credibility of the witnesses." The court did not address this particular contention but affirmed the trial court judgment that "all other matters complained of seem to be without merit and are overruled" and it denied Burleson's motion for a rehearing. The court's opinion noted that the defendant's testimony that he—a white man in East Texas in 1934—had given a "negro" a loan of ten dollars (a substantial sum at the time) "to go to supper" was "a bit incredible." The intimation is that the court found this incredible not just because Burleson, by his own statement, barely knew Clark and had no knowledge of his ability to repay a loan. The case set a precedent: white jurors and the courts would hold white men accountable for crimes against black citizens.[11]

As Clark testified, Allred Rangers Hines and McCormick had sought him out, and the case had made it to trial as a direct result of their initiative and tenacity in investigating cold cases. The Rangers' efforts were now resulting in convictions against members of the McClanahan-Burleson inner circle.[12]

Edward Clark was not the only African American victim of the McClanahan-Burleson gang for whom the Allred Rangers were able provide courtroom justice.

Curg Burleson would be tried and convicted by a jury for another offense, the theft of hogs from San Augustine county resident Ella Curl described in chapter 2. During Burleson's trial in this case, the defense's strategy was immediately apparent during cross-examination and laid out explicitly during the defendant's testimony. Curg claimed that his brother Tom (by then deceased) had sold him three hogs and told him that those hogs were located at Curl's house and that he, Curg, could pick them up there the next day. Curg further testified that he'd had a long conversation with Curl on the day that he took the hogs, during which he attempted to negotiate the trade of one of the barrows he was taking for her big sow. Her response to that claim was, "If Mr. Burleson wanted to trade me a barrow for an old sow, it must have been in his mind. . . . They just put the hogs in the wagon and left." She adamantly denied that any such conversation had taken place, even after repeated efforts under cross-examination by defense counsel to get her to change her story. Curl and her son also vehemently and repeatedly denied the defendant's claims that there were other "darkies" or "colored boys" present at her home when the defendant took her hogs, and she testified that no one there assisted the thieves or "got some slop . . . [and] loaded [the hogs] in the wagon," while Burleson and his companions remained seated and then drove away. Once again, an all-white East Texas jury accepted the testimony of two African Americans over that of three whites, and convicted Curg Burleson for a second time in 1935, sentencing him to two more years in a state penitentiary.[13]

The Texas Court of Criminal Appeals sustained Curg's argument that the trial court erred in not allowing the testimony of his mother-in-law, Sarah G. Steptoe. According to the defense counsel, she would have testified that she had overheard the transaction between Tom and Curg Burleson in which, Curg claimed, Tom had sold him the hogs. The justices concluded that her testimony *might* have provided the jury with reasonable doubt that Curg, along with Vandy and Calvin Steptoe, had intended to steal the hogs, although they also noted that the jury verdict might also have remained the same, depending on whether Sarah Steptoe were to have actually testified thusly and the jury to have found such additional testimony more credible than Curl's. The court reversed the initial judgment and remanded the case back to the trial court on this basis and did not rule on any of the other points of error, such as those relating to sufficiency of evidence. Such a scenario would have conveniently placed the responsibility for the victimization of Curl onto the deceased Tom Burleson who obviously could not be called to rebut such a claim or be held accountable for the theft. Regardless, Curl had testified that she had made no arrangements with Tom and that she was unequivocally the victim of a theft. Furthermore, Curg Burleson, by his own admission, had made no effort to ask Curl whether she had sold the hog to Tom before loading it up and taking it away without her consent, nor did he produce any sort of documentation to support his claim.[14]

It should be noted that the record is inconclusive as to whether or not Sarah Steptoe would have testified that she overheard the conversation Curg Burleson claimed he'd had with Tom. Her husband, Henry Steptoe, denied knowledge of it during his own testimony, despite apparent defense counsel efforts to elicit such a statement from him. The fact that her own son, Vandy, was also charged in the matter heightens the possibility that Sarah Steptoe might have perjured herself on his behalf, but in any event a jury had felt compelled to accept Curl's testimony over that of Curg Burleson and convicted him, defying common notions about East Texas white culture in that place and time.[15]

Like many of the San Augustine cases from this time, the final disposition in Curg Burleson's hog theft case is unknown. Burleson may have been retried, lost, and not attempted to appeal the second conviction, or, more likely, he may have entered into a plea arrangement with the state since the sentence in the hog theft case was two years, Burleson had earlier in the year been sentenced to six years for extortion, and such sentences typically ran concurrently (simultaneously rather than one term being added on at the end of another). It is also possible that the state chose not to retry this case since, shortly after it was reversed and remanded, Burleson's conviction and six-year sentence in the extortion case was upheld. The Curl theft case outcome remains a mystery, as no record of the post-remand adjudication has been located. Vandy Steptoe was eventually convicted in the theft of Ella Curl's hogs, and he was sentenced to two years in state prison for that.[16]

It was not only citizens of San Augustine who took note of, and benefited from, the dramatic changes that took place after the Allred Rangers arrived. The US Secret Service investigations into the beating of E. C. Cleveland had at first produced little evidence and even fewer witnesses willing to testify against the McClanahan-Burleson gang. But by the fall term of the federal district court in October 1935, that had changed. By the time operative-in-charge Edward Tyrrell met with US Attorney S. D. Bennett on October 2, 1935, to discuss how to proceed, the status of the defendants was very different than it had been during the previous term.[17]

While a number of rumors regarding his fate have been passed down over time, Tom Burleson died from blood poisoning resulting from the bullet wounds he sustained during the San Augustine shoot-out in December of 1934. Charlie

McClanahan had been convicted of murdering Edward Boone Brackett Sr. and sentenced to ninety-nine years in state prison. Joe Burleson was serving state prison sentences for multiple convictions, and several other members of the gang had cases pending that were likely to net them each multiyear prison terms. All of these developments were attributable to the efforts of the Allred Rangers, who had brought order to the community and initiated proceedings against members of the McClanahan-Burleson gang.[18]

Additionally during this time, the Allred Rangers had investigated the assault on Robert Ellis and filed charges that resulted in the indictment of Charlie and Wade McClanahan Sr. under state law. The witnesses in that case were Ellis, Charlie Welch, Monroe L. Burkett, Dr. J. H. Ellington, Herman Williams, a black boy named Price (first name unknown), and Elzie Edwards, a black woman. The inclusion of the last two witnesses—whose race was noted on the grand jury minutes form—was another instance where the Allred Rangers and the citizens of San Augustine defied the standard discriminatory practices of Jim Crow era justice.[19]

As a result of the flurry of state cases against gang members, Bennett again asked Tyrrell to agree to a continuance into another term of court. This time his rationale was that they should wait to see how the remaining state cases against the gang turned out. While Tyrrell was not pleased with the idea of delaying the case yet again, the circumstances involving the other cases led him to take a pragmatic approach in his response. Tyrrell told Bennett that he would defer to him in the matter, but he also suggested a potential strategy for eventually securing plea agreements from the defendants. He theorized that if all of the defendants in the federal assault case were convicted on state charges in other cases, they might be willing to plead guilty on the federal charges in exchange for concurrent sentencing, thereby avoiding the trouble and expense of a trial, which would be good for the federal government too. Bennett advised Tyrrell that the fall 1935 term of court was delayed until November 4 in Beaumont and said that he would take the matter under consideration then. On October 18, Bennett contacted Tyrrell to tell him that the case had been continued until the spring 1936 term of court and that therefore the witnesses should be advised that they would not need to appear before then. Tyrrell was becoming increasingly frustrated, but he resolved to hold firm and hang in until the next term to see justice served in the case.[20]

While the federal case was stalled, the state case involving alleged McClanahan-Burleson gang connection to counterfeiting was moving forward quickly in the courts. And Lee "Red" Jordan was the first defendant brought to trial for the armed robbery of Curtis Butler (see chapter 3). The trial commenced on September 9, 1935, in the district court of San Augustine County, under Cause Number 4879 (the official court designation for the case), with Allred Ranger Dan Hines in attendance. Hollis M. Kinard, the district attorney of Orange, was the counsel for the state, and A. L. Lowery of Nacogdoches was the counsel for the defendant. Kinard presented just two witnesses, Butler and I. J. Stone, for his primary evidence and a third, Mrs. Fred Rike, as a rebuttal witness. Lowery presented seven witnesses, including the defendant. The other six were Mrs. Lee Jordan, Cynthia Martin, Charlie Lynch, Walter J. Lakey, Ellie McDaniels, and Johnnie Stinson.[21]

Both Butler and Stone were of questionable character, although Stone was the only one with a criminal record. He was a convicted felon who had served a short sentence in a state penitentiary. The two men admitted that they had gone to San Augustine for an unlawful purpose, to acquire some counterfeit money. It was further established that neither man needed immunity nor was offered any immunity for testifying in the case. Both men testified in substantial detail regarding their personal knowledge of the events of July 2, 1934, and under cross-examination they not only proved consistent but also provided additional testimony supporting the case. In particular, Stone testified that the defendant had approached him outside the courthouse the week before the trial and offered him money if he and Curtis would testify that they could not identify Jordan. Stone also testified that Jordan had told him that he had already approached Curtis's father with a similar offer in an attempt to "get this thing squashed" and that "if they did not identify him he would get the money [to pay them off]."[22]

After failing to get the victim to admit that he might have consensually turned over his money to Jordan or Burleson, defense counsel focused on convincing the jury that the robber must have been a different redheaded associate of Jim Burleson (who also went by the nickname "Red"), despite the fact that Butler had already identified Jordan by sight in the courtroom. Lowery's first witness, Cynthia Martin, ran a rooming house "right on the corner." She testified that Burleson once had a room there and had come to see an unidentified man who also had a room there. She testified that "a redheaded fellow" who was not Lee Jordan had accompanied Burleson on that occasion. Martin could not verify the date in question, nor did she know the redheaded man's name until Lowery interjected "Red Daniels" into a question. Prosecutor Kinard's objection to that "leading and suggestive" question was sustained, although the witness thereafter continued to repeat that name in her testimony, along with that of "Red Chapman."

She asserted that she recalled knowing "Red Daniels" from the time that officers were searching for Clyde Barrow and his gang (Barrow's partner Bonnie Parker had relatives near San Augustine). Martin also testified that the victim had never reported the alleged crime to her, though she acknowledged that she could not specifically recall the victim ever having boarded with her either. Though her testimony was vague and she appeared unsure upon cross-examination, it is clear that the defense intended for the jury to assume that Martin was the proprietor of the boardinghouse where the alleged robbery occurred.[23]

The state's single rebuttal witness, Mrs. Fred Rike, was also a local boardinghouse proprietor. Rike testified that the victim, who she identified by sight and name, had boarded at her establishment on the date in question and that he had reported the robbery to her before he left the next morning, corroborating the core of his testimony. Two more defense witnesses, Lynch and Lakey (later convicted of moonshining and other offenses) also testified that Jim Burleson had another redheaded associate other than Lee Jordan who went by the nickname "Red," though they had no direct knowledge of the events alleged by the victim. Upon cross-examination, they could not deny Jordan's association with Jim and admitted that the two were often seen together when Jordan operated a café in town. When Jordan himself later admitted under cross-examination that he had purchased that café with a twenty-dollar loan from Jim, the defense strategy of trying to convince the jury that some other redhead must have been to blame for the robbery seemed to collapse.[24]

Then Lowery made an inexplicable move. He put the defendant's wife on the stand. The problem with this was that the extent of her testimony during direct examination was that she had only been home "from three o'clock that afternoon until about six o'clock on Monday" and was therefore unable to provide the defendant with an alibi as to his whereabouts at the time of the alleged robbery. In an additional blow to the defense, on cross-examination she was forced to admit that she had written a letter at the direction of the defendant in an attempt to influence the testimony of a potential witness. This testimony was very damaging to the defendant's credibility. Jordan's wife (and later Jordan himself) acknowledged during cross-examination that the letter was specifically intended to instruct the witness how to testify in regard to certain matters of fact and offered him financial compensation for doing so. Kinard as prosecutor was then able to have the letter entered into evidence, using Jordan's wife's testimony as the legal predicate instead of having to put the recipient of the letter (the source of the evidence) on the stand.[25]

If the defense counsel had not placed Jordan's wife or the defendant on the stand, the prosecutor would likely have been unable to introduce that letter since he had already rested his case. However, it is equally likely that he chose not to put the letter's recipient on the stand because he knew that Jordan's wife had written it on behalf of the defendant and that she was on the defense witness list. Either way, the contents of the letter appear to have influenced the jury's verdict more than any other evidence or testimony in the case.[26]

With the defendant's credibility undeniably harmed, the defense counsel Lowery turned to attacking the character of the victim. Both Johnnie Stinson and Ellie McDaniels provided vague testimony claiming that the victim's "reputation for truth and veracity" was "bad." On cross-examination, Stinson was forced to acknowledge that he'd had some sort of conflict with Butler in the past, though he insisted that it did not influence his decision to testify. Lowery failed to deliver any specific allegations or solid facts to explain the contention that the victim was making the whole thing up. Considering that Mrs. Rike's rebuttal testimony directly corroborated several of Butler's specific claims, in addition to refuting and undermining the testimony of more than one defense witness, any damage to the victim's character by the defense witnesses was probably minimal. The defense counsel then ended his presentation of evidence in the case with what was arguably another tactical mistake: he put the defendant on the stand.[27]

During the direct examination by Lowery, his own counsel, Jordan merely provided an account of his employment history around the time of the alleged robbery and then claimed that he had stayed home sleeping on the night in question (alone, with no corroborating witnesses). Upon cross-examination, Jordan was shown to have misrepresented certain facts, and he was forced to admit that he had attempted to "fix" a witness in the case, though he continued to deny robbing Butler and attempted to diminish the significance of his relationship with Jim Burleson. These assertions of innocence fell on deaf ears: the jury convicted Jordan of felony robbery and sentenced him to twenty years in a state penitentiary. The testimony in the trial of Lee "Red" Jordan reveals not only the evidence of his guilt in that particular case but also supports long-held perceptions regarding the existence of ongoing cooperative criminal activities guided and protected by way of an alliance between the Burlesons and McClanahans.[28]

— 9 —

THE HARDER THEY FALL

While Jordan's conviction was certainly a victory for the Allred Rangers, the pinnacle of their investigative efforts was undoubtedly the conviction of Charlie McClanahan for the murder of Edward Boone Brackett Sr. That trial in one of the best-known San Augustine murder cases came about thanks to the intrepid investigative efforts of McCormick and Hines, and the conviction was thanks to the prosecutorial acumen of Spot Sanders. Sanders, a former judge, had been picked by Governor Allred to prosecute the case, and Sanders kept the governor, himself a former prosecutor, regularly informed about progress throughout the process. While McClanahan's murder of the fifty-three-year-old former manager of the San Augustine Chamber of Commerce and former federal farm agent for Angelina County was not the last case to be tried in connection with the Rangers' cleanup of San Augustine, its successful prosecution was a valuable symbolic and practical victory against the gang. It demonstrated that even their top leaders were no longer immune to the law, and it reinforced public confidence in the efforts of the Allred Rangers. *The State of Texas v. Charles C. McClanahan* was the case that finally brought down the leader of the McClanahan-Burleson gang in San Augustine.[1]

There appears to have been no reasonable doubt of McClanahan's guilt and lack of justification for the killing, but his ties to corrupt local law enforcement officials and to intimidation of witnesses had long shielded him from successful prosecution. Less than two years earlier, McClanahan had been acquitted for the murder of a black man named Jack Garrett, whom McClanahan had shot to death inside the Clark-Downs store on November 10, 1928, allegedly because Garrett had insulted McClanahan's wife. Due to the unrecorded nature of jury proceedings, the reasoning behind the jury's verdict in that case is unknown. There were several witnesses in the Garrett case whose original testimony had led to McClanahan's indictment, including Bill Mitchell, John Davis, Gladys Womack, and Mrs. A. Jones, though no record of their testimony has survived. However, it comes as no surprise that local citizens were hesitant to participate in the trial of a man who appeared immune to prosecution and violently vindictive toward anyone who dared challenge that immunity. It was against that backdrop that two years later key witnesses refused to testify and citizens were reticent to serve on a jury against McClanahan in the Brackett case, which was therefore dismissed without prejudice within months of the murder. Fortunately for the citizens of San Augustine and for Brackett's family, justice delayed would not, in the end, be justice permanently denied.[2]

The trial of McClanahan, former postal carrier, deputy sheriff, Ferguson special Ranger, and de facto head of the McClanahan-Burleson gang of San Augustine, commenced in Carthage, Texas, on Monday, September 23, 1935. Judge T. O. Davis of Center presided over the trial in which E. C. Clabaugh Jr., J. Ball, R. Priester, Jess Brooks, J. I. Driscoll, Deason Bush, Loyd Davidson, Herbert Keeling, Wiley Roundtree, Emmett Copeland, Frank Jernigan, and O. B. Marshall, were selected from a venire of seventy-five Panola County citizens to serve as jurors. There were large legal teams on both sides. Spot Sanders led the prosecution, assisted by district attorneys Hollis Kinard of Orange and Wardlow Lane of Center, Panola County attorney Fred Whitaker, and three other attorneys: Ed McElroy and two identified in the press only by their last names, Woolworth and Turner. The defense was led by Steve King of Beaumont, the firm of Long and Strong of Carthage, and W. T. Davis from San Augustine.[3]

There was nothing particularly complicated about the crime itself (see chapter 2). Under normal circumstances, such a case would have been adjudicated swiftly, and the community might have been spared five more years of oppression. However, by the time McClanahan murdered Brackett, he had already evaded justice in a case where he had murdered another man, Jack Garrett, in full view of the public (see chapter 2). According to one of the jurors in that case, the jury had been too intimidated to convict McClanahan, which created the impression within the San Augustine community that he was untouchable. By the fall of 1935, however, that had all changed and justice was finally at hand.[4]

Hines and McCormick remained in Carthage during the week of the Brackett murder trial, and they may have been called as witnesses by the state. Other prosecution witnesses included the mortician who prepared Brackett's body for burial after the murder and John D. Clark, who testified as to the wounds inflicted by the shotgun blast. Brackett's widow testified that she was unaware of the previous disputes between McClanahan and her late husband. L. B. Mitchell provided details of the "near altercation" between the two in a drugstore that Brackett's daughter said she led him away from. Next, J. W. McKnight testified about being pistol-whipped and threatened by Charlie and Charlie's brother Wade and subsequently fleeing to South Texas, fearing for his life. W. A. Fussell, owner of the cotton gin across the road from where McClanahan had waited for Brackett, testified that he saw McClanahan there with a smoking shotgun at his shoulder immediately after he heard the shots fired and that he saw Brackett slumped over the steering wheel in his car as it rolled into the ditch nearby. Another eyewitness, Bud Hardin, confirmed that he had moved out of town immediately after the murder. Although his motives for the move were not explicitly referenced in the surviving news account, the implication from the context was that he had done so out of fear of being called to testify against McClanahan, having seen firsthand what the man was capable of and knowing past juries had failed to convict him.[5]

The first witness for the defense was E. W. Nations, a former Panola County commissioner and former Sabine County sheriff who had been convicted and sentenced to prison for a murder committed while in office but pardoned by Ma Ferguson. An insurance agent from Nacogdoches named Luther Cook, who claimed to be friends with both the victim and the killer, further claimed to have twice at the Redland Hotel heard Brackett discussing his efforts to get McClanahan fired from the post office. A Mr. Jackson, also of Nacogdoches, claimed to have overheard one of those conversations, although he elaborated by saying that Brackett's threats went beyond just getting McClanahan's job. McClanahan's wife told of a confrontation in which, she alleged, Brackett had pointed a gun at her husband, which may have been the time he recovered the stolen mule (although she made no mention of that, of course). The defense also called Roy V. Watson of Beaumont and sixteen-year-old Kirk Sanders of San Augustine, although Sanders testified that McClanahan had brought whiskey to try to get Sanders's father drunk and agree to testify for him.[6]

McClanahan eventually took the stand in his own defense, and, after answering some superfluous questions regarding his personal history, he elaborated on a claim for the origin of the "bad blood" with Brackett. McClanahan asserted that

Brackett, who was well-known for his personal, professional, and political disdain for the defendant, had asked McClanahan to accept the local postmaster position in place of Mrs. Cynthia Martin, who McClanahan asserted Brackett was conspiring to have removed. McClanahan then alleged that his refusal to join Brackett's conspiracy against Mrs. Martin was the reason for the deadly conflict between the victim and his killer. There's no evidence that anyone else corroborated that claim, at trial or otherwise. McClanahan then claimed that he was near Fussell's gin for legitimate and innocuous (and also uncorroborated) reasons that had nothing to do with Brackett when, he alleged, the victim saw him from his vehicle and then swerved toward him and fired two shots at him from a pistol, from a distance of about one hundred yards, and that he had only pulled out his shotgun (in a matter of seconds and while seated in a vehicle) and returned fire out of self-defense. The implausibility of that scenario given the physical circumstances, eyewitness testimony, and the direct evidence—Brackett's pistol tucked under his coveralls at the time of his murder—debunk McClanahan's version of those events.[7]

As is customary in the trial process, both sides presented the jury with their closing arguments, which consisted of five "eloquent and dramatic speeches" altogether. Wardlow Lane spoke for over an hour as he laid out the prosecution's argument that McClanahan was nothing more than a "cold-blooded, unreasonable, and way-lay murderer." Hollis Kinard painstakingly went through the evidence, from the origins of the conflict between Brackett and McClanahan through to the murder of Brackett on October 14, 1930. Spot Sanders and P. P. Long of Carthage for the prosecution also gave closing statements, the latter's declared by the local press as "the 'masterpiece' of his career."[8]

For the defense, Steve King portrayed his client as a victim who had been "persecuted under the rule of Alred's [sic] Texas Rangers." King declared, "This is just a question of trading rangers, and the second set got the best of the defendant through the hand of power." Fortunately for the victim, such politicized deflections of McClanahan's culpability for the murder did not distract the jury from the evidence. The persistence of the Brackett family, prosecutor Sanders, and the Allred Rangers finally paid off on Friday, September 27, 1935, when a Panola County jury found Charlie McClanahan guilty and sentence him to ninety-nine years in prison after just two hours of deliberation. McClanahan showed no emotion as Panola County district clerk W. D. Anderson read the verdict just after 3:00 P.M. Captain McCormick rushed to the Western Union office immediately following the announcement of the verdict and sent the governor a telegram informing him of the successful conviction. Governor Allred expressed his appreciation and congratulations to the Rangers and the prosecutors for their "splendid work" in bringing McClanahan to justice.[9]

The efforts of the Allred Rangers were central to that success, and the prosecutors who tried the case before the jury emphatically expressed recognition of this and appreciation for it. In his closing report to the governor on the case, Spot Sanders provided the governor an overview of the proceedings followed by his own expressions of admiration for the Rangers: "Especially was the state indebted to the rangers, for from the time I was engaged in the case until the verdict was announced the rangers were right with us, doing all within their power to get the true facts in the case, and much credit is due Captain McCormick and Dan Hines for their splendid work in this case."[10]

On October 1, 1935, three days after the trial ended, District Attorney Kinard sent the following commendation to the governor:

> Honorable James V. Allred
> Governor of Texas,
> Austin, Texas.
>
> Dear Governor:
>
> I wish to take this opportunity to say to you that I unhesitatingly give the credit to Captain J. W. McCormick and Ranger Dan Hines for the splendid victory in the McClanahan case in Panola County last week.
>
> The intelligent, fearless services of these fine officers have worked a condition in San Augustine County, which a year ago I thought impossible. They have unearthed many cases since they have been stationed in San Augustine, many of which involving corruption, viciousness and violence. We have tried many of these cases, and only one has been lost. I dare say that there are no two other officers in Texas or elsewhere who could have gone there and have so effectively obtained these remarkable results.
>
> The people of San Augustine County appreciate the high type of public service which Captain McCormick and Ranger Hines have rendered, and are grateful to you for sending them there.
>
> With every good wish, I beg to remain
> Yours sincerely,
> Hollis Kinard,
> District Attorney
> First Judicial District of Texas[11]

The prosecutors were not the only people praising the Allred Rangers for their work on the McClanahan case. Edward B. Brackett Jr., the son of the victim, wrote to the governor from his family's new home in Abilene to express his appreciation and commend his Rangers for their hard work on the McClanahan case. After responding, Allred forwarded the letter to the director of the newly created Department of Public Safety, under whose auspices and authority McCormick and Hines now worked. McClanahan did not appeal his conviction, possibly as a part of a plea arrangement in order to dispose of the many other felony charges still pending against him at that time. He served several years in prison before being released due to severe illness and died shortly thereafter in Lufkin, Angelina County, Texas, at fifty-one years of age and was buried there in Glendale Cemetery.[12]

It took five years and the intervention of Allred Rangers McCormick and Hines in addition to persistent efforts by the Brackett family, but, in the end, Charlie McClanahan did not escape justice for the murder of Edward Boone Brackett Sr. McClanahan's incarceration signaled the end of the oppression of San Augustinians by the McClanahan-Burleson gang. Thanks to the Allred Rangers and the newfound fortitude that their presence brought forth from the vast majority of San Augustine's citizens, the crime wave was over and its chief architect was behind bars. The gratitude of Brackett's family toward the Allred Rangers for making that justice possible and seeing it through to the end has not waned, even as they have pursued their lives and livelihoods in distant regions of the United States.[13]

Though Captain McCormick and Ranger Hines spent a tremendous amount of their time leading up to the McClanahan trial investigating that case, they still had to work on many other cases at the same time. During and after the trial, the Allred Rangers continued to file charges against dozens of McClanahan-Burleson associates and accomplices, as well as against some new public officials who had not gotten the message that the old times were really over, this time for good. Among other duties, they continued to investigate Jim Burleson's whereabouts, as Burleson had failed to appear, and his bond was revoked, making him a wanted fugitive in addition to the charges already filed against him. Burleson finally surrendered in the days immediately following the verdict in the Brackett murder case, to face charges for "robbery by the use of firearms," "assault to murder," and "threats to extort money." "[Burleson's arrest] winds up the gang of law violators who have been operating here a number of years," the *San Augustine Tribune* asserted, "[and] the general clean-up is a credit to the law officers sent here by the Governor and to the local officers and citizens who cooperated with them."[14]

Also adding to the Allred Rangers' workload were myriad responsibilities outside of San Augustine County, most notably when the International Longshoreman Association (ILA) Gulf Coast strike in October 1935 reached the Beaumont docks. Captain McCormick and five Rangers, including Hines, E. M. Davenport, Dick Oldham, H. P. Purvis, and Fletcher Albright, were ordered to Beaumont to "protect lives and property without taking sides." The police chief, mayor, and other local leaders requested state assistance due to recent and related violent strikes in Port Arthur, Texas, and Lake Charles, Louisiana, in which three men were killed. Numerous reports of "professional agitators," including "carloads of men headed from Houston to Beaumont" had heightened tensions in the city and strained the resources of local law enforcement agencies. Local authorities also appointed a group of fifteen citizens to act as mediators between the factions and requested a "federal conciliator" to lead that process. Including an ILA representative, they asked Governor Allred to close the ports until tensions had abated. Longshoremen's unions were divided, both racially and on the issues at hand, as black unions and some white ones sat out the strike. Beaumont did not, in the end, experience the level of violence that other involved port cities did during the strike, which ended in December that year. There is no indication that the Allred Rangers remained in Beaumont for very long, although Hines did oversee to two Rangers, Dick Oldham and John England, sent to Orange in November for the continuing longshoremen's strike.[15]

Another challenge the Allred Rangers faced on top of their daily responsibilities in San Augustine was the ongoing development and organization of the newly created Department of Public Safety, of which they were now a part. In November 1935, just three months after it officially came into existence, the new state agency was subjected to a major change in leadership. Due to Ranger chief Tom Hickman's failed attempt to raid the Top o' the Hill Terrace, an illegal but popular gambling hall and bar in his home turf of Fort Worth, at Governor Allred's behest the DPS commissioners sent Captain McCormick and Sergeant Sid Kelso, who had also participated into the initial foray into San Augustine back in January, to do the job. While an unknown informant to the illicit establishment had apparently thwarted a raid by Hickman in which no booze or gambling was discovered, McCormick and Kelso's venture four days later caught the notorious casino in full swing. Five men, including the proprietor and Hickman friend Fred Browning, were arrested for operating an illegal casino, and $8,000 worth of gambling equipment was confiscated.[16]

Hickman's reluctance to enforce state gambling laws, move to Austin, work out of his assigned office at DPS headquarters there, and produce a viable organizational plan for the Rangers as ordered had already undermined his relationship with Governor Allred, Acting Director Phares, and the DPS commissioners. The publicity surrounding McCormick's successful raid immediately following Hickman's failed attempt was a tremendous embarrassment for Hickman, but Phares and the commissioners had already decided to suspend him. Hickman's reluctance to enforce state gambling laws was evident not only in his failure to shut down Top O' the Hill Terrace but also in concentrated efforts to protect such establishments statewide.[17]

Having been instructed by the commissioners to develop a long-term strategic plan for organizing and stationing the Rangers across the state, Hickman apparently drafted a "shoestring" map that would have put every major city in the state (where gambling houses were most prevalent) under his jurisdiction while relegating all of the other Ranger captains exclusively to rural regions, including those immediately surrounding the major cities—where such activity was comparatively insignificant. Although Hickman's map was never officially submitted or approved by Phares or the commissioners, Hickman ordered all Rangers not to conduct any raids of gambling halls without his approval. He didn't really make an argument for such a dubious policy but instead simply asserted that he was "the only man on the force capable of handling [gambling enforcement]." Once suspended, Hickman vented to a Waco journalist on a train ride from Fort Worth to Austin, and the resulting publicity led the commissioners to demand Hickman's immediate resignation and then to fire him after he refused.[18]

Acting Director Phares then reorganized the DPS Texas Rangers Division, with commission approval. McCormick was appointed headquarters/senior captain in Austin; Hines was assigned as "Private (In charge)" of the re-designated Company A in San Augustine; Fred McDaniel remained as captain of Company B in Wichita Falls; R. C. Hawkins was appointed captain of Company C, now headquartered in San Angelo; and William McMurrey remained captain of Company D, in the Rio Grande Valley. That reorganization also involved or was preceded by a substantial reduction in manpower, as the new roster documented only twenty-four active Rangers at that point, down from thirty-four at the time of their transition to the DPS. While this reduced the force to nearly half the size of the legislatively approved forty officers, it is unclear whether the reduction was the result of terminations, layoffs, or resignations. Much as they had during their thirty-four years as the Ranger Force under the Adjutant General's Department, the new DPS Texas Rangers Division was often left to cover the vast state of Texas with only a handful of men.[19]

Despite the controversy behind the transition, San Augustinians were elated when their favorite Allred Ranger, McCormick, was promoted to the top Ranger post, and they were equally happy that Dan Hines was placed in command in San Augustine. The *Tribune* declared: "The entire citizenship of San Augustine will join the Tribune in congratulations to Captain McCormick in this deserved promotion which came to him in the line of duty. His sojourn in this county and the matchless manner in which he has handled the restoration of law enforcement here has made for him a friend of every law-abiding citizen in the county. Congratulations, and continued success to you, Captain!"[20]

While McCormick would now have statewide responsibilities that would reduce the amount of time he would be able to spend in San Augustine, Hines's command of the re-designated East Texas Ranger Company A ensured continuity in the ongoing investigations and trials. Hines's appointment to that post reassured local citizens that the relationships built over the preceding year would be maintained. Hines affirmed this when he unequivocally stated that the Allred Rangers would indefinitely continue to provide any and all assistance required by local authorities, including the recently appointed sheriff, Sublett Sharp.[21]

The trials of Charlie McClanahan (for the murder of Edward Boone Brackett Sr.) and Eron Harris and Noah Thacker (for their involvement in the murder of John Gann) were some of the highest-profile cases that the Texas Rangers sent by Governor Allred handled during their cleanup of San Augustine in 1935. However, those cases represented a small fraction of the many charges filed and gang members and associates indicted based on their efforts. Allred's Texas Rangers also investigated several other murders and a great number of lesser felonies and misdemeanor cases during their sweeping investigations in San Augustine during 1935 and 1936. In less than a year, more than forty defendants were indicted for more than one hundred different criminal offenses, including bootlegging, theft, extortion, and assault with the intent to murder. This represented a sea change for the San Augustine criminal justice system, which had been virtually dormant for many years. While not every crime that had occurred during the troubles would be adjudicated, the crime wave propagated by the McClanahan-Burleson gang was finally suppressed.[22]

Charlie was not the only McClanahan to be convicted of a felony. His brother Wade Sr. also served time in state prison, and Charlie's nephew Wade Jr. received a suspended sentence (probation) for election law violations. Wade Sr. had run

BEAUMONT, TEXAS, SATURDAY, MAY 9, 1936   THE BEAUMONT JOURNAL

Rangers Win Praise Of San Augustine In Clean-Up That Is High Spot In History Of State Police Force

Above are shown two reasons why crime does not pay in Texas—in fact teor, counting the two "assistants" in the center. The men are state rangers who have been given the main credit for | driving out during the past two years the criminal element in San Augustine, which had plagued the county for generations. | The middle photograph shows the brace of six-shooters of the latest pattern which were presented to Hines by the citizens of San Augustine last Christmas. On the guns are engraved messages of thanks. | Captain J. W. McCormick, now acting senior captain of rangers in Austin, is shown at the right. McCormick also received a brace of pistols from the citizens as a Christmas present.

Hines and McCormick with gift pistols, 1936. *Courtesy of Cherry Hale Hines Harrison.*

for constable in the July 1934 election, during which time he and his son stole a ballot box from the district clerk's office in an apparent attempt to influence the election results. McClanahan was nevertheless defeated in that race by Sublett Sharp, who went on to work closely with the Allred Rangers after their arrival, while McClanahan shot out the windows of several stores when he found out that the owners had not voted for him. The Allred Rangers investigated the case, and the two men were arrested in Leesville, Louisiana, in July 1935. Both Wade Sr. and Jr. pled guilty on September 2, 1935, a move that resolved three felony indictments for Wade Sr., including two for extortion. As more of the leading members of the McClanahan-Burleson gang were brought to justice, more local citizens reaffirmed their approval of, and admiration for, the Allred Rangers.[23]

The December 5, 1935, *San Augustine Tribune* heralded the accomplishments of the Rangers with an unambiguous headline: "San Augustine Now an Ideal County in Which to Reside." The huge article, presumably written by owner and editor Webster F. Hays and complete with a picture of a young James McCormick,

Texas Rangers with Governor James Allred (*seated at desk*), 1936, in his office at the State Capitol. Captain James W. McCormick (*far left*) shows off engraved pistol given to him by San Augustinians in December 1935. Many Gault looks over McCormick's shoulder from his left, while Dan Hines is standing at far right and Captain Roy Aldrich is the second Ranger to the right of McCormick. The identities of the other Rangers are not confirmed. *Photographer unknown. Photo courtesy of the Texas Ranger Hall of Fame and Museum, Waco.*

was poetic about the community's past, its social advancement, and the Texas Rangers who gave it back its tranquility and prosperity and its citizens' sense of pride. The piece unequivocally credited McCormick, Hines, and Bishop for bringing "peace and security to a community that had known much violence and constant jeopardy" and for doing so "in a few weeks." The time prior to the arrival of the Allred Rangers was described as "the blackest page in San Augustine," a time when "a tiny handful of despoilers . . . took advantage of a God-fearing and God-loving people and wrought havoc" and during whose "brief sojourn in power the building of a generation was undone and justice prostrated before the altar of greed and political degeneration." The bold tone demonstrates Hays's apparent lack of concern about offending a certain percentage of locals.[24]

The *Tribune* lamented that the "reign of violence by pseudo bad men . . . had awed the populace by their unscrupulous acts of violence" and sadly "took the lives of some of [San Augustine's] best citizens." But thanks to the "fearless and fair" Allred Rangers, San Augustine had been transformed into "one of the cleanest and best governed communities in the state." As to the proportion of popular local support, a subsequent article asserted that "the better element of the entire citizenship of the county [was] one hundred percent with [McCormick]." Hays had a reputation for treading lightly where local controversies were concerned, and as a businessman he would have been sensitive to the risk of offending a substantial portion of his customer base, so his willingness to make such strong statements in interpreting events underscores a key fact: while the McClanahan-Burleson gang had its sympathizers, they did not represent a sizable portion of the population.[25]

In addition to acclaim at numerous fairs, rodeos, and parades described earlier, in December 1935 McCormick and Hines received a tangible and enduring demonstration of public admiration from San Augustine: a set of custom engraved pistols for each, with their choice of caliber and model. On December 28, the *San Augustine Tribune* announced:

CITIZENS OF SAN AUGUSTINE HONOR BELOVED RANGERS
Redland Folks Show Hearty Appreciation
With Six-shooters for Christmas

Speaking of real Christmas spirit, consider the motive behind the handsome gifts which the citizens of San Augustine are presenting to Ranger Captain J. W. McCormick, Ranger Dan Hines, and Ranger D. L. Bishop.

Two fine pearl-handled .45's of the latest make and design are to be given Captain McCormick and Ranger Hines. Inscribed on the shooting irons will be the following: "In appreciation, from the citizens of San Augustine."

A sizeable gift of cash has been forwarded to Ranger Bishop whose service to the Redland City was not of as long duration as the other pair but whose work was appreciated nevertheless—Shelby Reporter, Center.[26]

While McCormick chose customized pearl-handled .45 Colt revolvers— long a popular model among law enforcement officers of that era—the younger Hines opted for Smith & Wesson Model 27 .357 Magnum revolvers. The .357 Magnum revolver had just been invented and would become a staple for law officers and gun enthusiasts. The inscription on Hines' pistols (the paper had it wrong): "From the Grateful Citizens of San Augustine, To Dan Hines, Ranger."[27]

In response to such outpourings of gratitude, the Allred Rangers were equally magnanimous. They responded in the *Tribune*, "We want to extend our sincere thanks. It makes our hearts glad to serve people of your type. Our sojourn in your little city will always be a bright spot in our life." The Allred Rangers recognized that their success had relied directly on the support and cooperation of San Augustine's citizenry, who had merely needed their faith in the local criminal justice system restored, at which point they stood to be counted in the fight to restore law and order to their community. They also recognized that the Rangers' continued support was essential to maintaining, over the long term, the order that had been established. McCormick and Hines too knew that there was more work still to be done.[28]

—10—

COMPLETING THE CLEANUP

By the beginning of 1936, San Augustine was at peace, and its courts (as well as the courts of surrounding jurisdictions) were producing convictions of dozens of McClanahan-Burleson gang associates for crimes against citizens of San Augustine, regardless of race. The fugitives who had escaped from the jail during Virgil Worsham's short tenure as sheriff had finally all been rounded up, and even they provided detailed accounts of just how bad the troubles had been. Ranger Dan Hines and Sheriff Sublett Sharp recounted that the information they received from Jeff Duffield—the black San Augustinian who was one of Joe Burleson's accomplices in the killing of Henry Clay—was "almost unbelievable regarding the depredations of the gang that had operated here over the past several years." One by one, the gang was being indicted, arrested, and prosecuted for those years of corruption and brutality.[1]

Mrs. M. A. Johnson led the first San Augustine grand jury session of 1936 and, like her predecessor, submitted a report to Judge F. Pat Adams when the session concluded. Johnson reported that the January session had lasted fifteen days, during which the grand jury had investigated approximately seventy-five cases, received testimony from approximately two hundred witnesses, and returned thirty-three true bills of indictment. She also noted that the jail was full yet well maintained and that it was the grand jury's observation that crime was on a steady decline throughout the county. Johnson also referenced complaints that the grand jury had received and investigated regarding the use of tax dollars by members of the commissioners' court. She stated that it was the jury's assessment that some commissioners had "been somewhat extravagant in the past," and the grand jury therefore admonished the court to be "more economical" with regard to future expenditures. Johnson closed, again like her predecessors, by thanking the Allred Rangers, the district attorney (Hollis Kinard), and the sheriff's department for their service to the community and grand jury. At a community meeting following the closing of the January session, several members of the public spoke out in support and appreciation for the Allred Rangers' efforts in their community. Among them were several grand jury members, such as Tom Norwood, who stated that he could "speak for the community as being 100 per cent behind the move to clean up crime" in San Augustine. The community had taken back control and was moving steadily forward in holding those responsible for the troubles accountable for their criminal acts.[2]

Some of the defendants indicted in 1935 didn't go to trial until early 1936. Among those, Jim Burleson was finally convicted in January for his role in the robbery of Curtis Butler, in connection with an attempt to obtain counterfeit money, and sentenced to five years in state prison. His case, however, would be reversed and remanded upon appeal to the Court of Criminal Appeals in Austin. The appellate court ruled that the trial court judge should have instructed the jury on the law of circumstantial evidence, as it applied to the evidence of the appellant's role in the alleged crime. No record survives as to whether Burleson went to trial again in the case or pled out or if the prosecution eventually dismissed the charges. In addition to the robbery case, Burleson was also indicted on a state charge of assault to murder and a federal assault charge for the attack on the Secret Service agent, E. C. Cleveland.[3]

Both at trial and in their appellate brief, the Burleson defense's arguments and theories were multitudinous and at times conflicting. The array of arguments (presented simultaneously) included (1) that Burleson had not been present when the alleged crime occurred; (2) that no crime had occurred at all; (3) that the victim was instead an "accomplice witness"; and (4) that the victim "got exactly what he went for—nothing." This last one was because, they argued, if Butler was robbed or swindled while attempting to buy counterfeit money, then he was a party to an act of "his own premeditated design" that "kicked back on him"—by implication, he had deserved what happened to him. But in making such arguments, the defense counsel specifically acknowledged Burleson's involvement in various criminal activities. They otherwise asserted that, in this case, he was not guilty of the particular crime for which he was charged.[4]

While the defense argued that the victim's testimony was "preposterous . . . flimsy and . . . ridiculous," they made no specific assertions about why he would invent the story, save that he was making up the part about being robbed at gunpoint because he had been victimized by trickery instead and was embarrassed. Jim Burleson's defense presented witness testimony in an attempt to support that contention, claiming that Butler had showed Mrs. Rike an envelope filled with blank paper. The defense relied on this allegation to advance the argument that Butler had been swindled rather than robbed. It should be noted that the person who stood to have benefited most from such a scenario—Lee "Red" Jordan—was not brought in to testify in the matter, and he had made no such claim during his own earlier trial or subsequent appeals. Furthermore, Mrs. Rike herself had made no mention of any such thing when she testified at Jordan's trial. It is not unreasonable to think that Burleson sympathizers had convinced her to add that part in at Jim's trial, though that is supposition. She had a personal connection to the local criminal activities and a related motive to retaliate against authorities, in that the Allred Rangers and local officers had arrested her husband and son for bootlegging just a few months earlier. While the final disposition of this case is unknown, Jim Burleson had also been convicted and sentenced to three years in another case that was either not appealed or not successfully appealed, meaning that his conviction in that case stood. He was transferred to the state prison in Hemphill in late 1936 after his trials early that year.[5]

In addition to the implied complicity between Red Jordan and Jim Burleson in the robbery of Butler, the McClanahans' protection of such criminal activities was also revealed. Whether it was Charlie McClanahan, Wade McClanahan Sr., or Wade McClanahan Jr. (all three were Ferguson-commissioned special Rangers), their alleged threats and refusal to take Butler's report along with the obvious fact that they never filed any charges against Jordan and Burleson (who were not indicted until nearly a year later and only as a result of the Allred Rangers' investigations) is compelling evidence of criminal collusion between the Burlesons and McClanahans. As with extortion victim Edward Clark, Butler testified that Hines and McCormick sought him out. Official records and news reports also verify that successful prosecution of the case was a direct result of their investigative efforts. While their success in helping to convict a growing number of the McClanahan-Burleson gang was a significant step in the process of restoring order, they would have to take down the gang's most violent members in order to establish a lasting peace and sense of security in the community.[6]

Several cases against Joe Burleson were still pending as of January 9, 1936. For unknown reasons, his name was still listed alongside Jeff Duffield's in the *Tribune*'s district court postings at that time, some six months after Burleson's acquittal for the murder of Henry Clay. It is plausible that the state found some grounds on which to retry him in the matter, though that is unknown. Though acquitted of the murder of Clay, Burleson was later convicted on multiple counts of extortion, charges to which he pled guilty. He was indicted altogether on nine state charges and one federal offense (for his participation in the attack on E. C. Cleveland, the Secret Service agent, in October 1934). In each case, the prosecution was the direct result of the Allred Rangers' efforts to reestablish law and order and examine cold cases that local officials had been unable, and in some cases unwilling, to investigate or adjudicate. Joe Burleson died in prison, evidently the victim of a stabbing by a fellow inmate. A female relative (an aunt, it would appear) claimed to know who committed the deed and swore vengeance, although she apparently never it carried out. Burleson's role in the San Augustine crime wave ended the day the Allred Rangers arrested him, which was his last day of freedom. Burleson was also charged with rape during this time, but is unclear what came of this. It likely was disposed of in a plea arrangement with any sentence to run concurrent to the rest.[7]

Another case tried in January was that of Robert Lee, for his part in the robbery of Fred Garrett (see chapter 6). Lee's accomplice and the alleged gunman in the crime, Wiley Green, pled guilty back in September 1935. Nevertheless, Lee decided to try his luck with a jury, and he tried to convince the all-white body that the incident was just a prank. District Attorney Hollis Kinard presented the state's case, while John R. Anderson of Center was counsel for the defense. The state's witnesses consisted of the victim and Sublett Sharp, who had been the constable in San Augustine at the time of the crime but was sheriff by the time the case went to trial. Garrett testified in detail about his activities before, during, and after the robbery that evening, and Sharp elaborated on his and Captain McCormick's investigative efforts after receiving the report.[8]

The defense produced twelve witnesses, although the defendant was the only one who could testify directly to the events in question. A black man, A. B. Wade, told of the defendants having given him a ride and having "pranked" him earlier that day. However, Wade acknowledged that he was not with them at the time of the alleged robbery of Garrett. J. L. Prince testified that the defendants had patronized his café earlier that evening, but that testimony also revealed that they had spent a lot of money drinking heavily while there and that his gun had gone missing from his car around the time they left. L. C. Cupit testified that the defendants had stayed at his house that night, saying that they had appeared passed out in the roadway around midnight and that Lee had given him three dollars to hold on to, with no explanation.[9]

When Lee took the stand, he testified that he had been driving through the area selling subscriptions to "Holland's Farm & Ranch magazine" and picked up Green along the road to San Augustine. Lee said that Green had agreed to pay him two dollars for a ride into town and that they sold magazine subscriptions along the way. He described their route as being "out the mail road from Grigsby . . . to Camp Worth and . . . across" into Blackjack and then into San Augustine. He testified that he often took items in trade in place of cash and that that day he had taken two radiators, a battery, and one chicken. Lee told of picking up A. B. Wade about three miles down from the Watson farm on the final leg that afternoon into San Augustine and described how they "took something off him . . . a ring" when they dropped him off but that it was all part of a "prank" and that they had returned the ring to Wade before they drove off. Lee claimed that he had sold some of the trade items after getting into town and that he had $7.50 on him when they arrived at Prince's café. He acknowledged that they had been there for some time drinking beer and said they left around 8:30 P.M. to give "two boys" a ride out to the demonstration farm to look for some girls that didn't end up being there, at which point they had returned to the café and continued drinking until about eleven.[10]

It was then that they had encountered Garrett and, according to Lee, decided to "have some more fun out of another negro." Lee testified that they had offered Garrett a ride and that he declined, at which point Lee "threw up his hands like that and said give me something," and Garrett threw five pennies in the car seat and ran off as Lee called after him that they didn't want his money. (Lee said that he had been the one wearing the hat and who had done the talking, not Green, as Garrett had testified). On the witness stand, Lee then claimed that Garrett had Green confused with him and that he (Lee) never had a gun and had tried to give Garrett the "five pennies" back, all claims that Garrett had already refuted in his testimony. Lee concluded that his "purpose in stopping in doing what [he] did to the negro was just to prank and picking at him." Lee repeated his assertion that Garrett had the roles and positions of the two defendants confused and that they had only meant to offer him a ride home and "pick at" him. Lee expressly denied having a gun, stealing the gun from Prince, and taking three dollars from Garrett, although regarding each he specifically only referred to himself and not to Green, who had already pled guilty to Garrett's accusations.[11]

The remaining defense witnesses had no direct knowledge of the alleged crime. Several offered testimony intended to bring the victim's reputation and character into question. Others (such as the defendant's grandfather) insisted that the defendant's "reputation for truth and veracity . . . was good." However, on cross-examination, those who impugned Garrett's character acknowledged that their testimony strictly relied on what they had heard about the victim from generally unnamed third parties who were not present to testify. Several of them offered blatantly racist assessments, such as commentary on whether or not Garrett was "as good as the average negro in San Augustine." The state then brought forward three rebuttal witnesses who had known Garrett personally for many years, including through business dealings, and these expressly refuted negative claims about his "reputation for truth and veracity," insisting that it was in fact good. In the end, the jury declined to believe that a reasonable and well-intended white person would conduct such a prank on a young black man in 1935, at 11:00 P.M., in a community where until very recently "highway robberies" of black San Augustinians had been common, if unprosecuted. Lee was convicted and sentenced to five years in a state penitentiary. White San Augustinian jurors affirmed once again that Jim Crow would no longer provide cover for white criminals who preyed on local black citizens.[12]

None of the McClanahan-Burleson gang members who were indicted in the beating of Secret Service operative E. C. Cleveland were convicted in that case. It was eventually dismissed in late July 1936 after the participants all had been convicted of more serious offenses in state court. Operative-in-charge Edward Tyrrell's reaction was one of resignation and ambivalence. He was frustrated that one of his operatives could be so brazenly beaten, especially by men possessing law enforcement credentials, without being held accountable. At the same time, he was tired of fighting against federal prosecutors who were supposed to be his allies, and he took solace in the fact that those involved were serving prison sentences, albeit for other, state-level offenses.[13]

Tyrrell concluded his final report on the case by asserting, "The action which was taken by this service at St. Augustine [sic] against these men was responsible for clearing up the conditions in that county." The breadth of this claim was likely not intended to minimize the efforts of the Allred Rangers but rather to reassure his boss that his and his men's efforts had not been in vain, despite the fact that the federal assault case ended up being dismissed. And it is a valid argument that the pressure brought to bear upon the McClanahan-Burleson gang by the existence of those charges, and the accompanying investigative process, played a positive, productive role in subduing the group's operations in San Augustine.[14]

Regardless of Tyrrell's assertions to his boss, the citizens of San Augustine knew exactly who they gave the credit for the improved conditions, and they continued to express their esteem and support for the Allred Rangers well into 1936. It was the year of Texas's centennial, and centennial celebrations were simultaneously used to honor the Allred Rangers. Judge F. Pat Adams published a letter of commendation specifically for Dan Hines, in which he gave Hines well-deserved credit for his key role in the cleanup and called him "a man of good moral character . . . sober, clean thinking, fearless, and, evidenced by his actions, . . . a desire to serve his fellow citizens in the suppression of law violations." That letter appeared in the *San Augustine Tribune* in addition to many articles that year detailing Hines's specific duties and actions throughout the cleanup. Further, the *Tribune* frequently made note of Hines's presence in town, "busy shaking hands with his many friends." Hines's local popularity was certainly good evidence of public sentiment toward the Allred Rangers' actions there.[15]

As captain of the East Texas Ranger company, Hines often had responsibilities that took him out of San Augustine briefly. Among more mundane cases, such as a series of robberies in Center, Hines led investigations into two high-profile, nationally reported murders during this time. The first was the 1932 disappearance of an entire family—parents and two young children—near Athens in Henderson County. In what became billed as "the Famous Patton Case," an elderly local farmer had murdered all four—ostensibly after a failed attempt to rape the young mother, buried the dismembered bodies near his home, and then, for the next four years, resisted local law enforcement efforts to gain a confession and information about the disposition of bodies. Two weeks after Hines's arrival, the murderer confessed and took Hines and other officers to the bodies. Patton was later convicted, sentenced to death, and executed.[16]

The second nationally publicized case solved by Hines, along with Captain McCormick, was the mysterious killing of a successful businessman and former elected official in Center. Marlie Childs, who suffered serious permanent disabilities related to childhood polio, was shot through his kitchen window one evening. Hines and McCormick discovered that the murder was the result of a conspiracy between Childs's young wife, Reable, and her even younger lover, nineteen-year-old Terrence Bramlett. Having carried on a secret affair for many months and with Childs's wealth in mind, the pair had devised a plan in which Reable sent Childs to the kitchen at a set time when Bramlett was posted outside with a rifle. The two confessed their conspiracy to Hines and McCormick and were convicted for the murder. Bramlett spent decades in prison and died alone in a government-subsidized nursing home after being finally rebuffed by Reable, who spent most of her five-year sentence in a traveling musical troupe of women prisoners known as the Goree Girls, was released, married three times—including to a wealthy Houston man, raised a daughter, and passed away in the summer of 2000.[17]

In addition to their increasing national profile and statewide popularity, McCormick and Hines remained immensely popular in San Augustine. In May 1936, approximately six thousand people attended a three-day centennial pageant, during which Dan Hines and San Augustinian Mrs. Otha Cobb Stark (both dressed in buckskins) led a colorful "giant" parade, followed by people dressed as "Indians on ponies, Spaniards, priests, Frenchmen, and soldiers," along with covered wagons, stagecoaches, buggies, and a ninety-one-year-old Confederate veteran (in uniform), John C. Mathes. Edward A. Clark represented Governor Allred to confer the "Rangerette Honor" on Mrs. Stark, crown Maggie Cobb as Miss San Augustine Centennial Queen, and officiate the historical pageant. The event featured a cast of over six hundred reenactors of East Texas history from the "Dawn of Creation" through the pre-Columbian period, the Spanish era, Anglo-American colonization, the revolution and Republic of Texas, and the Civil War to the present. There was also a special luncheon to honor Clark for his role in getting Governor Allred to send in the Rangers. In June, another banquet was held to honor McCormick and Hines, as well as local law enforcement officials. On the menu was venison procured by the editor of the *Tribune* in a South Texas hunt at then-famous Ingenhuett Ranch.[18]

The Allred Rangers' experience, professionalism, tenacity, and successes stood in stark contrast to the incompetence and corruption of the Ferguson-era Rangers. The Ferguson Rangers had assumed their posts through the "indifferent and ill-advised [process of] political patronage," leading many Texans to feel "resentment and embarrassment," while the Allred Rangers reflected the "colorful traditions and high ideals" that most Texans associated with the Rangers and were greeted accordingly with "enthusiasm [and] pride." The Allred Rangers moved swiftly across the state to "serve as shock troops in curbing widespread lawlessness," a practice that was met mostly with public support. Their efforts in San Augustine alone resulted in forty felons being convicted and sentenced to a combined 285 years in prison.[19]

While surviving eyewitnesses have sometimes confused details of 1930s events when interviewed decades later, most of their interpretations have been affirmed by official records and contemporary news reports from across the state. The final assessment is that prior to the arrival of McCormick, Hines, Leo Bishop, and other Allred Rangers, San Augustinians were under the control of a small group of corrupt and violent members of the McClanahan and Burleson families, which operated informally but together to control and commit local crime, including theft, counterfeiting, bootlegging, robbery, racketeering, extortion, and murder. In less than a year, the Allred Rangers restored order, reinvigorated the local criminal justice system, and returned control of the community back to legitimate local authorities.

The significance of the Allred Rangers' success in San Augustine was not only apparent to the citizens and the news media but also to the government officials responsible for ensuring peace and security throughout the state. In his official report submitted to the Forty-Fifth Texas Legislature in January 1937, Adjutant General Carl Nesbitt—who had relinquished command of the Texas Ranger Force to the new DPS almost a year and a half earlier—highlighted those events, an unusual contribution to an otherwise mundane bureaucratic document. "The most outstanding work was at San Augustine," he reported, "where Captain McCormick . . . and his men. . . . [were] very successful in suppressing lawlessness and bringing peace to that locality which had been in turmoil for years." Nesbitt included no other such editorializing in his long report, which primarily consisted of charts, tables, and financial data.[20]

There is little documentation of what happened to most members of the McClanahan-Burleson gang convicted of crimes as a result of the Allred Rangers' cleanup. Disgraced former sheriff W. C. Gary appears to have been one of the few high-level participants in the gang to return to San Augustine in any official capacity. He would serve as county surveyor and "commander of the home guard" there during World War II. But many of the key actors in their arrest and prosecution achieved success and even fame in the wake of the cleanup. Allred won a second term as governor of Texas, banking on the successful creation of the new Department of Public Safety, using the San Augustine cleanup as a prime example. From there, he was appointed to the federal judiciary, ran unsuccessfully for the US Senate, and returned to the federal bench for the remainder of his career. Native San Augustinian Edward A. Clark was appointed Texas secretary of state by Allred in November 1936 and went on to found what would become one of the largest and oldest law firms in Texas. Clark would also be a key figure in the ascendancy of Lyndon Baines Johnson, who, as president, appointed Clark as ambassador to Australia.[21]

Several of Allred's Texas Rangers also fared well. James McCormick, who was a famed lawman before the San Augustine cleanup, remained a captain under the new Department of Public Safety until 1939, then retired at the same time as Will Wright, who had served since the days of the Frontier Battalion. McCormick returned to his hometown of Wichita Falls, where he served as a juvenile officer until his retirement from that post in 1958. Daniel Hines retired from the Texas Rangers and left San Augustine in July 1936 to return to his ranching roots, accepting a position as manager of the 39,000-acre Stark Ranch in Orange, Texas. That position was undoubtedly far more lucrative—not to mention less dangerous—than working as a Ranger. Hines had spent the majority of his life in ranching and appears to have entered law enforcement after ranching employment became scarce in the early years of the Depression. He had even purchased an 800-acre ranch in Newton County while still working as a Ranger. During World War II, Hines volunteered as a home defense "guerilla" commander on the Texas Gulf Coast.[22]

In addition to managing a vast ranching enterprise, including what was then an experimental herd of Brahma (typically pronounced "*Bray*-mer") cattle from India, Hines became heavily involved in the professional rodeo circuit. Working for the legendary silent film cowboy Tom Mix, his son-in-law (Canadian cowboy legend Harry Knight), and their partner, Everett Coburn, Hines served as the arena director for every major rodeo in North America, from the Houston Fat Stock Show & Rodeo to the Cheyenne Frontier Days Rodeo in Wyoming, Calgary Stampede in Canada, and World Championship Rodeo at Madison Square Garden in New York City. It was there that Hines was "discovered" by playwright and journalist Damon Runyon. Runyon briefly described Hines's career, including the events in San Augustine, to his countless readers in one of his popular syndicated "personality profiles," in which he referred to Hines as "a sort of cow-country Sherlock Holmes." Hines retired from the Stark Ranch and the rodeo circuit around 1950, after which he worked as an independent rice farmer until his full retirement in the late 1960s.[23]

After Hines left the Rangers in July 1936, local officials and leading citizens of San Augustine requested that Captain McCormick be reassigned back to their community to ensure that the troubles did not reemerge without an Allred Ranger stationed there. The locals were particularly concerned that some of those convicted in the cleanup but whose prison terms would be expiring in the coming months and years would attempt to take control of the town again and retaliate against those who had supported the Rangers. Some of those individuals—Wade McClanahan Sr., in particular—were alleged to have threatened to do just that once free. McCormick, however, was not interested in moving back to San Augustine. He would stay in Wichita Falls, where he had served as sheriff, where he had frequently been stationed during his service as a Texas Ranger, and where his family lived.[24]

After McCormick declined the assignment, San Augustinians asked for the remaining original Allred Ranger who had come to their community, Leo Bishop, to return. Bishop had been looking to get away from his home and duty station of Del Rio because he had fallen on hard times financially and lost the family ranch, like so many did during the Depression. He jumped at the chance to return to San Augustine and was reassigned there from December 1936 until late 1939. Upon his return, the community showered Bishop and his family with gifts, including clothes and food in abundance, plus a set of ivory grips for his duty pistols.[25]

Bishop was overwhelmed with appreciation for their generosity but seemed to regret his decision to return. A month later he wrote to Governor Allred asking for assistance, expressing fear for his life and for the lives of his wife and children who he had brought there to live with him. Bishop was concerned that certain associates of the McClanahan-Burleson gang were still at large and claimed that they had threatened to retaliate for the prosecutions of their friends and family members. Besides reiterating his fears in great detail throughout the long letter, he asked that backup be sent so that he would not be forced to "kill some of the outlaw element." Fortunately such an event never transpired, and Bishop's "three-year hitch" in San Augustine was "largely uneventful." The former gangsters who had once run roughshod over black and white San Augustinians with impunity had apparently come to recognize that they had met their match in the Allred Rangers. Thanks to McCormick, Hines, Bishop, and many of their colleagues, the McClanahan-Burleson gang's stranglehold over the community had been broken, once and for all.[26]

Although white-on-white violence had been the impetus for local leaders to request state assistance and what dominated white newspaper coverage of the troubles in Jim Crow–era San Augustine, this was not the core criminal activity of the McClanahan-Burleson gang. Instead, it was the gang's constant victimization of African Americans, spanning perhaps more than a decade. The unsophisticated yet deadly organized crime syndicate eventually gained complete control of the community for at least the first half of the 1930s. For years members of the McClanahan and Burleson families and their associates oppressed the black community in San Augustine County under cover of Jim Crow restrictions on the rights of African American citizens to bring complaints or testify against white community members. When some white associates of certain black victims attempted to stand up to the gangsters for their crimes, they were met with sometimes deadly violence.

After many years of subjugation by the McClanahan-Burleson gang, white community leaders finally reached out for state assistance to overthrow the homegrown mobsters. Once the local black community became convinced that the white lawmen sent in by a newly elected progressive governor were truly there to protect them from the gang's abuses and retaliation, they came forward and testified to the extent of the gangsters' depredations over the years. Although local juries and grand juries remained exclusively white in accordance with Jim Crow traditions, they and the local courts nevertheless agreed to hear the black community's myriad criminal complaints against the gangsters, took them at their word as crime victims, and convicted the white offenders, one by one.

That collaborative effort between black and white San Augustinians and the Allred Rangers lifted the community out of the darkest era of its history, in an unprecedented defiance of period cultural norms. While all other aspects of Jim Crow segregation remained in force, some even longer there than elsewhere around the state, the community of San Augustine never again permitted whites to commit crimes against black citizens with impunity. The local criminal justice system was reinvigorated by the three-part collaboration and reinforced by the extended presence of a full-time Allred Ranger stationed there for an additional three years. Revelations of efforts by white citizens—including local and state officials—to ally with black citizens and provide them with the opportunity to seek redress in the courts are unprecedented in modern scholarship on Jim Crow–era Texas. That the events featured Texas Rangers makes them even more remarkable.

Altogether, the events that comprised the "troubles" and "cleanup" of San Augustine in 1935–36 represent a period of significant historical complexity. They involved the investigation and adjudication of hundreds of criminal cases, many of which were several years old and had not been previously reported to authorities or otherwise documented beforehand. Further, this took place in an environment where most of the local citizens were initially unwilling to come forward and complain, much less testify in open court, because they feared deadly retaliation. Nevertheless, in just under a year, the Allred Rangers drove out the McClanahan-Burleson gang leaders; convinced the citizenry, black and white, of their commitment to public safety for all; and then successfully investigated and helped prosecute hundreds of cases, ranging from simple assault, theft, and bootlegging to armed robbery, extortion, and murder. In collaboration with the law-abiding majority in the local black and white populations, the Allred Rangers were an essential catalyst for change in San Augustine, standing in stark contrast to the Ferguson Rangers, who had been a significant part of the problem—both there and in communities throughout the state. The vast majority of local citizens and the statewide news media lauded the Allred Rangers' efforts, which were also promoted by the Allred administration as validating the governor's state law enforcement reform policies, which faced plenty of opposition at the time.[27]

Local support was a notable aspect of the San Augustine cleanup because it was in contrast to reactions in many other communities where the Texas Rangers were sent to restore order during the same era. More often than not, officials elsewhere had been benefitting, directly or indirectly, from whatever vice the Rangers had been sent to eradicate. Corrupt governors such as the Fergusons often interfered with enforcement of state laws by state officers in order to ensure the political support of communities whose local economies depended to some degree on criminal enterprise. In response, Allred—a former prosecutor and state attorney general—succeeded in removing direct political influence over the Rangers by advocating for and signing into law the act creating the Public Safety Commission and Department of Public Safety.

Many Texas sheriffs had feared and opposed the creation of a new statewide law enforcement body. They resented what they saw as an infringement on their local authority. Some Ranger advocates thought that the changes would marginalize the lawmen and predicted that it would lead to the abolition of the force. One of these was historian Walter P. Webb, who published his treatise on Texas Rangers history the same year as the cleanup of San Augustine and the creation of the DPS. However, both groups of detractors would be proven wrong. Not only did the Rangers survive, they also entered the definitive phase in their decades-long evolution from paramilitary frontier defenders to elite modern criminal investigators who to this day bring state resources and expertise to assist often-underfunded local agencies throughout the state.[28]

The creation of the DPS removed gubernatorial authority for direct hiring of officers, a practice that had been abused. This change allowed for the professionalization of the Rangers, as not only was politics no longer the determining factor in their appointment, but also their ranks were no longer overturned every time a new governor was elected. The bureaucratization of the Rangers under the

DPS included established criteria for applicants and apolitical career opportunities. As a result, the organization was finally able to establish secure appointments of only qualified and experienced lawmen (and eventually women). Although it took several decades to come to pass, it was also due in part to that bureaucratization that the ranks of both the Rangers and Highway Patrol eventually became more racially diverse.[29]

Charles McClanahan's defense attorney's closing statement, "This is just a question of trading rangers," was prescient in a way that was not intended. Likewise historian Robert Utley's assessment is apt: the quality of Rangers during the early twentieth century directly reflected the sitting governor. There is little, if any, debate as to the corrupt nature of Ma and Pa Ferguson's combined four terms as governor of Texas. Nor is there substantial disagreement as to the contrast of James V. Allred's progressive tenure as governor. But the evolution that swept Texas law enforcement in the early and mid-twentieth century produced many unexpected outcomes that have often been overlooked. Among them is the Allred Rangers' cleanup of San Augustine, a previously forgotten "high spot" in the history of one of the most storied law enforcement agencies in the world.

NOTES

Introduction

1. East Texas is covered in a dense pine forest that local writers have long referred to as the Pine Curtain to signify the difference in life and culture there from the rest of the state. Gary Connor, "Life behind the Pine Curtain: The East Texas Redneck Special Forces," *Palestine Herald-Press,* March 2, 2013; Joe Holley, "Writer Captures Life behind the Pine Curtain," *Houston Chronicle*, July 18, 2014; Matt Joyce, "Pine Curtain of the Past," *Texas Highways*, January 2015.

   This book is built on a diverse array of evidence totaling over three thousand pages of primary source documents, the backbone of which consists of six complete trial transcripts from cases arising directly out of the cleanup, transcripts that are preserved at the Texas State Library and Archives Commission (TSLAC). Other sources include additional local and state court records and documents; federal agency records from the National Archives in College Park, Maryland; various related state records from James V. Allred's and Miriam Ferguson's papers at the TSLAC and the M. D. Anderson Library, University of Houston; hundreds of local and regional newspaper articles and some national magazine articles; eyewitness accounts of key actors and witnesses, from several memoirs and other published sources; and numerous interviews of eyewitnesses and other community members. Gathering these records occupied more than fifteen years of research.

2. "San Augustine Grand Jury to Probe Crime Wave under Protection of State Rangers," *Beaumont Enterprise*, January 7, 1935; "Rangers Win Praise of San Augustine in Clean-Up That Is High Spot in History of State Police Force," *Beaumont Journal,* May 9, 1936. From interviews I conducted with a cross-section of the community, including

some who were alive in the thirties and old enough recall events, I learned that locals refer to the years preceding the arrival of the Rangers as "the troubles." This book answers lingering questions within the community regarding the offenses committed and reveals citizens' attitudes toward the accused and the Allred Rangers, as the Texas Rangers were known during the Allred administration. The San Augustine troubles were the product of an ongoing criminal conspiracy to which most of the local citizens were opposed. The actions and efforts of the Allred Rangers (as opposed to their predecessors from the previous administration) were requested, endorsed, and immensely appreciated by the vast majority of San Augustinians, including local African Americans. In addition, these events were part of a watershed period in Texas Ranger history during which they completed their transition from a frontier defense force into modern law enforcement investigators. This process resulted in the creation of the Texas Department of Public Safety and the Rangers' integration into it.

3. Vista K. McCroskey, "San Augustine, TX (San Augustine County)," in *Handbook of Texas Online*, http://www.tshaonline.org/handbook/online/articles/hgs01; E. H. Johnson, "East Texas," in *Handbook of Texas Online*, http://www.tshaonline.org/handbook/online/articles/rye01.

4. McCroskey, "San Augustine, TX"; Donald E. Chipman, "Spanish Texas," in *Handbook of Texas Online*, http://www.tshaonline.org/handbook/online/articles/nps01; John V. Haggard, "Neutral Ground," in *Handbook of Texas Online*, http://www.tshaonline.org/handbook/online/articles/nbn02.

5. Gilbert M. Cuthbertson, "Regulator-Moderator War," in *Handbook of Texas Online*, http://www.tshaonline.org/handbook/online/articles/jcr01; Bruce A. Glasrud and Archie P. McDonald, eds., *Blacks in East Texas History* (College Station: Texas A&M University Press, 2008), vii–xiv; Crockett, *Two Centuries*, 331–54.

6. While elements that became recognized as components of Jim Crow appear to have been in place in certain urban communities in the South just prior to the Civil War, overall the antebellum South did not have need of Jim Crow–style laws and practices to maintain white supremacy: the slave codes (state laws implemented to enforce the institution of slavery) and a plantation culture that enforced chattel slavery had served that purpose. In the North, however, even urban domestic slavery involved greater interracial intimacy than was deemed appropriate during the antebellum period. Once chattel slavery was ended in the South through force of arms—as opposed to the economically driven political transition that took place in the North—white southerners needed means through which to maintain white supremacy. After the Compromise of 1877, when white former Confederates regained control of their local and state governments, southern states followed the North's example of racial segregation, and this and other means of subjugating black Americans below the Mason-Dixon Line would continue for nearly a century. Noted Jim Crow historian C. Vann Woodward pointed out that prior to the Civil War, "racial discrimination in political and civil rights was the rule in the ["free"] states and any relaxation the exception." Woodward further asserted, "The system was born in the North and reached an advanced age before moving South in force." C. Vann Woodward, The Strange Career

of Jim Crow, new ed. (New York: Oxford University Press, 2002), xi, 3–10, 17, 20, 31–32, 44–45, 65, 69. Long before Woodward studied US race relations, French political scholar Alexis de Tocqueville observed, "Race prejudice seems stronger in those states that have abolished slavery than in those where it still exists, and nowhere is it more intolerant than in those states where slavery was never known." Alexis de Tocqueville, *Democracy in America*, (1835; repr., New York: Harper & Row, 1988), 343–44.

7. There has been a decades-long discussion among scholars as to what exactly constitutes Jim Crow and disagreement as to exactly when and how it emerged in the South, including in Texas. Such debate aside, the core elements of racial subordination, segregation, discrimination, and deference were certainly present in East Texas from the late nineteenth throughout the early and mid-twentieth centuries. Robert M. Utley, *Lone Star Lawmen* (New York: Oxford University Press, 2007), 100–101; Randolph B. Campbell, *Empire for Slavery: The Peculiar Institution in Texas* (Baton Rouge: Louisiana State University Press, 1989); Andrew J. Torget, *Seeds of Empire: Cotton, Slavery, and the Transformation of the Texas Borderlands, 1800–1850* (Chapel Hill: University of North Carolina Press, 2015; Cary D. Wintz, foreword to *Blacks in East Texas History* (College Station: Texas A&M University Press, 2008), vii; Bruce A. Glasrud, introduction to *Anti-Black Violence in Twentieth Century Texas* (College Station: Texas A&M University Press, 2008), 1–4; Bruce A. Glasrud, "Jim Crow's Emergence in Texas," *American Studies* 15–16 (1974): 49–51, 56; Lawrence D. Rice, *The Negro in Texas: 1874–1900* (Baton Rouge: Louisiana State University Press, 1971), 53–54, 140–50; Barry A. Crouch and L. J. Schultz, "Crisis in Color: Racial Separation in Texas During Reconstruction," *Civil War History* 16 (1970): 37, 49; C. Vann Woodward, "The Strange Career of a Historical Controversy," in *American Counterpoint: Slavery and Racism in the North-South Dialogue* (Boston: Little, Brown, 1971), 234–60. See also C. Vann Woodward, "The Birth of Jim Crow," *American Heritage* 15 (1964): 52–55, 100–103; Joel Williamson, "The Separation of the Races," in *When Did Southern Segregation Begin?*, ed. John David Smith (Boston: Bedford/St. Martin Press, 2002), 61–63, 68–69, 81. For a study of Jim Crow in the North, see Leon F. Litwack, *North of Slavery: The Negro in the Free States, 1790–1860* (Chicago: Oxford University Press, 1965), 97–112; Richard C. Wade, *Slavery in the Cities: The South, 1820–1860* (New York: Oxford University Press, 1964), 266–77; August Meier and Elliott Rudwick, "A Strange Chapter in the Career of 'Jim Crow,'" in *The Making of Black America* (New York: Scribner, 1971), 2:14–19. For a study of Jim Crow in Texas, see Leonard Brewster Murphy, "A History of Negro Segregation Practices in Texas, 1865–1958" (unpublished master's thesis, Southern Methodist University, 1958).

8. My analysis of these events has been affected by their complexity and diversity and by chronological considerations, particularly since the resulting criminal cases, which numbered in the hundreds, often related to matters that had occurred several years prior. Further, the sheer volume of cases filed during the 1935 Texas Ranger cleanup of San Augustine required a broad survey, leading to several research and interpretive dilemmas. Adjudication of the relevant cases was not necessarily sequential (they were not necessarily completed in the order in which the crimes at issue occurred),

and not all cases have extant records. Finally, official documents are imbued with particular limitations, and the researcher must consider the source of records and the possibility that they may have been redacted.

9. "Etex Free-for-All Street Gun Battle Claims 3 Victims," *Dallas Morning News,* December 24, 1934; Alwyn Barr, *Black Texans: A History of African Americans in Texas, 1528–1995* (Norman: University of Oklahoma Press, 1973); Merline Pitre, *In Struggle against Jim Crow: Lulu B. White and the NAACP, 1900–1957* (College Station: Texas A&M University Press, 2010).

10. James R. Ward, "The Texas Rangers, 1919–1935: A Study in Law Enforcement" (PhD thesis, Texas Christian University, 1972), 210–47; Brownson Malsch, *Captain M. T. Lone Wolf Gonzaullas, the Only Texas Ranger Captain of Spanish Descent* (Austin: Shoal Creek, 1980), 119–21.

11. "Gambling Wide Open in Every City and Town," *Dallas Morning News*, January 6, 1935; "A New Ranger Force in Texas," *San Augustine Tribune*, January 24, 1935; Robert M. Utley, *Lone Star Justice: The First Century of the Texas Rangers* (New York: Oxford University Press, 2002), 228–29; "Radio Speech of Governor James V. Allred Regarding His Law Enforcement Program, March 22, 1935," James V. Allred Papers, Special Collections, University of Houston Libraries (hereafter referred to as "Allred's Radio Address"); James Randolph Ward, "The Texas Rangers, 1919–1935": A Study in Law Enforcement" (PhD thesis, Texas Christian University, 1972); Robert W. Stephens, *Lone Wolf: The Story of Texas Ranger Captain M. T. Gonzaullus* (Dallas: Taylor Publishing, 1979), 59–60; Ralph W. Steen, "Ferguson, James Edward," in *Handbook of Texas Online*, http://www.tshaonline.org/handbook/online/articles/ffe05; John D. Huddleston, "Ferguson, Miriam Amanda Wallace [Ma]"; Utley, *Lone Star Lawmen*, 110. Carol O'Keefe Wilson, *In the Governor's Shadow: The True Story of Ma and Pa Ferguson* (Denton: University of North Texas Press, 2014) indicates that the depth of the Fergusons' corruption was even greater than previously believed.

12. File #18208, *State of Texas v. Curg Burleson, 1935*; File #18219, *State of Texas v. Curg Burleson, 1935*, Statement of Facts (Texas Circuit Court of Criminal Appeals Records, Texas State Library and Archives Commission, Austin), 2, 4–5; File #18466, *State of Texas v. Robert Lee, 1936*, Statement of Facts, 1–11.

13. File #18208, *State of Texas v. Curg Burleson, 1935*; File #18219, *State of Texas v. Curg Burleson, 1935*, Statement of Facts, 2, 4–5; File #18466, *State of Texas v. Robert Lee, 1936*, Statement of Facts, 1–11; Woodward, *The Strange Career of Jim Crow*, xi, 3–10, 17, 20, 31–32, 44–45, 65, 69. Jim Crow laws and cultural barriers kept African Americans from associating with whites in virtually every venue. Over time, states enacted laws creating separate racial spheres for employment, housing, restaurants, retail establishments, public transportation, churches, schools, orphanages, prisons, doctors' offices and hospitals, funeral homes, morgues, and cemeteries. Black citizens without white permission were also denied access to government institutions and therefore had little legal protection or means of asserting their civil rights. This included prohibitions against voting, holding public office, or testifying against whites in criminal or civil courts. Even though the US Supreme Court eventually struck down specific statutes

forbidding such access, the culture of denying African Americans access to state and local legal systems remained. This meant that blacks victimized by whites could not bring charges against the latter or testify against whites in court, even in cases where other whites brought charges against their peers.

14. File #18208, *State of Texas v. Curg Burleson, 1935*; File #18219, *State of Texas v. Curg Burleson, 1935*, 2, 4–5; File #18466, *State of Texas v. Robert Lee, 1936*, Statement of Facts, 1–11.

15. Local tradition and recorded statements from historical participants and documents from the period hold that the crimes targeting black San Augustinians and other marginalized members of the community (poor people and petty criminals) began at least by the late 1920s. However, there are indications that such exploitation of Jim Crow may have first occurred decades earlier. See Joe F. Combs, *Gunsmoke in the Redlands* (San Antonio: Naylor, 1968).

16. The long-since-declassified daily reports of the period by the San Antonio office of the US Secret Service, now at the College Park, Maryland, headquarters of the National Archives and Records Administration, provide a detailed chronicle of these events and much more. Unfortunately, the many supplemental reports by field officers and other records have not been retained, but the daily reports provide long-forgotten details as to exactly when and why the Secret Service went into San Augustine in the first place (to investigate reports of counterfeiting), who they encountered, what transpired, how Secret Service agents and other federal officials responded, and the heretofore unknown yet substantial role that the Allred Rangers played in the resulting investigation.

17. "Etex Free-for-All Street Gun Battle"; Utley, *Lone Star Lawmen*, 152–53, 168–69.

18. Brackett interview.

19. When trying to make sense of the available records for cases adjudicated during this period, an understanding of how the US criminal justice system operates is essential. First, it should be noted that, for purposes of fiscal practicality and caseload management in a system that is perpetually underfunded and understaffed, it is a bureaucratic reality that not every single offense a person commits results in arrest, charges, and trial, even when substantial evidence exists to support prosecution. Prosecutors have to determine which cases present the highest likelihood of conviction at trial and represent higher offenses as well as considering other factors. Therefore, someone who has committed numerous misdemeanors and felonies may only be charged with certain offenses (or even just one, especially in cases of murder) that offer the best chance of conviction and the longest potential prison term. Second, the vast majority of charges filed are adjudicated by way of pleas and plea bargains. The prosecution typically offers a shorter sentence or probation or even a reduced charge and dismissal of other charges in exchange for the defendant's plea of guilty or no contest. So a person accused of several crimes may only be convicted of one, and a person accused of a felony may only receive a conviction for a misdemeanor or a lesser felony. A problem resulting from this is that little or no record is kept of the proceedings, thereby limiting future historical review of the matter, particularly because such cases are

typically no longer able to be appealed. The vast majority of cases arising out of the San Augustine cleanup were likely disposed of in this manner.

20. Further complicating research of the cases stemming from the Texas Rangers cleanup of San Augustine in 1935 is the fact that many of the cases were granted a change of venue from San Augustine to Shelby County, Nacogdoches, and other surrounding judicial districts. Unfortunately, the majority of Shelby County's court records were lost in a fire, making it difficult to ascertain the final disposition of any of the cases that were adjudicated there and not appealed. All of the complete court transcripts referred to in this study were located in the Court of Criminal Appeals records at the Texas State Library and Archives, except for a partial copy of one trial transcript that was located in a codefendant's case file (attached to his request for change of venue) in the San Augustine District Court records. In the case of San Augustine County, the results were mixed. Like most small counties, its records were sparse and largely inaccessible. It is also possible that relevant records were destroyed over the years. However, thanks to the efforts of local historian Harry P. Noble Jr. and other citizens, a grant was procured to have both the local court and newspaper records digitized. While the initial foray into the paper records yielded very limited results, a subsequent examination of the digital database brought forth a considerably higher quantity of useful data. Even then, only one partial trial transcript was found. Most of the records were incomplete and offered no significant insight into the facts of the cases filed as a result of the 1935 cleanup. However, they did corroborate long-standing assumptions regarding the exceptionally high volume of cases that were adjudicated during that period, including cases against all of the most notorious figures.

21. "Etex Free-for-All Street Gun Battle"; "San Augustine's Honor Visitors, Texas Rangers to Be Feted with Dance," *Dallas Morning News*, March 22, 1935; "San Augustine Rodeo to Celebrate Town's Return to Law, Order," *Dallas Morning News*, August 10, 1935; "Member Governor's Official Family to Crown Queen," *San Augustine Tribune* (undated news clipping in possession of the author); "Allred to Name Edward Clark as State Secretary," *Dallas Morning News*, November 6, 1935;

22. "Rangers Win Praise of San Augustine in Clean-up That Is High Spot in History of State Police Force," *Beaumont Journal*, May 9, 1936; J. L. Mathews to author (attaching an unpublished eyewitness account), May 21, 2001; "Governor Allred Predicts Better Enforcing of State's Laws," *San Augustine Tribune*, July 27, 1935; "Allred Uses Plane, Auto and Horse in Trip to Etex Rodeo," *Dallas Morning News*, August 11, 1935; "San Augustine Fair Opens Oct. 23," *San Augustine Tribune*, October 16, 1935. For detailed studies surrounding the evolution of state law enforcement during this period, see Ward, "Texas Rangers, 1919–1935"; and Stephen W. Schuster, IV, "The Modernization of the Texas Rangers" (master's thesis, Texas Christian University, 1965).

23. Utley, *Lone Star Lawmen*, 100–101.

24. Ibid., xii, 6–7, 9–11, 334–37; Ben H. Procter, "Great Depression," in *Handbook of Texas Online*, http://www.tshaonline.org/handbook/online/articles/npg01. Beginning in earnest with Oscar P. Colquitt in 1911, many governors began to exploit the prestige that Texas Ranger and special Ranger commissions brought throughout the state as

political capital, commissioning supporters with dubious or even nonexistent law enforcement credentials. That abuse of gubernatorial authority over the Ranger Force (then a division of the Adjutant General's Department) greatly diminished the Rangers' credibility. What's more, this occurred at a time when the Rangers were attempting to complete their evolution from paramilitary frontier defenders into modern lawmen and as they faced some of the most challenging events in their history—dealing with revolutionaries, thieves, and smugglers from both Texas and Mexico along the expansive international border in the Rio Grande Valley. Unfortunately for all concerned— and for Tejanos, in particular—those political appointees often did not live up to the traditional Ranger ideals. Many engaged in all manner of crimes in conjunction with their Ranger service, including theft, extortion, and murder. A substantial body of literature documents this. See, for example, Benjamin Heber Johnson, *Revolution in Texas: How a Forgotten Rebellion and Its Bloody Suppression Turned Mexicans into Americans* (New Haven: Yale University Press, 2003).

Chapter 1

1. Vista K. McCroskey, "San Augustine County," in *Handbook of Texas Online*, http://www.tshaonline.org/handbook/online/articles/hcs02; Vista K. McCroskey, "San Augustine, TX (San Augustine County)," in *Handbook of Texas Online*, https://tshaonline.org/handbook/online/articles/hgs01.

2. Bob Bowman, "The Oldest Town in Texas?," TexasEscapes.com, http://www.texasescapes.com/AllThingsHistorical/Oldest-town-in-Texas-BB109.htm; David G. McComb, "Urbanization," in *Handbook of Texas Online*, https://www.tshaonline.org/handbook/ online/articles/hyunw.

3. Margery H. Krieger, "Ais Indians," in *Handbook of Texas Online*, https://tshaonline.org/handbook/online/articles/bma15; George L. Crockett, *Two Centuries in East Texas* (Dallas: Southwest Press, 1932), v–vi, 1, 350–53; Combs, *Gunsmoke in the Redlands*, vii–viii, 1–13, 118–21; David La Vere, *The Texas Indians* (College Station: Texas A&M University Press, 2004), 3–5; F. Todd Smith, *The Caddo Indians* (College Station: Texas A&M University Press, 1995), 5, 7–9; F. Todd Smith, *From Dominance to Disappearance* (Lincoln: University of Nebraska Press, 2005), 5; "Caddo Mounds State Historic Site," http://www.thc.texas.gov/historic-sites/caddo-mounds-state-historic-site; McCroskey, "San Augustine County"; Randolph B. Campbell, *Gone to Texas: A History of the Lone Star State* (New York: Oxford University Press, 2003), 41–61; "Boundaries," in *Handbook of Texas Online*, https://tshaonline.org/handbook/online/articles/mgb02; John V. Haggard, "Neutral Ground," in *Handbook of Texas Online*, https://www.tshaonline.org/handbook/online/articles/nbn02.

4. "Boundaries"; Haggard, "Neutral Ground"; Combs, *Gunsmoke in the Redlands*, 1–2; Campbell, *Gone to Texas*, 41–61, 91–93.

5. Campbell, *Gone to Texas*, 109–10; Crockett, *Two Centuries in East Texas*, 90, 101–4, 154–60; Archie P. McDonald, "Fredonian Rebellion," in *Handbook of Texas Online*, https://tshaonline.org/handbook/online/articles/jcf01; Gregg Cantrell, *Stephen F. Austin: Empresario of Texas* (New Haven: Yale University Press, 1999), 179–88, 291.

6. Crockett, *Two Centuries in East Texas*, 91, 104–5; Harry P. Noble Jr., *Texas Trailblazers: San Augustine Pioneers* (Lufkin: Best of East Texas Publishers, 1999), 82; Crockett, *Two Centuries in East Texas*, 166–82; Cantrell, *Stephen F. Austin*, 300–38.

7. James L. Haley, *Sam Houston* (Norman: University of Oklahoma Press, 2002), 99, 103, 109, 162, 220, 222, 283, 364, 385; Stanley Siegel, *A Political History of the Republic of Texas, 1836–1845* (Austin: University of Texas Press, 1956), 51; Noble, *Texas Trailblazers*, 19, 58, 71, 83, 85, 95, 97, 114, 256, 265.

8. Campbell, *Gone to Texas*, 204–27; Cantrell, *Stephen F. Austin*, 300–38; Noble, *Texas Trailblazers*, 83–85; Crockett, *Two Centuries in East Texas*, 166–82.

9. Campbell, *Gone to Texas*, 204–27; Noble, *Texas Trailblazers*, 83–85; Crockett, *Two Centuries in East Texas*, 161–93; Richard B. McCaslin, *Fighting Stock: John S. "Rip" Ford of Texas* (Fort Worth: Texas Christian University Press, 2011), 4; Claude Elliott, "Henderson, James Pinckney," in *Handbook of Texas Online*, https://tshaonline.org/handbook/online/articles/fhe14; Rebecca J. Herring, "Cordova Rebellion," in *Handbook of Texas Online*, https://tshaonline.org/handbook/online/articles/jcc03; "Cherokee War," in *Handbook of Texas Online*, https://tshaonline.org/handbook/online/articles/qdc01; Herbert Gambrell, "Lamar, Mirabeau Buonaparte," in *Handbook of Texas Online*, https://tshaonline.org/handbook/online/articles/fla15.

10. Crockett, *Two Centuries in East Texas*, 193–203.

11. Campbell, *Gone to Texas*, 85–89; Crockett, *Two Centuries in East Texas*, 254, 268–70, 299–301; James D. Carter, *Masonry in Texas: Background, History, and Influence to 1846* (Waco: Committee on Masonic Education and Service for the Grand Lodge of Texas, 1958); William Preston Vaughn, "Freemasonry," in *Handbook of Texas Online*, https://tshaonline.org/handbook/online/articles/vnf01.

12. Campbell, *Gone to Texas*, 270–81, 307–10; Glasrud and McDonald, eds., *Blacks in East Texas History*; Carl H. Moneyhon, "Reconstruction," in *Handbook of Texas Online* https://tshaonline.org/handbook/online/articles/mzr01.

13. Margaret Swett Henson and Deolece Parmelee, *The Cartwrights of San Augustine: Three Generations of Agrarian Entrepreneurs in East Texas* (Austin: Texas State Historical Association, 1993), 249–62; Crockett, *Two Centuries in East Texas*, 346–49.

14. Crockett, *Two Centuries in East Texas*, 346–49.

15. Ibid.

16. Campbell, *Gone to Texas*, 310–12.

17. Ibid., Henson and Parmelee, *Cartwrights of San Augustine*; Ben H. Procter, *Just One Riot* (Austin: Eakin Press, 2000), 64–65; Woodward, *Strange Career of Jim Crow*, 27–28.

18. Utley, *Lone Star Justice*, 153–54.

19. Combs, *Gunsmoke in the Redlands*, 1–13, 14–88; C. F. Eckhardt, *Tales of Badmen, Bad Women, and Bad Places: Four Centuries of Texas Outlawry* (Lubbock: Texas Tech University Press, 1999), 168–72. Arch Price was an African American associate of the Borders who apparently operated as the Borders' enforcer within the black community of San Augustine County. As a result, most African Americans in the area held him in contempt, and white families too avoided association with him. Combs, *Gunsmoke in the Redlands*, 89.

20. John D. Carrell, "Shooting of Rangers in San Augustine County," commentary on "San Augustine County Courthouse," TexasEscapes.com, http://www.texasescapes .com/TOWNS/San_Augustine/San-Augustine-County-Courthouse-Texas.htm; "Limited. . . . Here's your Ranger Shootin," BaylorFans.com, http://www .baylorfans.com/forums/, accessed September 30, 2014; "Descendants of Samuel M. Williams, Sr." FamilyTreemaker.com/; "John Dudley White, Sr.," Officer Down Memorial Page, http://www.odmp.org/officer/14060-private-john-dudle y-white-sr.

21. Neal Murphy, "The Hanging," *Tadpole's Outdoor Blog*, February 17, 2013, https:// tadpolesoutdoorblog.wordpress.com/2013/02/17/the-hanging-by-neal-murphy.

22. Barr, *Black Texans*, 112–72.

23. Harold J. Weiss Jr. and Rie Jarratt, "McDonald, William Jesse," in *Handbook of Texas Online*, https://tshaonline.org/handbook/online/articles/fmc43.

Chapter 2

1. For a more detailed discussion of Jim Crow laws and practices in the post–Civil War South, including Texas, see Woodward, *Strange Career of Jim Crow*; Barr, *Black Texans*; and Douglas A. Blackmon, *Slavery by Another Name: The Re-enslavement of Black Americans from the Civil War to World War II* (New York: Anchor Books, 2008); "San Augustine Grand Jury to Probe Crime Wave under Protection of State Rangers," *Beaumont Enterprise,* January 7, 1935.

2. Sidney Lister Jr., interview by author, September 2, 2010; File #18208, *State of Texas v. Curg Burleson, 1935* (Texas Circuit Court of Criminal Appeals Records, Texas State Library and Archives Commission, Austin), 6, 8–10, 23; J. L. Mathews to author (email of unpublished eyewitness account), May 21, 2001; File #18202, *State of Texas v. Eron Harris, 1935*, Statement of Facts (Texas Court of Criminal Appeals Records, Texas State Library and Archives Commission, Austin), 107, 109–10; Sanders to Allred, February 22, 1935, James V. Allred papers, Special Collections, University of Houston Libraries, Houston [hereafter Allred papers].

3. *State of Texas v. Curg Burleson*, Statement of Facts, 2, 4–5. Clark's testimony did not specify what his arrangements were with his landlord, Frank Blount, including whether he still owed any debt to Blount from that current crop.

4. Ibid.

5. Ibid., 3–6.

6. *State of Texas v. Curg Burleson, 1935*, Statement of Facts, 1–6.

7. Ibid., 1–12, 23.

8. Ibid.; Lister interview; *State of Texas v. Curg Burleson, 1935*, 6, 8–10, 23; J. L. Mathews to author (email of unpublished eyewitness account), May 21, 2001; File #18202, *State of Texas v. Eron Harris, 1935*, Statement of Facts, 107, 109–10; Sanders to Allred, February 22, 1935, Allred Papers; Complaint and Affidavit for Warrant of Arrest for C. C. McClanahan, Precinct One, Justice of the Peace, San Augustine County, May 10, 1935.

9. File # 9685, *State of Texas v. Jeff Duffield, Joe Burleson, and Vandy Steptoe* (San Augustine County District Clerk Records, San Augustine Courthouse, San Augustine, Texas); Arlene Thomas interview by author, September 27, 2012; K. Austin Kerr,

"Prohibition," in *Handbook of Texas Online*, https://www.tshaonline.org/handbook/online/articles/vap01.

10. File # 9685, *State of Texas v. Jeff Duffield, Joe Burleson, and Vandy Steptoe*; Arlene Thomas interview; Kerr, "Prohibition."

11. File # 9685, *State of Texas v. Jeff Duffield, Joe Burleson, and Vandy Steptoe*; Arlene Thomas interview; Kerr, "Prohibition."

12. Howard Abadinsky, *Organized Crime*, 10th ed. (Belmont, Calif.: Wadsworth-Cengage Learning, 2013), 2; "Approve Rule of Rangers," *San Augustine Tribune*, March 28, 1935.

13. "San Augustine Farmer Slain," *Dallas Morning News*, October 15, 1930; Arlen Hayes, interview by author, May 17, 2001.

14. Arlen Hayes interview; "San Augustine Farmer Slain"; "San Augustine Man's Trial Began Monday," *Panola Watchman* (Carthage, Tex.), September 9, 1935; Edward Boone Brackett III, family papers, in possession of Edward Boone Brackett III, Oak Park, Illinois. The Brackett family papers include period news articles, government documents, court records, an unpublished memoir, a private investigator's reports, and notes compiled by descendants of E. B. Brackett Sr.

15. Arlen Hayes interview; "San Augustine Farmer Slain"; "San Augustine Man's Trial Began Monday," *Panola Watchman* (Carthage, Tex.), September 9, 1935; Edward Boone Brackett III, family papers; "Chronological Order of Events," Brackett family papers; unpublished memoir, Brackett family papers; "San Augustine Farmer Slain."

16. Arlen Hayes interview; "San Augustine Farmer Slain"; "San Augustine Man's Trial Began Monday," *Panola Watchman* (Carthage, Tex.), September 9, 1935; "Chronological Order of Events"; unpublished memoir, Brackett family papers.

17. Unpublished memoir, Brackett family papers; "San Augustine Man's Trial Began Monday."

18. Unpublished memoir, Brackett family papers; "San Augustine Man's Trial Began Monday."

19. Unpublished memoir, Brackett family papers; "San Augustine Man's Trial Began Monday."

20. "San Augustine Farmer Slain"; "San Augustine Killing," *Nacogdoches Sentinel*, October 17, 1930; "Well-Known San Augustine Citizen Shot from Ambush," *Redland Herald* (Nacogdoches), October 16, 1930; Arlen Hayes interview.

21. "San Augustine Farmer Slain"; "San Augustine Killing"; "Well-Known San Augustine Citizen Shot from Ambush"; Arlen Hayes interview; "San Augustine Slaying Trial at Carthage Opens," *San Augustine Tribune*, September 26, 1935; Motion for Continuance, *State of Texas v. C. C. McClanahan*, San Augustine County District Court, June 1, 1931.

22. File #4635, *State of Texas v. Charles McClanahan*, 1931, Jury Charge and Verdict Form (Digitized County and District Court Records, San Augustine County Historical Society, San Augustine, Texas); Lister interview. The jury for the Garrett case included E. Watson, Dick Price, J. R. Sharpston, Pete Clegg, R. M. Orton, G. C. Mitchell, Joe Miller, John McKinley, Sidney Lister Sr., H. H. Bate (correct spelling unknown), and Ida Wilkinson.

23. *State of Texas v. Charles McClanahan*, 1931, Jury Charge and Verdict Form; Lister interview.

24. "In Memory of Mr. Brackett," *San Augustine Tribune,* October 30, 1930.

25. Unpublished memoir, Brackett family papers.

26. Ibid.

27. Curtis Haley (San Augustine physician), interview with author, August 10, 2010; *State of Texas v. Eron Harris, 1935,* Statement of Facts, 171–93.

28. *State of Texas v. Eron Harris, 1935,* Statement of Facts, 5, 11, 15, 17–18, 22, 37, 47, 49–51.

29. Ibid.

30. File #18449, *State of Texas v. Noah Thacker, 1936,* Statement of Facts (Texas Court of Criminal Appeals Records, Texas State Library and Archives Commission, Austin), 12–14, 27–28.

31. Haley interview; *State of Texas v. Eron Harris, 1935,* 37.

32. *State of Texas v. Eron Harris, 1935,* 37–39, 47; File #18449, *State of Texas v. Noah Thacker, 1936,* Statement of Facts, 3, 12.

33. *State of Texas v. Eron Harris, 1935,* 3–4, 9–10, 14, 18, 30. 44–52; File #18449, *State of Texas v. Noah Thacker, 1936,* Statement of Facts, 33–34.

34. *State of Texas v. Eron Harris, 1935,* 44–52; File #18449, *State of Texas v. Noah Thacker, 1936,* Statement of Facts. 4, 33–34.

35. *State of Texas v. Eron Harris, 1935,* 31–33.

Chapter 3

1. File #18207, *State of Texas v. Lee Jordan, 1935,* Statement of Facts (Texas Court of Criminal Appeals Records, Texas State Library and Archives Commission), 2–11, 29.

2. Ibid.

3. Ibid., 2–11.

4. Ibid., 3,7.

5. Ibid., 7.

6. "Former Special Ranger and Son Arrested," *Dallas Morning News,* July 28, 1935; "Father, Son Sentenced for Ballot Box Theft," *Dallas Morning News,* September 2, 1935; "Smothers Slander Sheet with Facts and Slings No Mud Back at Opponent," *San Augustine Tribune,* August 13, 1936; Ranger-Endorsed Deputy Is Named Marshal in Etex," *San Augustine Tribune,* August 29, 1935; "San Augustine Asks for McCormick," *Wichita Falls Post,* September 23, 1936.

7. Daily Reports from San Antonio, vol. 40 (October 1, 1934–February 28, 1935), US Secret Service Records, National Archives and Records Administration, College Park, Maryland [hereafter Secret Service Daily Reports], 44–45. There are longstanding local rumors that a printing press was dumped locally near Cottingham Bridge around this time, but I found no records or eyewitness accounts to confirm this.

8. Ibid., 52, 57, 70–72, 78–79, 81–82, 92. Tyrrell and Moran had served in the agency for decades and were each eventually recognized for their storied careers. The district under Tyrrell's command was massive, extending from El Paso to Orange and from Brownsville to Austin, one of only forty-four Secret Service districts into which the entire nation was divided. To serve that immense region, he had, on average, six agents under his charge at any one time. Tyrrell had achieved some national acclaim and accompanying stature within the agency as one of the first two agents assigned to

protect the president of the United States (following the assassination of William McKinley in 1901). Tyrrell was also noted for having infiltrated the first Italian organized crime family in New York, commonly known the Black Hand. In an obituary it was stated that Tyrrell went undercover and "join[ed]" the gang, and his investigation led to the conviction of the founding patriarchs for counterfeiting. He accomplished all of this at a time when the Department of Justice unit that would eventually become known as the Federal Bureau of Investigation (FBI) was in its infancy, and the enigmatic J. Edgar Hoover was still in grade school; "Black Hand Nemesis, Edward Tyrrell, Dies," *Milwaukee Journal,* April 4, 1947. Moran guided the nation's second oldest federal law enforcement agency from 1918 until 1937, a period in which the agency expanded its counterespionage and intelligence duties during World War I, investigated government corruption during what came to be called the "Teapot Dome Scandal," and expanded its presidential protection duties and operations. Moran simultaneously fought off relentless machinations to usurp Secret Service duties and authority by the ambitious and politically ruthless Hoover and his ever-expanding FBI. "A Brief History of the FBI," http://www.fbi.gov/about-us/history/brief-history.

9. Secret Service Daily Reports, 60; Philip H. Melanson, *The Secret Service: The Hidden History of an Enigmatic Agency* (New York: Carroll & Graf, 2002), 16.

10. Secret Service Daily Reports, 79–80. None of the extant records identify Robert L. Ellis by race, though the Secret Service reports often refer to him as "Mr. Ellis," a formality that, at the time, was not typically extended to blacks. Additionally, under Jim Crow segregation blacks were typically only allowed to attend public events such as county fairs on designated days, when most local whites would then stay away. Combined with the fact that blacks were typically identified as such in most public records (such as the law enforcement reports and grand jury minutes) and whites were typically not, it is a fair presumption that Ellis was white.

11. Ibid.

12. Ibid., 80–81; "Sheriff Charged with Attacking U.S. Operative," *Dallas Morning News,* October 20, 1934; File #3747, *United States v. W. C. Gary et al.*: Grand Jury Report and Indictment (US District Court, Records of the Eastern District of Texas, Beaumont Division, National Archives and Records Administration, Fort Worth).

13. File #3747, *United States v. W. C. Gary et al.*; Secret Service Reports, 78–81, 92.

14. Secret Service Reports, 78–81, 92.

15. Ibid.; Melanson, *Secret Service,* 12–15, 37–45, 70, 78; Secret Service Daily Reports.

16. Secret Service Reports, 78–79, 84, 96; "Crime Control Acts—Further Reading," Law Library, http://law.jrank. org/pages/5853/Crime-Control-Acts.html.

17. Secret Service Reports, 85.

18. Secret Service Daily Reports, 92–96. The claim of Benavides having been the first Hispanic US Secret Service agent is based on a November 19, 1999, obituary in the San Antonio *Express News.* "Luis M. Benavides," FindAGrave.com, http://www .findagrave.com/cgi-bin/fg.cgi?page=gr&GRid=40191676.

19. Secret Service Daily Reports, 87, 95–97.

20. Ibid., 99–103.

21. Ibid., 102–5.

22. Ibid., 108, 112. I found no records that provide the first name of Deputy US Marshal Abernathy. He was only identified by his last name in the Secret Service reports, which also reflected a general disregard for Abernathy and his perceived lack of courage.

23. Ibid., 113.

24. Ibid., 113–14.

25. Ibid., 119. I found no records that recorded the first name of Commissioner Morris. He was only identified by his last name in the Secret Service reports.

26. Ibid., 118–19.

27. Ibid., 119.

28. Ibid., 241–75.

29. Ibid., 256–58.

30. Ibid., 274–75.

31. Ibid., 242, 274–75.

32. Ibid.; Sidney Lister Jr., interview by author, September 2, 2010; Harry Noble, interview by author, May 16, 2001; Arlen Hayes, interview by author, May 17, 2001; eyewitness no. 3 (who asked to remain anonymous), interview by author, May 17, 2001; J. L. Mathews to author, May 21, 2001; "Etex Free-for-All Street Gun Battle Claims 3 Victims," *Dallas Morning News*, December 24, 1934; "Rangers Sent to San Augustine," *Beaumont Enterprise*, January 5, 1935. A local genealogist confirmed Maxey's relationship to the Thomases for me through various court and census records, and San Augustine County Court Criminal Grand Jury minutes dated January 1, 1934, confirm that Tom Burleson was indicted for attempted murder of Felix Maxey on August 5, 1933. Suzanne Sowell email to author, December 3, 2017.

33. Sidney Lister Jr., interview by author, September 2, 2010

34. Ibid.; Harry Noble interview; Arlen Hayes interview; eyewitness no. 3 interview; J. L. Mathews to author, May 21, 2001; "Etex Free-for-All Street Gun"; "Rangers Sent to San Augustine."

35. "Etex Free-for-All Street Gun Battle"; eyewitness no. 3 interview; Jamie Burleson Dougherty, interview by author, May 17, 2001. The stone grave marker for J. Elbert Thomas indicates that he died on December 23, 1934, the day after he was shot. J. Elbert Thomas, Murry Beringer Thomas, and Maurice Asa Thomas are all buried in the San Augustine City Cemetery. See http://www.findagrave.com/.

36. Eyewitness no. 1 (who asked to remain anonymous), interview by author, May 15, 2001; eyewitness #2 (who asked to remain anonymous), interview by author, May 15, 2001; Lister interview; "Rangers Assisting Sheriff Worsham," *San Augustine Tribune*, January 10, 1935.

37. "Rangers Sent to San Augustine," *Beaumont Enterprise*, January 5, 1935; "Rangers Disarm Several Persons in San Augustine, *Dallas Morning News*, January 6, 1935; "Rangers Assisting Sheriff Worsham," *San Augustine Tribune*, January 10, 1935.

38. "Rangers Sent to San Augustine"; "Rangers Disarm Several Persons in San Augustine; "Rangers Assisting Sheriff Worsham"; "Radio Speech of Governor James V. Allred

regarding His Law Enforcement Program, March 22, 1935," James V. Allred Papers, Special Collections, University of Houston Libraries.

39. "A New Ranger Force in Texas," *San Augustine Tribune,* January 24, 1935; "Rangers Assisting Sheriff Worsham," *San Augustine Tribune,* January 10, 1935; Procter, *Just One Riot,* 66–68; Arlen Hayes interview; Harry Noble interview; eyewitness no. 3 interview; J. L. Mathews unpublished narrative document attached to email, May 21, 2001; Virgil B. Worsham, *A "Common Man's" Life Story: Including His Official Work and Accomplishments while Sheriff of San Augustine County* (San Augustine: V. B. Worsham, 1952), 77–79. Worsham's only source for validation of his actions at the time is a *Houston Post* article for which he was the only source. Furthermore, his claim is factually refuted in other records that clearly document that all of the McClanahans—the main instigators—still held their commissions when the Allred Rangers arrived later that month.

40. "3 Arrested in San Augustine," *Beaumont Enterprise,* January 9, 1935; "Rangers Car Shot into Tuesday Night," *San Augustine Tribune,* January 10, 1935. Frank Hamer left the Texas Rangers forever in 1932 after having openly and unsuccessfully opposed the Fergusons' return to the governor's mansion. In retaliation, the Fergusons appointed Estill Hamer to Frank's former position as senior captain, although he was not qualified. While Estill's appointment certainly exacerbated their disaffection for each other, the reason for their original estrangement remains a family secret. John Boessenecker, *Texas Ranger: The Epic Life of Frank Hamer, the Man Who Killed Bonnie and Clyde* (New York: St. Martin's Press,

Chapter 4

1. "Eight New Rangers Are Appointed by Adjutant General," *Dallas Morning News,* January 19, 1935; "Allred Uses Plane, Auto and Horse in Trip to Etex Rodeo," *Dallas Morning News,* August 11, 1935; "Allred to Name Edward Clark as State Secretary," *Dallas Morning News,* November 6, 1935; J. L. Mathews to author (attaching an unpublished eyewitness account), May 21, 2001. Allred Ranger Dan Hines's older sister was my great-grandmother, and although I never met Hines, this relationship is how I came to know of him and his career as a Texas Ranger and how I first became aware of the events discussed in this book.

2. "Report of the Adjutant General of the State of Texas from January 15, 1935, to December 31, 1936," Adjutant General Collection, Texas State Library and Archives Commission, Austin; Ward, "The Texas Rangers, 1919–1935," 228–29, 248–49; "Creating Department of Public Safety of the State of Texas and Public Safety Commission," Senate Bill Number 146, 44th Texas Legislature, 1935, General Laws of Texas, 448.

3. "Report of the Adjutant General of the State of Texas from January 15, 1935, to December 31, 1936"; Ward, "Texas Rangers, 1919–1935", 228–29, 248–49. Aldrich, in particular, was persona non grata with some of the leading Rangers of that era, including former adjutant general William Warren Sterling and Senior Captain Frank Hamer. Sterling and Hamer despised Aldrich not only because he was not a Texas native, lacked

practical experience, and had been unwilling to disavow the Fergusons, but most of all because they believed that Aldrich was self-serving and corrupt. William Warren Sterling, *Trails and Trials of a Texas Ranger* (William Warren Sterling, 1959), 130, 194–202, 426; Boessenecker, *Texas Ranger*, 342, 379.

4. "Report of the Adjutant General of the State of Texas from January 15, 1935, to December 31, 1936"; Ward, "Texas Rangers, 1919–1935," 228–29, 248–49. Despite Warren Sterling's personal lament regarding Wright's final term as a Ranger—written nearly two decades after Wright's death—no extant records have surfaced to indicate that Wright was unhappy with his appointment as a private. Given his age by that time, he may well have declined the opportunity to return as a captain. Even today some Texas Ranger commanders have been known to express a desire to return to working cases as rank-and-file rangers without the responsibilities that come with managing people. Sterling, *Trails and Trials of a Texas Ranger*, 416.

5. "Allred Predicts Better Enforcing of State Laws," *Dallas Morning News*, July 27, 1935; "Secretary of State: Edward Clark," *Athens (Tex.) Weekly Review*, November 26, 1936.

6. Boessenecker, *Texas Ranger*, 299–300, 446.

7. Ward, "Texas Rangers, 1919–1935," 191–94; "Eight New Rangers Are Appointed by Adjutant General," *Dallas Morning News*, January 19, 1935; "Enlistment, Oath of Service, and Description Ranger Force," January 18, 1935, Adjutant General's Records, Texas State Library and Archives Commission; eyewitness no. 5 (who asked to remain anonymous), interview by author, January 11, 2003; J. L. Mathews to author (attaching an unpublished eyewitness account), May 21, 2001; Chip McCormick, interview with author, November 2017; Procter, *Just One Riot*, 63–64.

8. Eyewitness no. 1 interview; eyewitness no. 2 interview; eyewitness no. 3 interview; eyewitness no. 4 (who asked to remain anonymous), interview by author, May 17, 2001; Jamie Burleson Dougherty, interview by author, May 17, 2001; J. L. Mathews to author, May 21, 2001; "Rangers Win Praise of San Augustine in Clean-up That Is High Spot in History of State Police Force," *Beaumont Journal*, May 9, 1936.

9. "Smothers Slander Sheet with Facts and Slings No Mud Back at Opponent," *San Augustine Tribune*, August 13, 1936; "Bad Negroes Who Broke Jail Captured," *San Augustine Tribune*, January 9, 1936.

10. Arlen Hayes interview; Procter, *Just One Riot*, 66; eyewitness no. 1 interview; Eyewitness no. 2 interview; eyewitness no. 3 interview; eyewitness no. 4 interview; Dougherty interview; Mathews to author, May 21, 2001.

11. Nelsyn Wade, interview by author, October 11, 2011. The Allred Rangers were taking every precaution not to allow a repeat of the Sherman Race Riot in 1930, during which a lynch mob burned down the Grayson County courthouse after Texas Rangers, including the legendary Frank Hamer, had used tear gas and even shot into the crowd to deny them access to their victim. Rumors had spread in Sherman claiming that the Rangers had been ordered not to use violence against the white lynch mob to protect a black man, so this time the Allred Rangers made it clear from the outset that they were under no such restrictions and possessed no compunction when it

came to the use of violence, if necessary. Jody Edward Ginn, "Rangers, Rioters, and Racism: The Official Record of the 1930 Sherman Race Riot" (doctoral research paper and book manuscript, University of North Texas, December 15, 2010).

12. "Ranger Captain Who Cleaned up San Augustine Said to Be Most Like Storybook Member of Force," *Beaumont Enterprise*, January 26, 1936; "Silver Guns Reward Ranger for 'Cleaning Up' of San Augustine," *San Augustine Tribune*, August 27, 1936. While the story is not substantiated by any documents of the time, Ranger Leo Bishop is rumored to have intimidated San Augustine criminals and gained some information and confessions by the use of a bullwhip, with the "interviewee" or suspect typically tied to a tree or up against the side of a building in an alley. However, it is most likely that such tactics occurred during his term alone there for a few years, well after the 1935 cleanup. It is also rumored that he once beat a black suspect that way and left him to die. Dougherty interview; Harry Noble interview.

13. "Smothers Slander Sheet with Facts and Slings No Mud Back at Opponent," *San Augustine Tribune*, August 13, 1936.

14. Jack Hollis and Josephine (Montgomery) Hollis, interview with author, September 27, 2012; Arlene (Price) Thomas and Patsy Thomas, interview with author, September 27, 2012; Panella (Curl) Davis, interview with author, September 28, 2012. The Burleson and Harris cases, the former involving the extortion and robbery of black citizens, and the latter the carefully orchestrated murder of John Gann, are of particular note because the conspiratorial nature of the crimes was revealed through witness testimony and because testimony reinforced the assertion that the gangsters engaged in all manner of common criminality, primarily against blacks and other marginalized citizens. They also demonstrate the lengths to which Allred's Rangers went in their investigations to locate victims in cold cases, people who previously had no hope of securing justice for crimes committed against them.

15. Dan Hines papers, in possession of Holly Harrison Waligura, Columbia, Texas; Leo Bishop papers, in possession of Betty and John Oglesbee, San Augustine, Texas. Black eyewitnesses I interviewed have insisted that, considering the circumstances of the time, their friends and relatives would not have been willing to talk with unknown white lawmen unless someone they knew and trusted acted as a mediator. They unanimously agree that the young man in these photos was likely that intermediary, but unfortunately his identity has not been established. Several members of the San Augustine African American community who examined the picture and were familiar with events of the time have suggested a likely candidate who had the requisite personal connections and motive for the role, but this remains supposition. Therefore, as to the "Two Rangers" label, we do not know whether the subject of the photos was actually a commissioned Ranger (which would have made him a historic first black Ranger). In any event, the young man pictured is the most likely candidate to have been the Allred Rangers' emissary to the local black community after their January 1935 arrival in San Augustine.

16. "Sheriff Resigns," *Dallas Morning News*, August 23, 1935; "Sheriff Is Named at San Augustine," *Dallas Morning News*, August 23, 1935; "Ranger-Endorsed Deputy Is Named Marshal in Etex," *San Augustine Tribune*, August 29, 1935.

17. "A New Ranger Force in Texas," *San Augustine Tribune*, January 24, 1935; "Statement of Governor James V. Allred to the Legislative Committee Investigation of the Department of Public Safety, San Antonio, December 13, 1935," Allred Papers.

18. John Burrows to governor, January 18, 1935, Allred Papers.

19. Fred T. Fisher to governor, February 12, 1935, G. Z. Moore to governor, February 12, 1935, both in Allred Papers.

20. William W. Wade to governor, February 12, 1935, Allred Papers.

21. M. A. Johnson to governor, February 18, 1935, Allred Papers.

22. "San Augustine's Honor Visitors, Texas Rangers to Be Feted with Dance," *Dallas Morning News*, March 22, 1935; "Road Meet Held in San Augustine; Street Dance Tonight Will Be Given in Honor of Texas Rangers," *Beaumont Enterprise*, March 22, 1935.

23. "Approve Rule of Rangers," *San Augustine Tribune*, March 28, 1935.

24. Telegram from Gov. James Allred to W. F. Hays, *San Augustine Tribune*, March 25, 1935.

25. Letter from Captain McCormick to the citizens of San Augustine, *San Augustine Tribune*, March 28, 1935.

26. "Radio Speech of Governor James V. Allred Regarding His Law Enforcement Program, March 22, 1935," Allred Papers; "Rangers Guard Slaying Trial," *San Augustine Tribune*, February 7, 1935; K. Austin Kerr, "Prohibition," in *Handbook of Texas Online*, https://www.tshaonline.org/handbook/online/articles/vap01.

27. "Moonshiners Slay Boys to Make Sure They Don't Tattle," *Dallas Morning News*, October 13, 1934; "Hillbilly Slaying of Two Etex Boys Thought Solved," *Dallas Morning News*, October 14, 1934; "Rangers Guard Slaying Trial," *San Augustine Tribune*, February 7, 1935.

28. "Rangers Guard Slaying Trial," *San Augustine Tribune*, February 7, 1935; "Texas Rangers Stand Guard as Trial for Murder of Two Boys Opens in San Augustine," *Beaumont Enterprise*, January 29, 1935; "Testimony Completed in Etex Murder Trial," *Dallas Morning News*, January 31, 1935; Harry P. Noble, "Murder in Sardis," *San Augustine Tribune* (undated manuscript in author's possession); "Jury Fails to Agree in Lee Parrish Case," *Dallas Morning News*, February 3, 1935; "Nine Jurors Selected in Lee Parrish Trial," *Dallas Morning News*, March 19, 1935; "10-Year Term Is Given E. Harris," *Beaumont Enterprise*, August 27, 1935; "Ten-Year Term Given in East Texas Killing," *Dallas Morning News*, August 27, 1935.

29. "Texas Rangers Stand Guard as Trial for Murder of Two Boys Opens in San Augustine," *Beaumont Enterprise*, January 29, 1935; Daily Reports from San Antonio, vol. 40 (October 1, 1934–February 28, 1935), US Secret Service Records, 141–242, 256–58, 274–75.

30. "Seven San Augustine Men Are Indicted in Beating Agent," *San Augustine Tribune*, March 7, 1935; File #3747, *United States v. W. C. Gary et al.*; Daily Reports from San Antonio, vol. 41 (March 1, 1935–November 30, 1935), US Secret Service Records, 17–18, 35.

31. "Seven San Augustine Men Are Indicted in Beating Agent," *San Augustine Tribune*, March 7, 1935; File #3747, *United States v. W. C. Gary et al.*; Daily Reports from San Antonio, vol. 41 (March 1, 1935–November 30, 1935), US Secret Service Records, 17–18, 35.

32. File #3747, *United States v. W. C. Gary et al.*; Daily Reports from San Antonio, vol. 41 (March 1, 1935–November 30, 1935), US Secret Service Records, 22, 26.

Chapter 5

1. File #3747, *United States v. W. C. Gary et al.*; Daily Reports from San Antonio, vol. 41 (March 1, 1935–November 30, 1935), US Secret Service Records [hereafter Secret Service Daily Reports], 33–34; "Seven San Augustine Men Are Indicted in Beating Agent," *San Augustine Tribune*, March 7, 1935; "San Augustine Man Jailed at Beaumont," *San Augustine Tribune*, March 14, 1935; "San Augustine Man's Bail Forfeited When He fails to Appear," *San Augustine Tribune*, March 14, 1935.
2. File #3747, *United States v. W. C. Gary et al.*; Secret Service Daily Reports, 33–34;
3. Secret Service Daily Reports, 34–35, 63.
4. Ibid., 37–38, 89.
5. Ibid., 62, 89.
6. Ibid., 62.
7. Ibid.
8. Ibid., 62, 89–90. Steptoe, a known McClanahan-Burleson associate and brother-in-law to the Burleson brothers, would later be convicted in state court of crimes committed in concert with the gang.
9. Ibid., 63, 67–68.
10. Ibid.; "San Augustine Man's Trial Is Postponed," *San Augustine Tribune*, March 14, 1935.
11. Ibid.
12. Ibid., 68, 90.
13. Ibid.
14. Ibid.
15. Ibid.
16. S. H. Sanders to James V. Allred, February 22, 1935, Allred Papers.
17. Ibid.
18. Ibid.
19. Ibid.
20. Sanders to Allred, March 1, 1935, Allred Papers.
21. Ibid.
22. Allred to Sanders, March 3, 1935, Sanders to Allred, March 26, 1935, Allred Papers.
23. Ibid.
24. Ibid.
25. Sanders to Allred, March 1, 1935, Allred Papers.
26. Sanders to Allred, March 19, 1935, Allred Papers.
27. Ibid.
28. Allred to Sanders, March 23, 1935, Allred to Kinard, March 23, 1935, Sanders to Allred, March 26, 1935, all in Allred Papers.
29. Sanders to Allred, March 26, 1935, Allred Papers.
30. Ibid.

31. "Officers Confiscate Liquor in Raids Last Saturday," *San Augustine Tribune*, February 2, 1935; Case # 9703 (Tandy Worsham) filed by H. S. Sharp, March 26, 1935, and #9789 (Waymon Worsham) filed by H. S. Sharp, February 16, 1935, San Augustine District Court Docket.

Chapter 6

1. Jack Hollis and Josephine (Montgomery) Hollis, interview with author, September 27, 2012; Arlene (Price) Thomas and Patsy Thomas, interview with author, September 27, 2012; Panella (Curl) Davis, interview with author, September 28, 2012; other interviews with members of the African American community in San Augustine who were alive and old enough to recall various events involved and wished to remain anonymous, September 26–27, 2012.
2. "Captain McCormick Presented with Fine Pistol," *San Augustine Tribune*, April 4, 1935; "Ranger Company C Stationed in San Augustine," *San Augustine Tribune*, May 16, 1935; Earle Thomas to James V. Allred, November 19, 1935, Leo Bishop family papers, private collection of John and Betty Oglesbee, San Augustine, Texas; C. B. Freeman to Allred, June 17, 1935, Allred to Freeman, June 28, 1935, Bishop to Allred, September 26, 1935, all in Allred Papers; "Citizens of San Augustine Honor Beloved Rangers: Redland Folks Show Hearty Appreciation with Six-Shooters for Christmas," *San Augustine Tribune*, December 27, 1935. Freeman and Allred were corresponding in regard to assigning Bishop to lead an investigation in the area, indicating that he had already been back there for some time and noting that he had "a great amount of experience in this particular section."
3. Daily Reports from San Antonio, vol. 41 (March 1, 1935 –November 30, 1935), 309, US Secret Service Records.
4. Ibid.
5. File #18466, *State of Texas v. Robert Lee, 1936*, Statement of Facts, 1–11.
6. Ibid.
7. Ibid.
8. Ibid.
9. Ibid.
10. "Five Men Break out of San Augustine Jail," *Dallas Morning News*, June 3, 1935.
11. "Sanders to Allred, February 22, 1935, Allred Papers; Nelsyn Wade, interview by author, October 11, 2011; "'Badlands' in San Augustine County Raided," *San Augustine Tribune*, June 3, 1935.
12. "Rangers Lead Two Raids, Seize Liquor at Port Arthur," *San Augustine Tribune*, June 20, 1935; Sanders to Allred, February 22, 1935, Allred Papers.
13. "Jim and Curg Burleson Surrender at Center," *San Augustine Tribune*, June 13, 1935; "Curg Burleson Captured in Dickens County," *San Augustine Tribune*, August 5, 1935; "Jim Burleson Surrenders," *San Augustine Tribune*, October 3, 1935.
14. "District Court Convened Monday," *San Augustine Tribune*, July 4, 1935.
15. "Report of the Grand Jury," *San Augustine Tribune*, July 26, 1935; "Special Court Opens Sept. 2," *Beaumont Enterprise*, August 16, 1935.

16. "Three Old Killings Revived by Ranger Clean-up of Etex," *Dallas Morning News*, July 11, 1935; "San Augustine County Ranger Probe Results in 5 Murder Indictments by Grand Jury," *Beaumont Enterprise*, July 12, 1935; "Grand Jury Returns Murder Indictments," *San Augustine Tribune*, July 11, 1935; "Former Texas Ranger Freed," *Lubbock Morning Avalanche*, July 27, 1935. Duffield was indicted locally, with Charlie and Wade McClanahan Sr., for assault and extortion of Della Brooks.

17. "Former Texas Ranger Freed," *Lubbock Morning Avalanche*, July 27, 1935.

18. Ibid.; "Sheriff Is Named at San Augustine," *Dallas Morning News*, August 22, 1935.

19. "District Court Opened Monday," *San Augustine Tribune*, January 9, 1935.

20. "Sanders Will Assist in Prosecution of McClanahan Case," *San Augustine Tribune*, July 18, 1935; Sanders to Allred, July 5, 1935, Allred Papers.

21. "Sanders Will Assist in Prosecution of McClanahan Case," *San Augustine Tribune*, July 18, 1935; Sanders to Allred, July 5, 1935, Allred Papers; Allred to Sanders, July 9, 1935, Allred Papers.

22. Sanders to Allred, July 8 and 16, 1935, Allred Papers.

23. Allred to Sanders, July 17, 1935, Allred to F. Pat Adams, July 17, 1935, Allred Papers; "Chas. McClanahan Moved to Center Jail," *San Augustine Tribune*, August 8, 1935.

24. Sanders to Allred, August 24, 1935, Allred to Sanders, August 29, 1935, Allred Papers; "San Augustine Man Held in Murder Has Nervous Breakdown," *Nacogdoches Sentinel*, June 28, 1935; Kent Calder to author (email with forwarded comments from William Seale), February 15, 2018.

25. Sanders to Allred, August 24, 1935, Allred to Sanders, August 29, 1935, Allred Papers.

26. Sanders to Allred, September 19, 1935, Allred Papers.

Chapter 7

1. File #18202, *State of Texas v. Eron Harris, 1935*, Statement of Facts, 1–3.

2. Ibid.

3. Ibid., 44–52; File #18449, *State of Texas v. Noah Thacker, 1936*, Statement of Facts, 33–34.

4. File #18202, *State of Texas v. Eron Harris, 1935*, Statement of Facts, 1–2, 44–52; Jamie Burleson Dougherty, interview with author, June 2010.

5. File #18202, *State of Texas v. Eron Harris, 1935*, Statement of Facts, 53–57.

6. Ibid., 57–184. The twenty-eight defense witnesses included H. B. Sparks, Almeta Steptoe, Herman Clark, Mrs. Eron Harris, Ada Burleson (wife of Joe Burleson), Doris Burleson (widow of Tom Burleson), J. M. Harris, Lee "Red" Jordan, Henry Peters, Rueben Peters, Opal Wells, Jimmie Hooper, Cleveland Wadsworth, Philip Rogers, Richard Hodges, Henry Hendricks, Fred Bradbury, Vance Davis, Maxie Moore, P. L. Sanders, Monroe Burkett, Dick Whitson, Clint Sheppard, Grady Beasley, John T. Leslie, Mark Sheppard, J. H. "Henry" Johnson, and Eddie Goodwin. The nine eyewitnesses were Henry and Rueben Peters, Wadsworth, Rogers, Hodges, Hendrick, Davis, Moore, and Goodwin.

7. File #18202, *State of Texas v. Eron Harris, 1935*, 57–184.

8. Ibid., 57–66, 155.

9. Ibid., 56, 59, 71–74.

10. Ibid., 15, 57, 90–105, 111–30, 135–45, 156–58.

11. Ibid., 107, 109–10.

12. Ibid., 69, 171–93; Curtis Haley, interview with author, August 10, 2010; File #18449, *State of Texas v. Noah Thacker, 1936*.

13. File #18202, *State of Texas v. Eron Harris, 1935*, Statement of Facts, 147–54.

14. File #18202, *State of Texas v. Eron Harris, 1935*, Brief for Appellant and Appellant's Motion for Rehearing; "Ten-Year Term Given in East Texas Killing," *Dallas Morning News*, August 27, 1935; "Third Arrest Is Made in Old Etex Slaying," *Dallas Morning News*, August 31, 1935; "Eron Harris Given 10 Years by Shelby Jury," *San Augustine Tribune*, September, 1935; "Eron Harris Gets 10 Years at Center," *San Augustine Tribune*, August 29, 1935; "Forced Confession Saves Man Thrice Sentenced to Die," *Dallas Morning News*, June 18, 1936.

15. Procter, *Just One Riot*, 71; eyewitness no. 6, interview with author, May 15, 2001; Harry Noble, interview by author, June 17, 2010; Jamie Burleson Dougherty, interview by author, May 17, 2001.

16. Procter, *Just One Riot*, 71; eyewitness no. 6 interview; Noble interview; Burleson interview; "Officers Confiscate Liquor in Raids Last Saturday," *San Augustine Tribune*, February 21, 1935; J. L. Mathews to author, May 21, 2001 (email of unpublished eyewitness account); "Five Men Break out of San Augustine Jail," *Dallas Morning News*, June 4, 1935.

17. Virgil B. Worsham, *A "Common Man's" Life Story: Including His Official Work and Accomplishments while Sheriff of San Augustine County* (San Augustine: V. B. Worsham, 1952), 79–83; "Silver Guns Reward for 'Cleaning Up' of San Augustine," *San Augustine Tribune*, August 27, 1936. Worsham's claims regarding Leo Bishop are of note since nearly forty years after the event, Bishop himself claimed to have orchestrated the sting on the disgraced sheriff. Extant contemporary records, including some documents produced in his own hand, demonstrate that Bishop had been reassigned from San Augustine months before the jailbreak and subsequent sting operation took place. Procter, *One Riot*, 71.

18. Worsham, *"Common Man's" Life Story*, 60, 66–79, 82–83, 89, 95–97; "Sheriff Resigns," *Dallas Morning News*, August 23, 1935; "To the Citizenship of San Augustine County," *San Augustine Tribune*, September 1935.

19. Worsham, *"Common Man's" Life Story*, 60, 66–79, 82–83, 89, 95–97; "Sheriff Resigns"; "To the Citizenship of San Augustine County"; "Citizens of San Augustine Honor Beloved Rangers" *San Augustine Tribune*, January 2, 1935; "Road Meet Held in San Augustine; Street Dance Tonight Will Be Given in Honor of Texas Rangers," *Beaumont Enterprise*, March 22, 1935; "San Augustine Now an Ideal County in Which to Reside," *San Augustine Tribune*, December 5, 1935; "Rangers Win Praise of San Augustine in Clean-up That Is High Spot in History of State Police Force," *Beaumont Journal*, May 9, 1936.

20. "Sheriff Worsham Resigns," *San Augustine Tribune*, August 29, 1935; "Sheriff Resigns"; "Sheriff Is Named at San Augustine," *Dallas Morning News*, August 23, 1935;

"Ranger-Endorsed Deputy Is Named Marshal in Etex," *San Augustine Tribune*, August 29, 1935; "Jim Greer Made First Deputy Sheriff," *San Augustine Tribune*, September 9, 1935.

21. "Sheriff Worsham Resigns"; "Sheriff Resigns"; "Sheriff Is Named at San Augustine"; "Ranger-Endorsed Deputy Is Named Marshal in Etex"; "Jim Greer Made First Deputy Sheriff"; "Street Dance Makes Big Hit: Thousands of People Attend," *San Augustine Tribune*, May 2, 1935.

22. Sheriff Worsham Resigns"; "Sheriff Resigns"; "Sheriff Is Named at San Augustine"; "Ranger-Endorsed Deputy Is Named Marshal in Etex"; "Jim Greer Made First Deputy Sheriff"; "Street Dance Makes Big Hit: Thousands of People Attend," *San Augustine Tribune*, May 2, 1935.

23. "San Augustine Rodeo," *San Augustine Tribune*, July 11, 1935; "Allred to Open Rodeo August 10," *San Augustine Tribune*, August 8, 1935; "East Texas Championship Rodeo to Open Here Saturday," *San Augustine Tribune*, August 8, 1935; "San Augustine Rodeo to Celebrate Town's Return to Law, Order," *Dallas Morning News*, August 11, 1935; "Allred Uses Plane, Auto and Horse in Trip to Etex Rodeo," *Dallas Morning News*, August 11, 1935; "Governor Opens Rodeo Program: Allred Acclaimed by Town Where He Sent Rangers Some Months Ago," *Beaumont Enterprise*, August 11, 1935.

24. "San Augustine Rodeo"; "Allred to Open Rodeo August 10"; "East Texas Championship Rodeo to Open Here Saturday"; "San Augustine Rodeo to Celebrate Town's Return to Law, Order"; "Allred Uses Plane, Auto and Horse in Trip to Etex Rodeo"; "Governor Opens Rodeo Program"; "Ranger Borrows Horse, Ties Calf inside 3 Seconds," *San Augustine Tribune*, July 11, 1935. Hines was an experienced rodeo performer and director who had recently set a world record for breakaway calf roping, at Wingate's Ranch in Fannett, while riding a horse owned by Sheriff W. W. Richardson of Jefferson County. On July 4, 1935, Hines had lowered the previous record of 3.2 seconds to a lightning fast 2.8 seconds in front of a crowd numbering more than three thousand.

25. "Governor Opens Rodeo Program"; "Two-Day Rodeo Thrills Thousands of Visitors," *San Augustine Tribune*, August 11, 1935; "San Augustine Rodeo to Celebrate Town's Return to Law, Order"; "Allred Uses Plane, Auto, and Horse in Trip to Etex Rodeo."

Chapter 8

1. "Texas Rangers and Highway Patrol Combined under New State Police System Today," *Beaumont Enterprise*, August 10, 1935; "Rangers Lone Wolf Days End," *Beaumont Enterprise*, August 4, 1935; "Creating Department of Public Safety of the State of Texas and Public Safety Commission," Senate Bill Number 146, 44th Texas Legislature, 1935, Gammel's General Laws of Texas; Utley, *Lone Star Lawmen*, 158–60, 166–73.

2. "Texas Rangers and Highway Patrol Combined under New State Police System Today"; "Rangers Lone Wolf Days End"; "Creating Department of Public Safety of the State of Texas and Public Safety Commission"; Utley, *Lone Star Lawmen*, 158–60, 166–73.

3. Minutes of the first Texas Department of Public Safety Commission meeting, August 10, 1935, Allred Papers; "Report of the Adjutant General of the State of Texas from January 15, 1935, to December 31, 1936," Adjutant General's Department records, Texas

State Library and Archives Commission; Ward, "Texas Rangers, 1919–1935," 228–29, 248–49; "Creating Department of Public Safety of the State of Texas and Public Safety Commission."

4. Minutes of the first Texas Department of Public Safety Commission meeting; "Creating Department of Public Safety of the State of Texas and Public Safety Commission."

5. Minutes of the first Texas Department of Public Safety Commission meeting.

6. Ibid.

7. "Texas Rangers and Highway Patrol Combined Under New State Police System Today."

8. For a more detailed discussion of Jim Crow laws and practices in the post–Civil War South, including Texas, see Barr, *Black Texans*, and Blackmon, *Slavery by Another Name*.

9. File #18219: *State of Texas v. Curg Burleson, 1935*, Statement of Facts, 6–9; File #9689, *State of Texas v. Curg Burleson, March 2, 1935*, Docket Sheet, San Augustine District Court Records, San Augustine, Texas.

10. File #18219: *State of Texas v. Curg Burleson, 1935*, Statement of Facts, 10–20.

11. Ibid., Appellant's Motion for Rehearing (p. 14), Brief for the State (p. 2), Opinion (p. 3), and Opinion on Motion for Rehearing (p. 4); "Curg Burleson Given 6 Years in Pen," *San Augustine Tribune*, July 11, 1935.

12. "Father, Son Sentenced for Ballot Box Theft," *Dallas Morning News*, September 2, 1935; Jamie Burleson Dougherty, interview by author, May 17, 2001; Lonn Taylor to author, March 9, 2005; File #18219, *State of Texas v. Curg Burleson, 1935*, Statement of Facts, 3–6.

13. "Father, Son Sentenced for Ballot Box Theft"; Dougherty interview; Lonn Taylor to author, March 9, 2005; File #18219, *State of Texas v. Curg Burleson, 1935*, Statement of Facts, 3–6; "Two More Convictions Follow Ranger Cleanup," *Dallas Morning News*, September 11, 1935.

14. File #18208, *State of Texas v. Curg Burleson, 1935*, Brief for Appellant and Opinion.

15. Ibid.

16. "District Court Opened Monday," *San Augustine Tribune*, January 9, 1935.

17. *United States v. W. C. Gary et al.*, Grand Jury Report and Indictment, US District Court, Records of the Eastern District of Texas, Beaumont Division, National Archives and Records Administration, Fort Worth; Daily Reports from San Antonio, vol. 42 (December 1, 1935–March 30, 1936), US Secret Service Records.

18. Daily Reports from San Antonio, vol. 42 (December 1, 1935–March 30, 1936), US Secret Service Records, 634.

19. Minutes of the Grand Jury, July Term 1935, San Augustine District Court Records, San Augustine, Texas.

20. File #18208, *State of Texas v. Curg Burleson, 1935*, Brief for Appellant and Opinion, 634–35; File #3747, *United States v. W.C. Gary et al.*; Daily Reports from San Antonio, vol. 40 (November 31, 1934–February 28, 1935), 119, US Secret Service Records; "Fugitive Is Returned to San Augustine," *Nacogdoches Daily Sentinel*, March 19, 1935.

21. File #18207, *State of Texas v. Lee Jordan, 1935*, Statement of Facts (Texas Court of Criminal Appeals Records, Texas State Library and Archives Commission), Index.

22. Ibid., 2–15.
23. Ibid., 15.
24. Ibid., 15–19, 28–30.
25. Ibid., 20–22, 27–28.
26. Ibid.
27. Ibid., 24–26.
28. Ibid.

Chapter 9

1. Charlie McClanahan did not appeal his ninety-nine year sentence for the murder of Brackett, thus, unfortunately, no trial transcript was preserved. However, extensive prosecutorial records and other primary documents involving the case can be found in Governor Allred's papers and private collections. McClanahan's trial was arguably the apex of the cleanup, as it involved the conviction of the de facto leader of the McClanahan-Burleson gang and produced the longest prison sentence of those prosecuted as a result of the Allred Rangers' investigations. Allred monitored the progress of the case closely, and the surviving records, especially correspondence between the prosecutors and the governor, demonstrate the level of involvement by particular Allred Rangers in that case.
2. File #4635: *State of Texas v. Charles McClanahan, 1931,* Jury Charge and Verdict Form.
3. "San Augustine Man's Trial Began Monday," *Panola Watchman* (Carthage, Tex.), September 9, 1935; Edward Boone Brackett III, family papers. Questionable spelling of many of the names discussed in the following paragraphs comes from several newspaper articles.
4. Sidney Lister Jr., interview by author, September 2, 2010.
5. Ibid.; "San Augustine Man's Trial Began Monday," *Panola* Watchman (Carthage, Tex.), September 9, 1935; Edward Boone Brackett III, family papers.
6. "San Augustine Man's Trial Began Monday"; Brackett family papers.
7. "San Augustine Man's Trial Began Monday"; Brackett family papers; "McClanahan Gets 99 Years in Murder Trial," *Panola Watchman* (Carthage, Tex.), October 3, 1935; "San Augustine Farmer Slain," *Dallas Morning News,* October 15, 1930; "San Augustine Killing," *Nacogdoches Sentinel,* October 17, 1930; "Well-Known San Augustine Citizen Shot from Ambush," *Redland Herald* (AU: place of publication?), October 16, 1930; Arlen Hayes, interview by author, May 17, 2001.
8. "McClanahan Gets 99 Years in Murder Trial."
9. "San Augustine Man's Trial Began Monday," *Panola Watchman* (Carthage, Tex.), September 9, 1935; "McClanahan Gets 99 Years in Murder Trial," *Panola Watchman* (Carthage, Tex.), October 3, 1935; Edward Boone Brackett III, family papers; McCormick to Allred via Western Union, September 27, 1935, Allred to McCormick, October 1, 1935, Sanders to Allred, September 30, 1935, James V. Allred Papers, Special Collections, University of Houston Libraries.
10. Sanders to Allred, September 30, 1935, Allred Papers.
11. Kinard to Allred, October 1, 1935, Allred Papers.

12. Allred to Edward Boone Brackett Jr., October 4, 1935, and Sanders to Allred, September 30, 1935, Allred Papers; "McClanahan Gets 99 Years in Murder Trial," *Panola Watchman* (Carthage, Tex.), October 3, 1935.

13. Allred to Edward Boone Brackett Jr., October 4, 1935, and Sanders to Allred, September 30, 1935; "McClanahan Gets 99 Years in Murder Trial."

14. "C. C. McClanahan Given 99 years at Carthage," *San Augustine Tribune*, October 3, 1935; "Jim Burleson Surrenders," *San Augustine Tribune*, October 3, 1935.

15. "Six Texas Rangers Are Ordered to Beaumont for Dock Strike Duty," *Beaumont Enterprise*, October 24, 1935; "Orange Quiet as Rangers Patrol," *Beaumont Enterprise*, November 19, 1935; F. Ray Marshall, *Labor in the South* (Cambridge: Harvard University Press, 1967), 204–8; Ruth A. Allen, George N. Green, and James V. Reese, "Strikes," in *Handbook of Texas Online*, http://www.tshaonline.org/handbook/online/articles/oeso2.

16. Utley, *Lone Star Lawmen*, 180–82; "Rangers Stage Gambling Raid," *San Augustine Tribune*, November 14, 1935. Fed up with Hickman's stalling, on October 31, 1935, Allred demanded that he immediately conduct a raid of Top O' the Hill Terrace. Only Hickman, Allred, Ed Clark, and Phares were aware of the assignment. Hickman hastily put together a team including two plainclothes highway patrolmen, the wife of one, and Doris Wheeler, the widow of the highway patrolman who had been murdered by Bonnie Parker and Clyde Barrow in 1934. Mrs. Wheeler later reported that the circumstances surrounding the botched raid led her to believe that someone had tipped off the proprietor prior to their arrival. When confronted after the failed raid, Hickman vehemently denied that possibility at first, then switched to insisting that someone other than himself—the only one involved known to be friends with the proprietor and having expressed opposition to the related laws that he was responsible for enforcing—must have done so. Transcripts of sworn testimony from the 44th Legislature, Texas House of Representatives committee investigating the firing of Captain Tom R. Hickman, December 3, 1935, Allred Papers.

17. Transcripts of committee investigating firing of Hickman.

18. Transcripts of committee investigating firing of Hickman; Utley, *Lone Star Lawmen*, 180–82.

19. "Texas Ranger Division roster of organizations and locations of officers . . . December 10, 1935," vertical files, Tobin & Anne Armstrong Texas Ranger Research Center, Texas Rangers Hall of Fame, Waco.

20. "Captain McCormick Promoted to Head of Texas Rangers," *San Augustine Tribune*, November 14, 1935.

21. Utley, *Lone Star Lawmen*, 180–82; "Rangers Stage Gambling Raid," *San Augustine Tribune*, November 14, 1935; "Captain McCormick Promoted to Head of Texas Rangers," *San Augustine Tribune*, November 14, 1935; "New Ranger Chief Is Well Known in this City as Fearless Officer," *San Augustine Tribune*, December 19, 1935; "Two Stills Taken in San Augustine; Dan Hines Made Head of Ranger Force Located in East Texas," *Beaumont Enterprise*, January 6, 1936; "Capt. McCormick Visits Here First of the Week," *San Augustine Tribune*, March 3, 1936.

22. "Smothers Slander Sheet with Facts and Slings No Mud Back at Opponent," *San Augustine Tribune*, August 13, 1936; "Ranger-Endorsed Deputy Is Named Marshal in Etex," *San Augustine Tribune*, August 29, 1935.

23. "Former Special Ranger and Son Arrested," *Dallas Morning News*, July 28, 1935; "Father, Son Sentenced for Ballot Box Theft," *Dallas Morning News*, September 2, 1935; "San Augustine Asks for McCormick," *Wichita Falls Post*, September 23, 1936.

24. "San Augustine Now an Ideal County in Which to Reside," *San Augustine Tribune*, December 5, 1935.

25. Ibid.; "Captain McCormick Here," *San Augustine Tribune*, January 9, 1936; Harry Noble, interview by author, May 16, 2001.

26. "Citizens of San Augustine Honor Beloved Rangers," *San Augustine Tribune*, December 28, 1935.

27. "Captain McCormick Presented with Fine Pistol," *San Augustine Tribune*, April 4, 1935; "Citizens of San Augustine Honor Beloved Rangers"; Jody Edward Ginn, "Justice Comes to the Redlands," *Texas Heritage* 3 (Fall 2007): 17; Procter, *Just One Riot*, 73; "Citizens Honor District Court Officials with Venison Banquet," *San Augustine Tribune*, January 28, 1937. There has been much misinformation printed in newspaper articles and journals regarding the pistols given to the Texas Rangers by San Augustinians, particularly in regard to the caliber and model of each and the wording of the inscriptions. Dan J. Hines's pistols belong to his youngest daughter, have been exhibited in several public venues since 2001, and are currently housed at the Texas Rangers Hall at the Buckthorn Museum in San Antonio. A pair of pistols on loan to the Texas Ranger Hall of Fame and Museum in Waco are McCormick's, according to his grandson.

28. "Aprreciation [sic]," *San Augustine Tribune*, December 28; "Citizens Honor District Court Officials with Venison Banquet."

Chapter 10

1. "Bad Negroes Who Escaped Jail Captured," *San Augustine Tribune*, January 9, 1936.

2. "Report of the Grand Jury," *San Augustine Tribune*, January 31, 1936; "District Court Proceedings," *San Augustine Tribune*, January 31, 1936.

3. Report of the Grand Jury"; "District Court Proceedings"; "Sheriff Reports Capture of Stills," *San Augustine Tribune*, January 2, 1936; "Two Stills Taken in San Augustine: Dan Hines Made Head of Ranger Force Located in East Texas," *Beaumont Enterprise*, January 6, 1936; "District Court Opened Monday," *San Augustine Tribune*, January 9, 1936; File #18451, *State of Texas v. Jim Burleson, 1935*, Opinion, Texas Court of Criminal Appeals Records, Texas State Library and Archives Commission. The final disposition in the state assault to murder case is unknown, but there exists no record of a trail or dismissal that, combined with Jim Burleson's eventual multiyear prison stint, would indicate that a plea agreement was reached.

4. File #18451: *State of Texas v. Jim Burleson, 1935*, Brief for Appellant.

5. Ibid.; File #18451, *State of Texas v. Jim Burleson, 1935*, Statement of Facts, 13–15; File #18207, *State of Texas v. Lee Jordan, 1935*, Brief for Appellant and Appellant's Motion

for Rehearing, Statement of Facts, 30; "Officers Confiscate Liquor in Raids Last Saturday," *San Augustine Tribune*, February 21, 1935; "Burleson and Thacker to Hemphill Jail," *San Augustine Tribune*, undated clipping in possession of the author; "Fred Rike's Place Closed by Injunction," *San Augustine Tribune*, July 16, 1936.

6. File #18207, *State of Texas v. Lee Jordan, 1935*, Brief for Appellant and Appellant's Motion for Rehearing; File #18451: *State of Texas v. Jim Burleson, 1935*, Statement of Facts, 13–15.

7. "District Court Opened Monday," *San Augustine Tribune*, January 9, 1935; File #3747, *United States v. W. C. Gary et al.*, Grand Jury Report and Indictment, US District Court, Eastern District of Texas, Beaumont Division, National Archives and Records Administration, Fort Worth); "Son, Father Sentenced for Ballot Box Theft," *Dallas Morning News*, September 2, 1935; Jamie Burleson Dougherty, interview with author, May 17, 2001; Lonn Taylor email to author, March 9, 2005; File #18219, *State of Texas v. Curg Burleson, 1935*, Statement of Facts, Texas Court of Criminal Appeals Records, Texas State Library and Archives Commission, 3–6.

8. "Two More Convictions Follow Ranger Cleanup," *Dallas Morning News*, September 11, 1935; File #18466, *State of Texas v. Robert Lee, 1936*, Statement of Facts.

9. File #18466, *State of Texas v. Robert Lee, 1936*, Statement of Facts.

10. Ibid.

11. Ibid.

12. Ibid.

13. File #3747, *United States v. W. C. Gary et al.*; Daily Reports from San Antonio, vol. 40 (November 31, 1934–February 28, 1935), 119, US Secret Service Records; "Fugitive Is Returned to San Augustine," *Nacogdoches Daily Sentinel*, March 19, 1935.

14. Daily Reports from San Antonio, vol. 41 (March 1, 1935–November 30, 1935), 635, US Secret Service Records.

15. "District Judge Commends Hines for Good Work," *San Augustine Tribune*, February 1936 (exact date unknown); "Dan Hines Here," *San Augustine Tribune*, February 1936 (exact date unknown).

16. "A Welcome Visitor," *San Augustine Tribune*, February 1936 (exact date unknown); Allan Sigvard Lindquist, *Jess Sweeten, Texas Lawman* (San Antonio: Naylor, 1961), 73–120; "Latest Patton Confession Admits Killing McGeehee," *Athens (Tex.) Weekly Review*, March 19, 1936; "Bones Exhumed as Suspect's Wife Watches," *Dallas Morning News*, March 15, 1936.

17. "Texas Rangers Solve Center Mystery Killing," *San Augustine Tribune*, April 30, 1936; "Mrs. Childs Confesses to Conspiracy to Kill Her Husband," *San Augustine Tribune*, May 7, 1936; "Testimony Starts in Death Trial of Mrs Reable Childs," *San Augustine Tribune*, September 17, 1936; "Two to 25 years Given to Mrs. Childs in Killing Charge," *San Augustine Tribune*, September 24, 1936; "Killer at the Casement," *True Detective Mysteries* 27, no. 3: 42–44, 95–98; Bob and Doris Bowman, "A Murder and a Music Legend," in *Historic Murders of East Texas* (Lufkin: Best of East Texas Publishers, 2003), 187–97.

18. "Thousands to View Centennial Celebration," *San Augustine Tribune*, May 28, 1936; "Festivities Open in San Augustine: 6000 Turn out for Parade and First Performance of Pageant," *Beaumont Enterprise*, May 30, 1936; "Member Governors Official Family to Crown Queen," *San Augustine Tribune*, undated news clipping in possession of the author; "San Augustine's Pageant Delayed by Bad Weather," *Dallas Morning News*, May 28, 1936; "Citizens Honor District Court Officials with Venison Banquet," *San Augustine Tribune*, January 28, 1936; "Full Mount Deer on Display in S.A. Tribune Office," *San Augustine Tribune*, June 11, 1936.

19. "Silver Guns Reward for 'Cleaning up' of San Augustine," *San Augustine Tribune*, August 27, 1936; "A New Ranger Force in Texas," *San Augustine Tribune*, January 24, 1935; Utley, *Lone Star Lawmen*, 170–72.

20. Carl Nesbitt, Report of the Adjutant General of the State of Texas from January 15, 1935, to December 31, 1936, Texas State Archives and Library Commission.

21. "San Augustine, Texas" (photograph captioned "W. C. Gary, county surveyor and commander of the local home guard, making a speech over the public address system in front of the courthouse"), Library of Congress Prints and Photographs Division, http://www.loc.gov/pictures/item/2017852234; Floyd F. Ewing, "Allred, James Burr V," in *Handbook of Texas Online*, http://www.tshaonline.org/handbook/online/articles /fa142; Jon P. Newton, "Allred to Name Edward Clark as State Secretary," *Dallas Morning News*, November 16, 1935; "Edward Clark Named Secretary of State," *San Augustine Tribune*, November 16, 1936; Jon P. Newton, "Clark, Edward Aubrey," in *Handbook of Texas Online*, http://www.tshaonline.org/handbook/online/articles /fcluv); "Many Famous Characters Played Roles in City's Past," *Times Record News* (Wichita Falls, Tex.), May 31, 2009.

22. Dan J. Hines to Allred, June 30, 1936, Allred Papers; "A Welcome Visitor," *San Augustine Tribune*, June 25, 1936; "Hines Named as Manager of Stark Estate," *Beaumont Enterprise*, July 1936 (exact date unknown); "Texas 'Guerillas' Ready for Defense," *Hyde Park Herald* (Chicago), February 1942; "Quick Shooting Texas 'Guerillas' Are Defense Minded," *Mt. Adams Sun* (Bingen, Wash.), February 6, 1942.

23. "Dan Hines Rated as 'Discovery' at Great Madison Square Garden Rodeo in New York City," *Beaumont Enterprise*, October 24, 1941; Cherry Hines Harrison (daughter of Dan Hines), interview with author, July 1, 2000.

24. "San Augustine Asks for McCormick," *Wichita Falls Post*, September 23, 1936.

25. Bishop to Allred, September 26, 1935, Allred Papers; "Ranger Bishop Moving to San Augustine," *San Augustine Tribune*, October 8, 1936; "Citizens Showing Their Appreciation of Bishop," *San Augustine Tribune*, October 28, 1936; "To the People of San Augustine County," *San Augustine Tribune*, October 15, 1936.

26. Bishop to Allred, January 27 and January 29, 1937, Allred Papers; "To the People of San Augustine County; Procter, *Just One Riot*, 73.

27. "Silver Guns Reward for 'Cleaning up' of San Augustine," *San Augustine Tribune*, August 27, 1936; Utley, *Lone Star Lawmen*, 166–78; "Radio Speech of Governor James V. Allred regarding His Law Enforcement Program, March 22, 1935," Allred Papers. The limited volume and type of records surviving in San Augustine is far from unique,

as most localities lack the resources necessary for maintaining closed case files for decades on end. Additionally, it is not common practice anywhere for local courts to produce or maintain complete trial records even in the short term, unless specifically requested (and financed) by a party to the case for continued litigation purposes. Therefore, the counties that served as new venues in the San Augustine cases had almost no related records remaining at all. The next step in the research process was to explore the appellate court records. However, if an appeal is not filed or a hearing is not granted, then it is unlikely that the trial record will be preserved for future examination. And since trials are the exception, not the rule, and appeals are even more rare, that means that there will be few opportunities to preserve detailed accounts and witness testimony for posterity. As would be expected, then, the Court of Criminal Appeals records at the Archives Division of the Texas State Library in Austin turned out to be the most productive source for detailed data on the trials coming out of the San Augustine cleanup.

28. "Texas Rangers Far from Through Says New Safety Chief," *Beaumont Enterprise*, May 20, 1936; Utley, *Lone Star Lawmen*, 186–89.

29. Utley, *Lone Star Lawmen*, 171.

BIBLIOGRAPHY

Archival Sources

Allred, James V. Papers. Special Collections, University of Houston Libraries, Houston.

Bishop, Leo. Family papers. Private collection of Betty and John Oglesbee, San Augustine, Texas.

Brackett, Edward Boone, III. Family papers. In possession of Edward Boone Brackett III, Oak Park, Illinois.

Childs, Marleta. Family papers. In possession of Marleta Childs, Lubbock, Texas.

Harrison, Cherry Hale Hines. Family papers. In possession of Cherry Hale Hines Harrison, Alleyton, Texas.

Hines, Dan. Papers. In possession of Holly Harrison Waligura, Columbia, Texas.

McCormick, Chip. Family papers. In possession of Chip McCormick, Spicewood, Texas.

Texas. Adjutant General's Department. Records. Texas State Library and Archives Commission, Austin.

——. Circuit Court of Criminal Appeals. Records. Texas State Library and Archives Commission, Austin.

——. Governor's Office. Records. Texas State Library and Archives Commission, Austin.

——. San Augustine County. County Clerk Criminal Court Records. San Augustine Courthouse, San Augustine.

——. San Augustine County. District Clerk Criminal Court Records. San Augustine Courthouse, San Augustine.

Tobin & Anne Armstrong Texas Ranger Research Center, Texas Ranger Hall of Fame and Museum. Waco.

United States. District Court. Records of Eastern District of Texas, Beaumont Division. National Archives and Records Administration, Regional Depository, Fort Worth.
———. Secret Service. Records. National Archives and Records Administration, College Park, Maryland.

Books and Miscellanea

Abadinsky, Howard. *Organized Crime.* 10th ed. Belmont, Calif.: Wadsworth-Cengage Learning, 2013.
Alexander, Bob. *Rawhide Ranger, Ira Aten: Enforcing Law on the Texas Frontier.* Denton: University of North Texas Press, 2011.
Anderson, Gary Clayton. *The Conquest of Texas: Ethnic Cleansing in the Promised Land, 1820–1875.* Norman: University of Oklahoma Press, 2005.
Barr, Alwyn. *Black Texans: A History of African Americans in Texas, 1528–1995.* 2nd ed. Norman: University of Oklahoma Press, 1996.
Blackmon, Douglas A. *Slavery by Another Name: The Re-Enslavement of Black Americans from the Civil War to World War II.* New York: Anchor Books, 2008.
Boessenecker, John. *Texas Ranger: The Epic Life of Frank Hamer, the Man Who Killed Bonnie and Clyde.* New York: St. Martin's Press, 2016.
Bowman, Bob, and Doris Bowman. *Historic Murders of East Texas.* Lufkin: Best of East Texas Publishers, 2003.
"A Brief History of the FBI." Federal Bureau of Investigation. http://www.fbi.gov/about-us /history/brief-history.
Brown, John Henry. *The History of Texas from 1685 to 1892.* St. Louis: L. E. Daniel, 1892.
———. *Indian Wars and Pioneers of Texas.* Austin: L. E. Daniel, 1880.
Campbell, Randolph B. *Gone to Texas: A History of the Lone Star State.* New York: Oxford University Press, 2003.
Cantrell, Gregg. *Stephen F. Austin: Empresario of Texas.* New Haven: Yale University Press, 1999.
Carter, James D. *Masonry in Texas: Background, History, and Influence to 1846.* Waco: Committee on Masonic Education and Service for the Grand Lodge of Texas, 1958.
Collins, Michael L. *Texas Devils: Rangers and Regulars on the Lower Rio Grande, 1846–1861.* Norman: University of Oklahoma Press, 2008.
Combs, Joe F. *Gunsmoke in the Redlands.* San Antonio: Naylor, 1968.
Cool, Paul. *Salt Warriors: Insurgency on the Rio Grande.* College Station: Texas A&M University Press, 2008.
Cox, Mike. *The Texas Rangers: Wearing the Cinco Peso, 1821–1900.* New York: Forge Books, 2009.
———. *Time of the Rangers: Texas Rangers from 1900 to the Present.* New York: Forge Books, 2009.
Crockett, George L. *Two Centuries in East Texas.* Dallas: Southwest Press, 1932.
Deshields, James Thomas. *Border Wars of Texas.* Tioga: Herald, 1912.
Eckhardt, C. F. *Tales of Badmen, Bad Women, and Bad Places: Four Centuries of Texas Outlawry.* Lubbock: Texas Tech University Press, 1999.

Fehrenbach, T. R. *Lone Star: A History of Texas and the Texans*. New York: MacMillan, 1968.

Frost, H. Gordon, and John H. Jenkins. *"I'm Frank Hamer": The Life of a Texas Peace Officer*. Austin, Tex.: Pemberton Press, 1968.

Ginn, Jody Edward. "Justice Comes to the Redlands." *Texas Heritage* 3 (Fall 2007).

Glasrud, Bruce A., and Archie P. McDonald, eds. *Blacks in East Texas History*. College Station: Texas A&M University Press, 2008.

Graybill, Andrew R. *Policing the Great Plains: Rangers, Mounties, and the North American Frontier, 1875–1910*. Lincoln: University of Nebraska Press, 2007.

Haley, James L. *Sam Houston*. Norman: University of Oklahoma Press, 2002.

Handbook of Texas Online. Austin: Texas State Historical Association. https://tshaonline .org/handbook.

Harris, Charles H., III, and Louis R. Sadler. *Texas Rangers and the Mexican Revolution: The Bloodiest Decade, 1910–1920*. Albuquerque: University of New Mexico Press, 2004.

Henson, Margaret Sweatt, and Deolece Parmelee. *The Cartwrights of San Augustine: Three Generations of Agrarian Entrepreneurs in East Texas*. Austin: Texas State Historical Association, 1993.

Jackson, Joaquin, and James L. Haley. *One Ranger Returns*. Austin: University of Texas Press 2008.

Johnson, Benjamin Heber. *Revolution in Texas: How a Forgotten Rebellion and Its Bloody Suppression Turned Mexicans into Americans*. New Haven: Yale University Press, 2003.

La Vere, David. *The Texas Indians*. College Station: Texas A&M University Press, 2004.

Malsch, Brownson. *Captain M. T. Lone Wolf Gonzaullas, the Only Texas Ranger Captain of Spanish Descent*. Austin: Shoal Creek, 1980.

Mason, Tyler. *Riding for Texas: As Told by Col. Edward M. House to Tyler Mason*. New York: Reynal & Hitchcock, 1936.

McCaslin, Richard B. *Fighting Stock: John S. "Rip" Ford of Texas*. Fort Worth: Texas Christian University Press, 2011.

Melanson, Philip H., and Peter F. Stevens. *The Secret Service: The Hidden History of an Enigmatic Agency*. New York: Carroll & Graf, 2002.

Noble, Harry P., Jr. *Texas Trailblazers: San Augustine Pioneers*. Lufkin: Best of East Texas Publishers, 1999.

Oglesbee, John, and Betty Oglesbee. *Images of America: San Augustine County*. Chicago: Arcadia, 2010.

O'Neal, Bill. *Reel Rangers: Texas Rangers in Movies, TV, Radio, and Other Forms of Popular Culture*. Austin: Eakin Press, 2008.

Paine, Albert Bigelow. *Captain Bill McDonald: Texas Ranger*. New York: J. J. Little & Ives, 1909.

Parsons, Chuck. *Captain John R. Hughes: Lone Star Ranger*. Denton: University of North Texas Press, 2011.

Portal to Texas History. https://texashistory.unt.edu/.

Procter, Ben H. *Just One Riot: Texas Rangers in the 20th Century*. Austin: Eakin Press, 2000.

Samora, Julian, Joe Bernal, and Albert Peña. *Gunpowder Justice: A Reassessment of the Texas Rangers*. Notre Dame: University of Notre Dame Press, 1979.

Siegel, Stanley. *A Political History of the Republic of Texas, 1836–1845*. Austin: University of Texas Press, 1956.

Smith, F. Todd. *The Caddo Indians*. College Station: Texas A&M University Press, 1995.

———. *From Dominance to Disappearance: The Indians of Texas and the Near Southwest, 1786–1859*. Lincoln: University of Nebraska Press, 2005.

Stephens, Robert W. *Lone Wolf: The Story of Texas Ranger Captain M. T. Gonzaullus*. Dallas: Taylor Publishing, 1979.

Sterling, William Warren. *Trails and Trials of a Texas Ranger*. Norman: University of Oklahoma Press, 1959.

Texas Ranger Hall of Fame and Museum. "Timeline." http://www.texasranger.org/history /Timespecial.htm.

Utley, Robert M. *Lone Star Justice: The First Century of the Texas Rangers*. New York: Oxford University Press, 2002.

———. *Lone Star Lawmen: The Second Century of the Texas Rangers*. New York: Oxford University Press, 2007.

Ward, James R. "The Texas Rangers, 1919–1935: A Study in Law Enforcement." PhD diss., Texas Christian University, 1972.

Webb, Walter Prescott. *The Texas Rangers: A Century of Frontier Defense*. New York: Houghton Mifflin, 1935.

Weiss, Harold J. Jr. *Yours to Command: The Life and Legend of Texas Ranger Captain Bill McDonald*. Denton: University of North Texas Press, 2009.

Wilkins, Frederick. *Defending the Borders: The Texas Rangers, 1848–1861*. Abilene, Tex.: State House Press, 2001.

———. *The Highly Irregular Regulars: Texas Rangers in the Mexican War*. Austin: Eakin Press, 1990.

———. *The Law Comes to Texas: The Texas Rangers, 1870–1901*. Abilene, Tex.: State House Press, 1999.

———. *The Legend Begins: The Texas Rangers, 1823–1845*. Abilene, Tex.: State House Press, 1996.

Wilson, Carol O'Keefe. *In the Governor's Shadow: The True Story of Ma and Pa Ferguson*. Denton: University of North Texas Press, 2014.

Woodward, C. Vann. *The Strange Career of Jim Crow*. New ed. New York: Oxford University Press, 2002.

Worsham, Virgil B. *A "Common Man's" Life Story: Including His Official Work and Accomplishments while Sheriff of San Augustine County*. San Augustine, Tex.: V. B. Worsham, 1952.

INDEX

References to illustrations appear in italic type.

Wilkinson, Henry J. "Judge," 34, 55, 93
Wilkinson, Ida, 158n22
Williams, Herman, 117
Williams, Sam, 23
Wilson, Ben T., 82
Wilson, Frank J., *48*
Womack, Gladys, 36, 122
Woodward, C. Vann, 150n6

World War I, 23, 142–43, 160n8
Worsham, Tandy, 88, 92, 105, 167n31
Worsham, Virgil B., 59, 76–77, 88, 92–93, 96, 100, 105–7, 134, 162n39, 169n17
Worsham, Waymon, 88, 105, 167n31
Wright, William L., 61, 143, 163n4

Young, Sharp, 59

CPSIA information can be obtained
at www.ICGtesting.com
Printed in the USA
BVHW031116291019
562247BV00020B/60/P